Qu... Educating Citizens

Academic · Civ
Editori
Pedag
Conce
Editorials · Der
Responsibility
Assess · Com
Enhance · Pow

Qu

Quick Hits
for Educating
Citizens

Edited by JAMES L. PERRY and STEVEN G. JONES

Foreword by THOMAS EHRLICH

SHARON J. HAMILTON and ROBERT H. ORR, Consulting Editors

INDIANA UNIVERSITY PRESS

Bloomington and Indianapolis

This book is a publication of

Indiana University Press
601 North Morton Street
Bloomington, IN 47404-3797 USA

http://iupress.indiana.edu

Telephone orders   800-842-6796
Fax orders   812-855-7931
Orders by e-mail   iuporder@indiana.edu

The paper used in this publication meets the minimum
requirements of American National Standard for
Information Sciences—Permanence of Paper for
Printed Library Materials, ANSI Z39.48–1984.
Manufactured in the United States of America

Library of Congress Cataloging-in-Publication Data

Quick hits for educating citizens / edited by James L.
    Perry and Steven G. Jones ; Sharon J. Hamilton and
    Robert H. Orr, consulting editors.
        p. cm.
    Includes index.
    ISBN 0-253-21867-5 (pbk. : alk. paper)
    1. Student service—United States. 2. Student service—
United States—Curricula. 3. Political participation—
United States. I. Perry, James L. II. Jones, Steven G.
    LC220.5.Q53 2006
    378.1'03—dc22
                                        2005031633

1 2 3 4 5   11 10 09 08 07 06

CONTENTS

3 Service Learning and Educating Citizens

4 Assessing Student Learning

5 Departmental and Disciplinary Approaches to Educating Citizens

FACET DIRECTORS' WELCOME

SHARON J. HAMILTON AND ROBERT H. ORR

Welcome to *Quick Hits for Educating Citizens*, the fourth volume of Quick Hits sponsored by the Indiana University Faculty Colloquium on Excellence in Teaching (FACET).

Founded in 1989, FACET is a growing community of more than four hundred faculty dedicated to and recognized for excellence in teaching and learning. The first volume, *Quick Hits* (1994), resulted from a collection of ideas from these award-winning faculty for engaging students in learning. Intended for our own membership, it caught national attention when it was referenced in the *Chronicle of Higher Education,* and completely sold out its initial and subsequent printing. *More Quick Hits* (1998) repeated the pattern established by *Quick Hits* and became immediately popular. A more targeted volume, *Quick Hits for New Faculty* (2004), while retaining the "quick hits" nomenclature, moved towards a more contextualized and scholarly approach to engaging students, providing further resources and applications. This fourth volume, targeted for faculty who are interested in strategies for involving students in civic engagement, marks an important departure for our Quick Hits series. For the first time, almost half of our contributors are from outside FACET membership, and represent institutions across the United States. Our two editors, James Perry and Steve Jones, are not FACET members, but work very closely with FACET through the FACET Leadership Institute and the American Democracy Project. And, while retaining the Quick Hits name for recognition as a FACET volume, we offer much more fully articulated and developed essays in order to be as helpful and as informative about the suggested strategies as possible. FACET members are advocates for creating engaging environments for learning in their classrooms, across the University, and in the community. We concur with Robert Hutchins that "The death of democracy is not likely to be an assassination from ambush" but rather "a slow extinction from apathy, indifference, and undernourishment." Civic engagement is proving to be one major source of intellectual nourishment for our students as they learn what it means to be a citizen of a democracy, and a citizen in their community.

This volume provides a wealth of resources for faculty in search of strategies and suggestions for involving their students in service-learning activities in the community. It makes the statement that democracy matters, that engagement in the community is essential to maintain our democratic values, and that civic engagement plays a significant role in educating our citizens. FACET is both proud and privileged to sponsor this collection of essays.

FOREWORD

Thomas Ehrlich

This splendid volume weaves together three primary strands in my professional past—Indiana University, teaching, and civic engagement.

I came to Indiana University as its president in 1987, convinced that this great university—with close to 100,000 students on eight campuses—is absolutely vital to the state of Indiana and to the preparation of its youth for lives of civic engagement, both in their local communities and in the broader communities of state, nation, and world. "One University with Eight Front Doors" was a mantra we used in those days to capture an essential truth—IU is an institution of opportunity, enabling Hoosiers throughout the state, and many from other regions as well, to gain the understanding and skills needed to empower them to use their talents and to realize their ambitions.

Like other great public universities, IU must ensure both access and excellence in everything it does. No arena is more important than teaching and learning, and in no arena was I more struck by the dedication of the faculty. In the early 1990s, Eileen Bender, a wonderful professor of English at IU South Bend, came to me with a proposal to start a new program called FACET that would bring together the best teachers from each IU campus. Under Professor Bender's leadership, the program flourished. It not only honored outstanding IU teachers, it also helped those teachers spread the benefits of their good teaching to other faculty throughout the university on all its campuses.

One of the first tangible results of FACET was a volume called *Quick Hits*. It was the brainchild of a group of FACET faculty who wanted to enable college and university faculty everywhere to gain the insights and understandings that seasoned FACET faculty had developed after years of experience. Much to our pleasure, the book proved to be a big success, and it was followed over time with two sequels, one especially for first-time teachers. This is the fourth in the series, and in time I expect others will be published.

The aim of this volume of Quick Hits, like its predecessors, is to help overcome the greatest single challenge in promoting good teaching—it evaporates once exposed to students. As a result, good teaching is left undocumented and, therefore, unavailable for others to build on or to learn from. As Lee Shulman, president of The Carnegie Foundation has said, teaching should be "community property." The Quick Hits series is not based on an underlying grand theory of good teaching. Rather, it is prepared on the simple premise that all faculty want to improve their teaching and that sharing the classroom-tested experiences of master teachers is a particularly useful way to further that objective.

Quick Hits serves an important need. One of the most troublesome weaknesses in higher education is the lack of preparation faculty members receive before plunging into the classroom as teachers. Some may have exposure as teaching assistants in graduate school, but even that exposure is too rarely supervised by a teaching mentor with anywhere near the care and attention given to the supervision of research. Although a few universities, including IU, now sponsor "future faculty" programs for some of their graduate students, many faculty members, especially in professional schools, have no exposure at all. I well remember being told that I would teach Contracts and International Law in my first year on the Stanford Law School faculty forty years ago, and heard not a word abut how I would do so—let alone an expression of concern from my colleagues about how well I would teach. Even today, the quality of teaching in higher education is too often a secret except to students who may have little incentive to do more than express relief to their peers when they are finally free of an inadequate teacher.

When my wife, Ellen, and I left Indiana University—the first strand of my past that's woven into this book—we returned to California to be closer to our family of children and grandchildren. I then returned to teaching, the second strand—this time on the campus of San Francisco State University. Over the next five years, I taught a number of different courses, all designed to promote the civic engagement of undergraduates. This was an opportunity to help students gain the understanding, skills, and motivation they needed to be responsible and engaged citizens of their communities. A number of those courses involved community-service learning, the strategy of integrating academic learning with community service using various modes of structured reflection. In the process, students come to understand how they think about what they feel and how they feel about what they think. This volume of Quick Hits provides important insights on how to enhance the civic dimensions of community-service learning.

When I returned to California, I did not anticipate that I would have the good fortune to add a new chapter to my professional life at The Carnegie Foundation for the Advancement of Teaching, one focused on civic engagement of undergraduates, which is the third strand of my academic adventure and the major theme of this book. Beginning in 1997, as part of a new Carnegie Foundation initiative, Anne Colby and I, together with Elizabeth Beaumont and Jason Stephens, spent several years examining how America's undergraduates are being prepared for lives of moral responsibility and civic engagement. We studied twelve campuses, ranging from a research university to a community college, that are particularly focused on the moral and civic responsibly of their students and reviewed courses and programs at many other campuses as well. The results of our work were published in *Educating Citizens* (Jossey-Bass 2003), the book that gives the title to this volume.

In writing *Educating Citizens,* my colleagues at the Carnegie Foundation and I found much to encourage us. But we also found, as survey data confirms, much more interest in individual civic engagement—cleaning up a park, tutoring a kid, serving at a community kitchen—than interest in trying to bring about systemic change through the only means we have in this country, politics. And we found no campus that prioritized political engagement, broadly defined to include all public policy making, as well as partisan politics. In response, we have been examining courses and programs aimed particularly at what is needed for political engagement. We are pleased that our work shows that faculty and administrators who want to make a difference in this arena can do so.

No one can predict today exactly where our students will be in the decades ahead or what they will be doing. But we can be sure that our democracy will face difficult challenges and that its strength will depend on an educated and engaged citizenry. And we can prepare our students for their roles as citizens in conscious and deliberate ways, based on the wisest learning from our best teachers. That is the goal of this fine book.

THOMAS EHRLICH
SENIOR SCHOLAR
THE CARNEGIE FOUNDATION FOR THE ADVANCEMENT OF TEACHING
AND PRESIDENT EMERITUS, INDIANA UNIVERSITY

ACKNOWLEDGMENTS

We owe debts to many who have helped us move this book quickly from idea to reality. Sharon Hamilton and Bob Orr, our consulting editors and the Indiana University Faculty Colloquium on Excellence in Teaching's (FACET) leaders for the past five years, got the project off the ground by recruiting us as editors. They helped facilitate Indiana University Press's publication of the book, the fourth volume in the highly successful Quick Hits series. After the project formally got under way, Sharon and Bob provided much appreciated encouragement and guidance.

This book is embedded in a larger national initiative, the American Democracy Project, which is sponsored by the American Association of State Colleges and Universities (AASCU) and the *New York Times*. George Mehaffy, AASCU's vice president, has been a continuous source of inspiration because of his commitment to re-orienting the way universities educate citizens and his optimism about the payoffs from this work.

Janet Rabinowitch, director of IU Press, Greg Domber, project manager, and all the Press staff have been highly supportive and professional throughout the process. The Center for Service and Learning and the School of Public and Environmental Affairs, our academic units at IUPUI, were congenial homes for pursuing this project. In particular, we would like to acknowledge the support of Robert Bringle and Julie Hatcher, director and associate director of the Center for Service and Learning. Our campus leadership, Chancellor Charles Bantz and Executive Vice Chancellor William Plater, who value community engagement, created both the climate and infrastructure that encouraged us to pursue this project.

Alison Morris of the FACET staff deserves special credit for doing much of the hard work. Ali organized and standardized the formats of the essays as they arrived, facilitated communications with authors, and tended to last-minute details. Kim Lane, Ali's supervisor, was gracious to share Ali's time and talents with us for this endeavor.

JIM PERRY AND STEVE JONES
INDIANAPOLIS

INTRODUCTION
WHY "EDUCATING CITIZENS"? WHY NOW?

Steven G. Jones and James L. Perry

This volume in the Quick Hits series focuses on educating citizens, providing a rationale for making civic education an intentional component of the curriculum, as well as offering successful models of curriculum-based civic education activities from faculty across the disciplines. We believe civic engagement is a timely theme for the Quick Hits series. Colleges and universities are reassessing their roles in preparing future citizens for engagement in civic and political life. Three leading associations of colleges and universities—the American Association of State Colleges and Universities (AASCU), the National Association of State Universities and Land Grant Colleges (NASULGC), and the Association of American Colleges and Universities (AAC&U)—are independently pursuing efforts to enhance the attention their member organizations give to civic engagement (Kellogg Commission on the Future of State and Land Grant Universities 2000; AAC&U n.d.). The missions of other associations of higher education institutions, such as Campus Compact, revolve exclusively around promoting civic engagement. In addition, the Carnegie Foundation for the Advancement of Teaching has two major projects, Higher Education and the Development of Moral and Civic Responsibility Project and the Political Engagement Project, devoted to understanding and improving how higher education institutions educate their students for lives of civic and moral responsibility (Carnegie Foundation for the Advancement of Teaching).

Increasing interest in and concern about civic engagement, particularly among our youth, is manifest in other arenas. The 2004 presidential election sparked increased interest in political issues from college-aged students. Many public and private colleges and universities have recommitted themselves to their civic engagement missions. Regional accrediting bodies, such as the North Central Association (2003), have made institutional service and engagement core criteria for the accreditation of institutions of higher education. The Carnegie Foundation for the Advancement of Teaching, which is responsible for the Carnegie Classification System, is embarking on a pilot project to include a classification for community engagement (Carnegie Foundation).

The service-learning movement in higher education continues to grow, with many colleges and universities institutionalizing service learning through service-learning offices and service-learning requirements. Professional associations are identifying civic, as well as technical, competencies, in their professional standards. Despite these trends, some faculty are likely to see civic engagement as the work of only a few academic units or as an inherent by-product of a college education—they do not see a need to intentionally integrate education for civic engagement into their teaching. Research indicates, however, that where teaching and learning activities are not intentionally linked to learning objectives, the learning we want for our students is unlikely to occur (Chickering and Gamson 1987; Eyler and Giles 1999; Hutchings and Wutdorf 1988). Consequently, this volume provides a rationale for educating students for civic engagement and includes concise, helpful advice and models from successful college teachers on incorporating civic-engagement activities into courses. Like previous Quick Hits volumes, this volume is organized with brief articles linked to specific topics related to civic engagement.

What Do We Mean by "Educating Citizens"?

We take as a starting point Colby, Ehrlich, Beaumont, and Stephens' (2003) volume, *Educating Citizens: Preparing America's Undergraduates for Lives of Moral and Civic Responsibility*. Although "educating citizens" means many things to many people, we agree with Colby, et al.'s observation:

> If today's college graduates are to become positive forces in this world, they need not only to possess knowledge and intellectual capacities but also to see themselves as members of a community, as individuals with a responsibility to contribute to their communities. *They must be willing to act for the common good and capable of doing so effectively* [italics added]. (7)

In other words, educating citizens means providing students with the knowledge, skills, and experiences needed "to act for the common good." Of course, not every educator will agree with this interpretation of educating citizens. For some, educating citizens simply means educating students about the nature and functions of political institutions. For others, it means preparing students to become agents of social change, particularly for oppressed or underrepresented groups. Individual articles in this volume represent each of those perspectives. What they share is an emphasis on educating students to be *active* participants in our local, national, and global communal life.

Elements of Good Teaching for Educating Citizens

The individual contributions in this volume not only present individual approaches to educating students for citizenship, but, collectively, reflect best practices for faculty to emulate. As readers of this volume will see, elements of good teaching for educating citizens include:

Intentionality: "Acting for the common good" is not necessarily a natural by-product of undergraduate education. We must be intentional in our efforts if we want to prepare students for active civic and political participation (Colby et al. 2000, xl). This means involving students in learning activities that require them to think about their individual and group roles in contributing to the common good.

Engagement/Active Learning: In order to prepare students for active civic and political participation, we must provide them with active, engaged learning experiences (Kolb 1984; Sax 2000, 16–17). As Colby, et al. point out, "if used well these student-centered, or active pedagogies, can have a positive impact on many dimensions of moral and civic learning as well as on other aspects of academic achievement" (Colby, et al. 2003, 136). All of the contributions in this volume involve active-learning strategies to one degree or another, ranging from active reading and analysis of current events to active participation in the community through service learning and other forms of community-based learning.

Meaningfulness: Another characteristic shared by the contributions in this volume is that the teaching and learning strategies are meaningful. That is, they integrate civic-learning activities with students' personal and professional goals and interests (Long 2002). The learning activities are not seen as an "add on" to coursework, but as a vital component to the students' personal, career, and academic development.

Demonstrable Outcomes: Good teaching and learning always results in demonstrable outcomes (Angelo and Cross 1993). There is a measurable change in students' knowledge, skills, attitudes, dispositions, etc. as a result of their learning experience(s). One of the reasons we included chapters on goals and objectives and assessment is because faculty may not always know how to define or measure those learning outcomes.

Integrated Teaching and Learning: Finally, educating citizens requires that students realize not only the importance of active civic and political participation for its own sake, but that the critical thinking, communication, quantitative research, professional, and other skills they are developing are essential components of active citizenship (American Association of Colleges and Universities 2002). Consequently, they learn that being a nurse, for example, is not only a personal career, but is also a profession that makes unique, specialized contributions to the "common good" (Sullivan 2005, 14, 288–290).

Organization of the Book

The primary audience for *Quick Hits for Educating Citizens* is full- and part-time university faculty from every discipline. The contributors have made a special effort to illustrate how the curricular and co-curricular activities they describe and discuss are relevant for many different disciplines and professional fields. The book should also be useful for the larger community of people interested in the knowledge, skills, and dispositions students acquire, not just faculty. Administrators, student affairs professionals, institutional research staff and others will find valuable and useable ideas in this book.

Reflecting the interests of the different audiences that will use the book, we have organized it into seven chapters. We begin with an introductory section that puts the reasons and content of the book into the perspective of larger developments in our society and higher education. In our introduction, we discuss several important questions: What developments in society at large are driving the movement toward renewal of civic education in our colleges and universities? How have universities come together to respond to perceived needs? What does educating citizens entail?

In chapter 1, "Tips for First Timers," contributors help readers to cope with the inevitable challenges associated with getting started. This chapter presents ideas for simple classroom activities to get started, anecdotes about others' initial mistakes and how to avoid them, tips for creating a classroom climate that pays off for civic learning, and ideas for setting goals and how to use them for course planning and assessment.

Chapter 2, "Classroom Activities," presents an extensive array of classroom techniques that engage students in the development of citizenship outcomes. Contributors discuss many general pedagogical strategies for educating citizens, including using theatre to dramatize civic learning, writing op-eds and letters to the editor as ways to motivate students to discover public issues, and observing and simulating public institutions. In addition to explicating general pedagogical strategies, several essays illuminate effective tactics that have been used nationally on many campuses, including Public Achievement, Democracy Lab, and Democracy Matters.

"Service Learning and Educating Citizens" (chapter 3) presents a range of ideas about engaging students in contemporary social and political issues outside of the classroom. Service learning is viewed by many as a particular pedagogy that unites concepts and theory with service and reflection to reinforce both academic and civic learning. Contributors cover issues ranging from using service to form civic attitudes and sensitivity to social justice, to maximizing the value of reflection, to employing service learning as a capstone experience.

Chapter 4, "Assessing Student Learning," turns to questions that inevitably arise both as a result of universal expectations about accountability and from particular concerns about whether interventions to change student civic understanding, motivations, and dispositions make a difference. Contributors present strategies for assessing particular interventions, as well as ways to use the National Survey of Student Engagement for course planning and assessment.

We would be remiss if we left the impression that educating citizens is the domain of individual faculty. Our view is that responsibility for educating citizens is quite the opposite. Each and every faculty member can make a difference. More importantly, faculty must act in concert with colleagues in their disciplines, departments, and schools. Chapter 5, "Departmental and Disciplinary Approaches to Educating Citizens," makes precisely these points. This chapter provides examples of the collective work of faculty through their academic departments, exploring the notion of the engaged department. We believe the transformation and institutionalization of civic education in higher education is dependent upon departments, disciplines, and individual faculty accepting responsibility for educating citizens. Thus, this chapter conveys messages central to higher education's long-term success to transform itself.

Chapter 6, "Educating Citizens through Research," discusses another powerful tool available for engaging students in civic and public life. It includes descriptions of participatory action research and other forms of community-based research as examples of how can we use the research process to enhance civic engagement.

The concluding chapter, "Overcoming Barriers to Educating Students for Citizenship," acknowledges that efforts to transform the way we educate citizens will encounter barriers. One of the foremost is that many faculty believe civic education is the domain of select disciplines and academic units. This chapter addresses a range of barriers, giving particular attention to how civic engagement relates to "nontraditional" civic disciplines, e.g., engineering, science, and technology, by providing examples of courses from those disciplines that integrate civic engagement activities.

References

American Association of State Colleges and Universities. American Democracy Project. http://www.aascu.org/programs/adp.

Angelo, T. A., and K. P. Cross. 1993. *Classroom assessment techniques: A handbook for college teachers.* 2nd ed. San Francisco: Jossey-Bass.

Association of American Colleges and Universities. 2002. *Greater expectations: A new vision for learning as a nation goes to college.* Washington, D.C.: Association of American Colleges and Universities.

Association of American Colleges and Universities. AAC&U Civic Engagement Project. http://www.aacu.org/issues/civicengagement/index.cfm.

Campus Compact. Website. http://www.compact.org.

Carnegie Foundation for the Advancement of Teaching. Classification of Community Engagement Pilot Project. http://www.carnegiefoundation.org/Classification/community-engagement.html.

———. Higher Education and the Development of Moral and Civic Responsibility Project. http://www.carnegiefoundation.org/MCR/index.htm.

———. Political Engagement Project. http://www.carnegiefoundation.org/PEP/index.htm.

Chickering, A., and Z. Gamson. 1987. Seven principles of good practice in undergraduate education." *AAHE Bulletin* 39, no. 7:3–7.

Colby, A., T. Ehrlich, E. Beaumont, J. Rosner, and J. Stephens. 2000. Higher education and the development of civic responsibility." In T. Ehrlich, ed., *Civic responsibility and higher education,* xxi-xliii. Phoenix, Ariz.: Oryx Press.

Colby, A., T. Ehrlich, E. Beaumont, and J. Stephens. 2003. *Educating citizens: preparing America's undergraduates for lives of moral and civic responsibility.* San Francisco: Jossey-Bass.

Ehrlich, T., ed. 2000. *Civic responsibility and higher education.* Phoenix, Ariz.: Oryx Press.

Eyler, J., and D. E. Giles, Jr. 1999. *Where's the learning in service-learning?* San Francisco: Jossey-Bass.

Hutchings, P., and A. Wutdorff, eds. 1988. *Knowing and doing: Learning through experience.* San Francisco: Jossey-Bass.

Kellogg Commission on the Future of State and Land-Grant Universitites. 2000. *Renewing the covenant: Learning, discovery, and Engagement in a new age and different world.* Washington, D.C.: National Association of State Universities and Land-Grant Colleges.

Kolb, D. 1984. *Experiential learning: Experience as the source of learning and development.* Englewood Cliffs, N.J.: Prentice Hall.

Long, S. 2002. *The new student politics: The wingspread statement on student civic engagement.* Providence, R. I.: Campus Compact.

North Central Association of Colleges and Universities. 2003. *Handbook of accreditation.* 3rd ed. Chicago: The Higher Learning Commission. Also available online at: http://www.ncahigherlearningcommission.org/download/Handbook03.pdf..

Sax, L. 2000. Citizenship development and the American college student. In T. Ehrlich, ed., *Civic responsibility and higher education,* 3–18. Phoenix, Ariz.: Oryx Press.

Sullivan, W. M. 2005. *Work and integrity: The crisis and promise of professionalism in America.* 2nd ed. San Francisco: Jossey-Bass.

Quick Hits for Educating Citizens

TIPS FOR FIRST TIMERS

Easy to Use and Easy to Do

PAMELA JEAN OWENS
UNIVERSITY OF NEBRASKA OMAHA

Before students can venture forth into engaged civic action in response to their education, they first must recognize the links between what they are studying and how they might act as engaged citizens. I make it a practice to have at least one activity which pushes my students to make such links in every course I teach. As I see it, the key to incorporating a civic engagement activity in every class is to make the activities easy for the teacher to assign and score, and easy for the students to understand and complete. First time civic engagement activities should allow the student to earn credit simply for completing the activity; the activities should require a relatively small amount of time, compared to the amount of work for the entire course.

First timers might start with a single course, but I encourage the discipline of pushing yourself as an educator to find the civic engagement links to every class you teach and to devise an activity that highlights those links, even in classes where you can't imagine squeezing anything else into your schedule.

Here are some simple activities that have worked well for me:

"YOUR SUBJECT in the News"

I am convinced this activity can fit just about any subject matter. Here is how it works, using some of my courses as examples:

- Students watch for and report on news stories in which knowledge related to the subject being studied improves understanding of the event reported.
- For example, in "Introduction to World Religions," students divide into groups, each of which focuses for the semester on a particular world religion. Each student must watch for news articles in which knowledge of "their" religion is necessary in order to understand contemporary world events. Similarly, in "Introduction to Native American

Studies," groups follow a particular tribe for the semester and watch for news involving that tribe.

- How to make it work:

  - Post on-line a simple form students print out to turn in with their news stories. Here they record the title of the article, the news source and date, the connection to the course material, a summary of the key points of the story in light of these connections, and a concluding paragraph discussing follow-up stories for which an interested person would watch.

  - Students sign up for dates on which to present the "News Briefing" segment of class. I make these the very first item on the day's agenda. In the past I have used a paper sign-up sheet or calendar, but now I use an on-line Discussion Board for the sign-ups. Having the sign-up calendar on-line has saved countless requests of "Can I see the sign-up sheet again? I've forgotten what day I signed up for."

  - I require students to turn in at least two stories (both with an analysis form), but to present only once. In a smaller class, students could present more often. If class size prohibits having every student present to the whole class, then giving the oral news briefing might have to be done in discussion sections or might have to be optional, perhaps for extra credit.

- Keeping this activity going throughout the semester, not just making it apply to one portion of the course, shows students that their course material continually engages the world, not just at designated moments called "political" or "relevant" or "controversial."

- The students' brief presentations become the teachable moments in which to make real-life connections, pointing to what we are studying as it intersects the civic arena throughout the world. This approach makes opportunities for the connections which would not have made it into the prepared syllabus, because they are connections to events which had not yet happened as the syllabus was being written. The paragraph or two of my planned lecture that is sacrificed is a small price to pay for the self-awareness of engagement between the course content and the real world which students regularly report when filling out their end of term course evaluation forms.

"*YOUR SUBJECT* in the News" as a Closure Activity

In some courses the "In the News" Activity lends itself to expansion into an activity to bring closure to a course. For example, with "Indians in the News":

- After a semester of hearing news reports from Indian Country, we form several inter-tribal councils (the number would depend on your class size) with students distributed among the councils to maximize the number of tribes represented in each council.

- The task of each council is to consider the news of Indian Country presented over the semester and then formulate a statement of the five most pressing issues for Native Americans in the coming decade. Representatives of each council read the statements in our closing class session. I suggest they write their statement in the form of an editorial which might be printed in the newspaper *Indian Country Today*.

- Any course in a discipline which has pressing issues facing it for the future is a likely candidate for this expanded activity.

Martin Luther King Day Assignment

- MLK day falls early in the second semester and students often see it as just an extra day off. I offer extra credit to students who attend a MLK day event of any kind. They are to use the Discussion

Board for their responses. They write a thoughtful response to the event they attended and draw a connection to the topic of our class if they see one. Even when they don't find a connection, they have practiced the idea of making such connections and that, in itself, is a habit I am trying to help them develop.

Election Season Activity

- Identify the campaign issues relating to your subject matter. Surely almost every academic discipline has a stake in the outcome of at least one race in every election season: scientific research and its funding, education, women's issues, minority issues, church/state issues, economic issues, international affairs, etc.

- Students choose a race to analyze (or you can assign one) and make a list of the issues addressed which relate to the chosen subject. Sometimes a race in another state offers the most interest, depending on the issues. The race need not be one in which the students themselves would be voting, although it can be if that race is most relevant.

- Students search each candidate's web site for his or her position on the issues chosen.

- They report their findings in a chart, with the first column listing the issues and subsequent columns showing the positions of the various candidates on each issue, leaving a blank when a candidate makes no mention of an issue being examined.

- Imagining themselves as someone for whom these issues are the deciding factors, they argue for the candidate they consider the better choice.

- To receive credit for the assignment, the student must clearly lay out the issues, correctly present the views of each candidate, and then give a well-argued rationale for the candidate selected.

- As with most civic engagement assignments, the only wrong answers are ones which are poorly presented or poorly argued.

Let Students Take the Bait before You Set the Hook

Nadia Rubaii-Barrett
Binghamton University

Exposing students to civic engagement does not have to begin with a large scale project. Introductory experiences should emphasize the positive aspects and numerous rewards associated with being an involved member of the community, rather than the long hours and hard work that may accompany engagement. Civic engagement occurs when three conditions are met: the individual is motivated to get involved, the individual has skills and resources which permit involvement, and the individual has access to avenues for participation (Verba, Schlozman, and Brady 1995). In an introductory level course, it is not safe to assume that students meet any, let alone all, of these conditions. The more assistance instructors provide in each of these areas, the more likely students will have a positive experience which may, in turn, lead to continued engagement in the community.

Some students in an introductory class may demonstrate high levels of motivation for civic participation, and a small percentage may have long histories of volunteerism which pre-date their college years. Most students, however, will not have the experience or motivation, and may be overwhelmed by an unstructured or large-scale assignment requiring them to get involved in the community. For those with no prior experience, the instructor may need to combine providing assistance with generating a sense of motivation, in addition to helping students identify what they have to offer and how to connect with groups in the community.

The key is to have students experience the rewards of their involvement *before* they are asked to give too much of their time and energy. So, rather than ask students to spend numerous hours over the course of an entire semester volunteering their time for a community group, I keep things simple and I use class time for students to get their initial exposure. Although the time commitment is kept to a minimum and I make the arrangements for the class, students must still "step outside the box" in terms of their physical location and the nature of their activities. They must get out of the classroom, off campus, and into the community, and they must interact directly with people other than the in-

structor and their fellow students. I arrange to have one class session scheduled for an off-campus location where students can interact face-to-face with others in the community. It is essential that this off-campus session place students in a position of *interacting with* not simply passively observing members of the community.

In my introductory American government course, I ask each student to bring one item of clothing (in good shape) which they are willing to donate to a person in need. Rather than simply collect these items or have a representative of the homeless shelter pick them up, the class takes a trip to the shelter to deliver the items. Simply donating money or other items—without also sharing one's skills and ideas and without making connections with individuals engaged in civic life—will most likely not translate into sustained civic engagement (Kirlin and Kirlin 2002). Thus, I arrange in advance for the students to be able to participate in the distribution of items so they can talk with and experience the appreciation of those who receive the items.

Prior to this activity, I provide students with factual information about the shelter and the homeless population in the community. I also assign readings from the discipline related to the topic. We do *not* discuss this material before the visit, nor do I caution students about what they should expect. I want students to be as unbiased and honest in their reactions as possible and to not be swayed by what I or anyone else tells them to expect or to feel. I do, however, provide some basic guidelines and my expectations regarding respectful conduct.

Following that initial experience, which is eye-opening for many students, they are required to reflect on the experience and to discuss the experience in the context of the previously assigned readings. The most effective forms of reflection are somewhat structured and guided by the instructor to ensure that students are challenged to consider issues more critically, connect the experience with their studies, place the experience in the context of community, and continuously assess and re-assess their perceptions and beliefs (Eyler, Giles, and Schmiede, 1996). These reflections take the form of in-class discussions, individual journal entries, and a follow-up assignment.

The follow-up assignment requires that every student get involved in *one* of several ways. They may volunteer additional hours for the shelter or the accompanying soup kitchen; they may research the needs of the homeless in the community and communicate their concerns to public officials, or they may organize a forum (on or off campus) to bring together speakers on the topic of homelessness. For these activities, they are encouraged to work in groups once they select which assignment option they wish to pursue. The idea behind the follow-up assignments is to keep students involved and talking about the issues. Giving them options allows them an opportunity to discover that engagement may take many forms.

The same or a similar activity could be used as part of a class in any discipline, although the reading materials and follow-up assignments might vary. After the initial experience described above, students in an art course might produce and provide artwork to either decorate the shelter or be sold at an auction to generate funds for the shelter; students in an architectural design course might volunteer their expertise to prepare plans for an expansion or re-design of the shelter facilities; and students in a marketing course could prepare brochures or posters advertising shelter services or fundraising events. In each case, the additional assignments require some interaction with members of the community.

Student feedback from this type of experience illustrates that these smaller scale efforts are quite effective in generating enthusiasm about participation in the community. Students are more excited and less hesitant about continued involvement once they have had an initial positive experience. Student reactions to this initial experience have been overwhelmingly positive. Their

The short, highly structured service activities act as "bait" that lures students into the community and allows them to experience a positive aspect of engagement.

journal entries and course evaluations include comments such as: "I had no idea that I could make such a difference in someone else's life," "The handouts were just boring facts until I saw the faces of some of those people at the shelter," and "I never would have dared to go there on my own, but now my roommate and me [*sic*] go help out regularly." Some comments indicate an increased identification with and commitment to the community following the experience, which suggests support for Campbell's assertions that an individual's sense of their own identity is a social construct which is "influenced, shaped, and achieved through relationships, experiences, participation, and discourse" (690).

An individual experienced in the art of fishing knows that you must patiently allow a fish to take the bait before setting the hook and reeling in the line. The short, highly structured service activities act as "bait" that lures students into the community and allows them to experience a positive aspect of engagement. For many, this experience hooks them on the benefits of engagement and sets them on a path to continued involvement in their communities.

References

Campbell, K. B. 2005. Theorizing the authentic: Identity, engagement, and public space. *Administration & Society* 36:668–705.

Eyler, J., D. E. Giles, Jr., and A. Schmiede. 1996. *A practitioner's guide to reflection in service-learning: Student voices & reflections.* Nashville, Tenn.: Vanderbilt University.

Kirlin, J. J. and M. K. Kirlin. 2002. Strengthening effective government-citizen connections through greater civic engagement. *Public Administration Review* 62:80–85.

Verba, S., K. L. Schlozman, and H. E. Brady. 1995. *Voice and equality: Civic voluntarism in American politics.* Cambridge, Mass.: Harvard University Press.

Strong at the Seams: Joining Academic and Civic Interests

Diane Chin, Ann M. Feldman, Megan Marie, and Candice Rai
University of Illinois at Chicago

Educators who plan civic engagement programs soon stumble over the sturdy roots of the clichéd notion that academia is a domain distinct from "the real world." After a few semesters on campus, it is easy to forget that the aims and interests shaping the everyday pursuits of faculty and students really do differ from the day-to-day concerns of people who live and work in the off-campus community. The rediscovered differences may be so stark that the task of finding mutual ground on which to build a program appears discouragingly difficult.

Hope dawns with the realization that meaningful engagement does not require creation of a bland utopia in which all difference disappears. Instead, as we have learned while developing the Chicago Civic Leadership Certificate Program (CCLCP), commitment to engagement motivates the invention of partnerships in which differing interests dovetail. When we thoughtfully and creatively join dissimilar interests and aims, we create relationships that endure because they are strong at the seams.

CCLCP, funded by a Learn and Serve America matching grant from the Corporation for National and Community Service, is a three-year pilot program with one year under its belt as of May 2005. CCLCP offers a cohort of undergraduates five different academic courses over five semesters while sending them into the city to practice what faculty preach. We believe that by taking course content to the street and, simultaneously, applying off-campus experience to a critique of "book learning," students will learn more, and learn it in greater depth, than they would simply by attending even the most brilliantly taught traditional class. And while absorbing disciplinary knowledge, students accomplish valued goals for our partner non-profit organizations. In the longer run, CCLCP adds value to higher education by fostering in our students habits of mind that encourage and enrich lifelong engagement with civil society.

As we look ahead to CCLCP's second year, can we claim to have crafted a perfectly articulated program? Do our students, community partners, and faculty experience campus and community as a smooth continuum of academic and community-based experiences? Certainly not, although perfect mutuality remains a cherished goal. We do believe, however, that we have hit on a method of realizing the vision of campus-flowing-into-community-flowing-into campus for the betterment of both.

The key is to be clear, first, about the foundational concepts of one's discipline and, second, about the ways in which those concepts attain incarnation outside the classroom. The prime pedagogical move is to enable students to transport disciplinary concepts into an arena in which those ideas can (and do, every day, without our help) drive tangible accomplishment. Such pedagogy is extended and completed by our partners, off-campus community service professionals who daily breathe life into a discipline's body of knowledge.

Clarity about foundational concepts develops when program faculty talk to each other and agree on the disciplinary essentials that students must learn to enact "out there." Understanding exactly how essential disciplinary knowledge plays out off campus develops when faculty listen to community partners. Community partners, in turn, must become familiar with and supportive of the academic goals faculty set for students. (Happily, we have found our community partners as eager to help students attain academic success as they are to put students to work on behalf of their civic missions.) The intention of all this thinking, talking, and listening is to help everyone concerned, including students, develop and share a vision of how academic aims and civic mission might fit together to create a structure strong enough to support both.

Here's what happens when the pieces fit:

1. The first year of CCLCP consists of a sequence of two writing courses, remodeled into service-learning courses that encourage civic engagement. Our First-Year Writing Program helps students understand and accomplish writing by teaching them to analyze a completed or proposed piece of writing in terms of its situation, genre, language, and consequences.

2. This understanding of writing was called into play when one of our community partners needed a fact sheet explaining a program for grade-school

children. To produce a useful document, the student writer needed to: fathom the expectations, needs, and resources of both the partner organization and its primary audience (mostly low-income, Latino families); grasp the capacities and limitations of the "fact sheet" genre; make choices about style, tone, and vocabulary; and anticipate the consequences of writing so as to pursue the positive and avoid the negative.

3. A tall order for a first-year college writer—but achievable because key disciplinary principles were introduced and variously exemplified in the classroom. Writing instruction occurred before, during, and after ongoing off-campus experience in which the student tested her developing rhetorical knowledge by doing "real work."

4. The *simultaneity* of on- and off-campus learning in CCLCP is tremendously important because, as mentioned, a student's struggle to apply disciplinary concepts in the "real world" teaches the deep meaning of the concepts far better than endless hours of classroom instruction ever could. Moving the lesson to a venue in which the outcome of student effort counts for more than a mere grade— well, that's a strategy with real pedagogical power. And real risk.

5. The risk, of course, is that a seam joining campus to community will pop if, through lack of instruction, student work falls short of a community partner's expectations, or if a partner overlooks the importance of students' engaging with an academic discipline as well as with an agency's mission. All through the stresses of the semester, perfecting the campus-community dovetail requires continual awareness and an unhesitating, yet delicate touch. Both are enacted in continual, respect-

ful communication among instructors, students, and community partners. This three-way communication absorbs incredible quantities of time, yet cannot be foregone: when seams split, the failure most often can be traced to a communication lapse.

6. CCLCP faculty meet formally with community partners several times during summer and immediately before the opening of each semester to share aims and ideas and make plans for student projects. But a few planning meetings are not enough to transform community service professionals into co-teachers, or college teachers into seasoned community workers who understand what's happening on the ground: we find we must continually share our perspectives, ideas, problems, and solutions.

We believe civic engagement can be implemented across the curriculum. The second year of our program now involves faculty from the College of Urban Planning and Policy Administration. As word of our program spreads around the university, our director is finding it increasingly possible to interest faculty from other disciplines in future iterations of CCLCP. We feel our program's academic breadth is almost limitless because at the vital center of every discipline is a set of ideas that live even more robustly outside the core texts. We imagine students "doing" political science, history, botany, accounting, computer programming, statistics, theater, literature in a way that teaches them to think in disciplinary terms *and* work with people in communities that face real challenges and offer important life lessons. The ongoing task of our and every civic engagement program is to smooth the junctures of campus and community, to reveal human enterprise made beautifully whole.

Can't We All Just (Dis)Agree?

JENNIFER S. SIMPSON
INDIANA UNIVERSITY–PURDUE UNIVERSITY FORT WAYNE

The ability of students and an instructor to disagree on contentious social issues is an important component of civic engagement. Civic learning includes "tolerance of perspectives different from one's own . . .

and the capacity to conduct moral discourse across points of view" (Colby, Ehrlich, Beaumont, and Stephens 2003, 16). In a classroom that includes civic engagement-related learning outcomes, students must be "encouraged to think independently," and to disagree with each other and the instructor (Colby et al. 2003, 16). Students must become familiar with the practice of "moral argumentation," and of "acknowledging agreement where it exists; considering alternative positions to common debates; and avoiding simple dichotomies" (Colby et al. 2003, 145). This essay articulates pedagogical strategies for supporting disagreement linked to contentious social issues in the context of civic engagement–related learning outcomes.

Civic engagement principles do not support argument in the form of competitive debate, the necessity of one uniform conclusion, or the desirability of persuasion. Rather, civic engagement principles support listening for the sake of understanding, complexity, and collaborative dialogue. In such a framework, classroom discussion is a chance to take risks, articulate new ideas, come to grips with one's own lack of evidence, ask questions, seek clarification, ask why and why not, and consider multiple perspectives on any one issue, including those that may at first be difficult to hear. Finally, to engage with others on difficult issues in the face of strong disagreement, and to do so class meeting after class meeting, requires a regard for and concern with others in the classroom. Such practices require a cognitive and affective commitment not only to dialogue itself, but also to those with whom one is in dialogue.

In addition to institutional support for a range of viewpoints, it is crucial for individual faculty to take stock of our own comfort level with disagreement in the classroom.

Finding a balance between the articulation of sharply different viewpoints, and course content and learning objectives is difficult. How can instructors structure learning so that students begin to see thoughtful disagreement as central and routine to their learning? At one level, an instructor can make students aware of existing institutional support for such disagreement and difference; at a second level, he or she can integrate difference and disagreement into all aspects of their class.

At my institution during the 2004 presidential election, individuals on campus removed public notices when those announcements advertised events to which they were opposed. In response, the chancellor and vice chancellor for academic affairs wrote a letter that states in part, "As members of the IPFW academic community, we are obliged to respect the opinions of others, even if we disagree, and to hear them out in the spirit of mutual respect and shared commitment to the pursuit of knowledge." My departmental mission includes educating students "as concerned, caring citizens in a democracy." What are the sources of support for difference and disagreement at your institution? How can we communicate to students that a university education involves grappling with viewpoints different from one's own? It is useful to locate institutional support for constructive disagreement, and to discuss these documents with students. Students often have no way of being aware of such priorities unless we tell them they exist.

In addition to institutional support for a range of viewpoints, it is crucial for individual faculty to take stock of our own comfort level with disagreement in the classroom. How do we respond when students disagree, raise an issue about which we have strong feelings, or assert viewpoints on social issues about which we have little knowledge? Particularly when instructors feel unfamiliar with sharp differences in the classroom and with facilitating related conversations, it can be useful to begin such dialogue with topics with which we are familiar and feel more at ease discussing. In short, instructors might construct a few class sessions around contentious social issues that feel approachable, and then evaluate: Who was comfortable? Who was not? What did I do? How did I feel? Who spoke up? Who did not? What did students learn? What did I learn?

Instructors can also create a classroom environment that normalizes the relevance of different viewpoints to the learning process. The syllabus, assignments, and readings all offer opportunities for integrating disagreement into the learning process. Syllabi might include guidelines for disagreement and dialogue. Readings can encourage consideration of a range of viewpoints or an awareness of democratic practices and the components of dialogue (Guttman and Thompson 2004;

Opposing Viewpoints, Resource Center). Finally, assignments can require analysis of two or more different perspectives. In this way, disagreement and multiple viewpoints become central to all aspects of learning.

In addition to reconsideration of the syllabus, readings, and assignments, it is possible to structure in-class time so that the instructor integrates different viewpoints into group work and class discussion. Instructors might begin the semester with students discussing their experiences with conflict related to difficult social issues in class. Students might individually write down: What are their experiences with disagreement in class? How did disagreement feel? What were the outcomes? In pairs, students can discuss what they wrote. Finally, as a class, students can articulate guidelines for disagreement that the class will rely on over the semester. These guidelines can also be posted on a class website. This process signals the desirability of disagreement, and the idea that such dialogue requires thoughtfulness.

A second classroom strategy is engaging and validating students' differing perspectives. When students do in-class group work, I will often ask them to write their answers to focused questions, such as "What does this article say about the media, race, and crime?" In addition to each group writing responses on paper, students then write group responses on the board. Students might put an "A" by statements on which group members agree, and a "D" by those on which group members disagree. Once all groups have done this, there may be 20 or 30 statements on the board. I then ask students to engage each other. Regarding what is on the board, what

needs clarification? Where do they have questions for each other? Where do they disagree and why? In some cases, I will put what they have written on the board on the class website as a way of validating their knowledge. We can return to conversations, pick up assertions they have made and discuss them from a different angle. Students become eager to articulate their own ideas and to understand others'. This process of articulation, questioning, disagreeing, clarifying, and listening can become a way of learning.

Disagreement and sharply different opinions in classroom settings rarely come in comfortable or contained packages. Rather, such conversations are unpredictable, leak out where we did not even see the possibility of a hole, disappoint, and disturb. Instructors can work at building a classroom environment in which constructive disagreement related to difficult social issues is central to the learning process, and in doing so, can communicate the idea that such dialogue is possible and has concrete benefits, both pedagogical and democratic.

References

Colby, A., T. Ehrlich, E. Beaumont, and J. Stephens. 2003. *Educating citizens: Preparing America's undergraduates for lives of moral and civic responsibility.* San Francisco: Jossey-Bass.

Gutmann, A. and D. Thompson. 2004. *Why deliberative democracy?* Princeton, N.J.: Princeton University Press.

Opposing Viewpoints Resource Center, Greenhaven Press. http://www.galegroup.com/OpposingViewpoints/.

Doing It Right: Reflections on Experience

THOMAS A. P. SINCLAIR
BINGHAMTON UNIVERSITY

Civic engagement is becoming a vital part of the development of higher education curricula. Students want their education to be relevant and to make a difference. Community organizations with limited managerial capacity are under pressure to deliver their services in increasingly complex environments, and they want to draw upon the resources of students and faculty

at their local universities to help them. Faculty and administrators view civic engagement as one strategy to bridge the gap between town and gown. While the potential benefits are high, more than any other classroom experience, a service-learning project demands careful planning and high levels of commitment from you for it to contribute to the civic engagement of students and/or community members. Service-learning projects merge service activities with learning objectives (Eyler and Giles 1999, 3–5). The learning experience affects real people in tangible ways and reflects upon your students, your program, and you. This essay offers tips for planning and implementing service-learning projects that will improve the chances that everyone involved will have a positive experience. While I work with master's level public administration students, many of these tips will apply to any in-depth, classroom-based service-learning projects.

Planning

Many community-based organizations contact university faculty looking for expertise and assistance. These requests may cover almost any discipline or profession. A historical district might seek help in developing an inventory of a neighborhood's historical assets, or a small airport might want an economic impact assessment completed, or an environmental group might want to assess the health of a local watershed. Indeed the list of possible service projects exceeds any department's capacity to complete them. Consequently, faculty members can afford to be selective about choosing projects that match their courses' learning objectives.

When evaluating a potential project, ask yourself and the requesting group some key questions.

• Are there direct and specific linkages between the project and your course objectives? Assess whether the required course readings will help the students complete their project. If they do not, then you should consider revising the course or the project, or wait for another project that better fits your course objectives.

• Do project deadlines line up with your academic calendar? If most of the project work occurs early in the semester, you may overload students early on. On the other hand, if the project is due after the semester is over, the students will not be available to help with any last minute tasks required to complete it.

• Does the proposed project enjoy the full support of the stakeholders who will need to be involved to make it happen? You do not want your students to become participants in difficult political battles.

No matter how exciting the project sounds, do your homework before committing a class to a project.

You may assume that a match between your course objectives and the scope of the project along with your good will, extraordinary energy, commitment to the ideals of service learning, and knowledge of the subject matter is sufficient to make a project succeed. While necessary, these are not sufficient conditions for success. Study the growing literature on service learning (Jacoby & Associates 1996; Eyler and Giles 1999; Kenny, et al. 2002) and, if you have one, talk with staff in your university's service-learning office. Assess whether the work that students will do falls within the scope of human subjects review at your university. Even "small" community-based learning projects will take significant preparation, and time in-class and during your office hours. If you intend to involve all your students in a course, think through how you and the participating organization will provide a consistent and meaningful experience for 15–40 students. Solving that problem by creating more than one service-learning project in a course multiplies the logistical and pedagogical issues that you will need to address.

Implementation

When you design a community-based learning project, you are creating an organization staffed by part-time employees with varying levels of commitment and, as a colleague noted, you have no control over the hiring process. Take time to prepare your students for their service work by introducing them to the basic rules of conduct, decorum, dress, team work, and ethics. Debrief students frequently as they work with their organizations or clients. If you approach these matters systematically as part of your course objectives, your students will be more effective participants in the project, and you will limit conflicts or uncomfortable situations.

No matter what level of experience your students have, you should expect them to make uneven contributions to the project, with varying degrees of enthusiasm and ability. Your project should have sufficient "slack" so that it does not depend on outstanding contributions from every student.

A service-learning project requires you to balance project outcomes with course objectives. These projects are like dissertations, they look easy when you are designing them, but executing those designs often entails scaling them back to a more manageable size. For example, because it almost always takes considerable effort for student teams to organize themselves, it often takes longer to conduct interviews or participate in meetings than you might expect. Be careful not to orient your course (and possibly student assessment) around unattainable project expectations. One semester, I promised to help a small county develop a performance-based budget using twenty five graduate students as liaisons with the different county departments. In contrast, one of my colleagues had her students conduct just one brief analysis as part of a strategic planning course. Guess which professor got the rave reviews? It was not the one whose students needed to travel to interviews and have frequent contact with preoccupied department heads to finish their assignments!

Make sure that the staff in the participating organization who will be working with your students are prepared. Orient them to the course objectives, and the students' roles in the project. Manage all critical operational communications with organizational staff yourself, and be very precise with your students if they need to give a consistent message to organizational personnel or clients. The success of a project depends upon your detailed knowledge of the communications between students and organizational personnel and your ability to correct misperceptions quickly and effectively.

Build redundancies into your community-based projects. If your project depends upon everything working like clockwork, it may be threatened by relatively minor problems. Inevitably, team members will miss assignments or make mistakes and have to redo tasks. Organizational staff will get sick, or not return telephone calls. You will make mistakes too. Mistakes are easy to correct when you are working alone, but not when an entire class is conscientiously repeating an error. Careful preparation will reduce problems, but you should expect mistakes, so create flexible processes that identify problems quickly and facilitate their correction.

Conclusion

Service-learning projects are outstanding tools for bringing together students and communities and engaging them in a joint learning activity. The more you combine careful planning with flexible implementation, the greater your chances are of providing your students and participating organizations with positive outcomes and a memorable learning experience.

References

Eyler, J. and D. E. Giles, Jr. 1999. *Where's the learning in service-learning?* San Francisco: Jossey-Bass.

Jacoby, B., ed. 1996. *Service-learning in higher education: Concepts and practices.* San Francisco: Jossey-Bass.

Kenny, M. E., L. A. K. Simon, K. Kiley-Brabeck, and R. M. Lerner. 2002. *Learning to serve: Promoting civil society through service-learning.* Boston: Kluwer.

Matching Goals to Students' Interests

NADIA RUBAII-BARRETT
BINGHAMTON UNIVERSITY

Effective civic engagement is as much about addressing the individual needs of one's students as it is about serving the needs of a community. If one of the goals is to encourage students to stay involved beyond the duration and scope of class activities, they must develop a sense that the engagement is meaningful and rewarding, not simply a fulfillment of a course requirement. In my experience, students and the community gain so much more, and the relationship is much more likely to continue after the semester, when I have students conduct self-assessment activities early in the semester, then discuss with them how to use those self-assessments to identify appropriate volunteer activities that will advance their personal and professional goals *and* contribute to the community.

When designing civic engagement activities for your class, it is important to consider which outcomes are most important. Perry and Thomson (2004) identify fifteen potential outcomes or benefits that may accrue to individuals performing the service, the beneficiaries of the service, or institutions and the broader communities. Their focus is on large-scale civic service programs, such as AmeriCorps. Programs of this magnitude may realistically strive to achieve measurable improvements in the quality and quantity of service provided to the target populations, or to realize institutional or community-wide changes, in addition to the benefits accrued to student participants. Courses that incorporate community-based learning as a central pedagogical feature may also aspire to go beyond individual student benefits to make a noticeable contribution to the community, although their ability to do so may be limited (Barber 1997). When designing community engagement activities that will serve only as one component of a course, an instructor would be well advised to focus on the outcomes which more directly affect the student.

Student benefits from civic engagement may take many forms, including increased skills, a heightened sense of civic responsibility, greater self-esteem, increased tolerance for diversity, a sense of satisfaction, improved mental or physical well-being, or more educational opportunities (Perry and Thomson 2004), or a greater sense of empowerment (Schwerin 1997). It is unrealistic to expect that all or even most of these would be achieved through an individual service activity or that they are of equal importance to all students. Depending on the subject matter of the course, the instructor's goals, and the students' goals for themselves, some outcomes may be of higher priority than others.

In a political science or public administration course, having the student develop or enhance their sense of civic responsibility may be deemed most important, whereas a class in sociology may identify increased tolerance for diversity as the most desired outcome of the service. An engineering course may place greater emphasis on skill development and application. Within the context of an instructor's expectations for a course, there are also considerations about individual student needs and motivations.

When I first began requiring community service activities as a component in my courses on public administration and public policy, I allowed students to select almost any service activity and simply required documentation of hours they contributed and a paper on what they learned in relation to the course material. This was a largely unsatisfactory process for everyone involved. Undergraduate and graduate students alike seemed unable to identify appropriate activities and to make meaningful connections to the course. Students who volunteer in the community in the absence of en-

thusiasm and motivation cannot possibly reflect well on the university, nor are they likely to generate any long-term commitments to engagement.

I have found that it is important to spend time on the front end to identify students' interests, interaction preferences, and attitudes about issues and groups before asking them to get involved in the community. This information is then used to identify goals and objectives for the service activity, and to determine an appropriate activity.

To obtain information about students' interests and attitudes, I provide students with a list of five to 10 issues facing the community and I ask them to "[r]ank the following issues in terms of their importance to the community" and "[r]ank the following issues in terms your interest in them." For those issues at the top of both lists, each student answers an additional set of questions. These questions assess the student's knowledge of the current status of that issue in the community, understanding of and/or experience with the public and private entities involved in the issue, and personal views regarding how the issue should be addressed. Documenting the students' perceptions on the issues at this stage gives them a basis for comparison to assess how their views may have changed as a result of their community involvement.

Once the list of potential issues has been narrowed, the next step is to determine appropriate goals and define the scope of the service activity. Self-reflection and self-assessments are the most valuable tools in this process. Carr-Ruffino (2003) provides several useful instruments to gauge students' values and comfort with diversity. Student preferences for methods of learning and types of interactions can be assessed through well-established tests such as the Learning Styles Inventory (Kolb 1984) or the Keirsey Temperament Sorter, an abbreviated version of the Myers Briggs Type Inventory (Keirsey and Bates 1984). In addition, I ask students to self-evaluate their writing, research, presentation, and interpersonal skills. Alternatively, students can be given assignments which allow the instructor to assess these skills. Finally, students are asked to list key aspects of their educational and/or professional aspirations.

I review the results of these varied assessments and then meet with the student to identify civic engagement activities which would best meet the student's needs and interests, while also serving a useful, albeit limited, function for the community. In small, graduate courses, I meet individually with each student to discuss the results of their assessments. In larger, undergraduate classes, I meet with groups of students who identify similar sets of strengths, weaknesses, and interests, to discuss service options that would meet their needs.

Students are encouraged to build upon their strengths, but to also address at least one weakness. That is, the service activity should allow them to spend much of their time and energy in ways which they feel comfortable and have interest. A small amount of the activity should force them to work on improving skills or expanding their experiences to address their self-identified weaknesses. Consider the situation where the assessments indicate that a student who has administrative aspirations has strong research and writing skills, but is an introvert who is terrified of public speaking and has had little or no experience interacting with public officials. In this case, I would encourage the student to select a project for which most of the work would take the form of research and writing a report, but that would include one short presentation to a small audience or several meetings with agency officials, to either gather information or to share the results of the research.

One of the obstacles to civic engagement is that students may not know how or where to begin. Self-assessments can give students direction and focus for their service activities. In my experience, when students approach the service activity with a sense of purpose, their passion is more likely to flow from the experience, and they are more likely to continue their engagement in the future.

References

Barber, B. R. 1997. Afterword. In R. M. Battistoni and W. E. Hudson, eds. *Experiencing citizenship: Concepts and models for service-learning in political science*, 227–235. Washington, D.C.: American Association for Higher Education.

Carr-Ruffino, N. 2003. *Managing diversity: People skills for a multicultural workplace*. Boston: Pearson.

Keirsey, D. and M. Bates. 1984. *Please understand me: Character & temperament types*. Del Mar, Calif.: Prometheus Nemesis Book Co.

Perry, J. L. and A. M. Thomson. 2004. *Civic service: What difference does it make?* Armonk, N.Y.: M. E. Sharpe.

Schwerin, E. 1997. Service-learning and empowerment. In R. M. Battistoni and W. E. Hudson, eds., *Experiencing citizenship: Concepts and models for service-learning in political science*, 203–214. Washington, D.C.: American Association for Higher Education.

Setting Service-Learning Goals

Lisa Dicke and Gera McGuire
University of North Texas

To effectively design a service-learning course faculty members should carefully consider the learning objectives that are desired. Below are several perspectives, each of which pursues a different set of learning objectives.

Perspectives on Service-Learning
Community Service

This perspective recognizes the benefits of service to students and to the community through partnerships with local nonprofits. Among the learning objectives are helping students develop feelings of personal efficacy and stronger ties with their community. Grassroots organizations may be able to build administrative capacities and initiate projects that could not otherwise be pursued.

Moral Development

Service learning can be used to create experiences that promote moral development through the recognition of others, respect for collaboration, and stewardship. In light of technological advances that have isolated people and left them with fewer social skills, the learning objectives include helping students become more aware of the needs of others. Empathy is an "emotional response to a perceived need [which] is a result of the perceiver adopting the perspective of the person in need" (Batson 1991, 83). Projects that provide opportunities for students to adopt the perspective of another are most likely to be helpful.

Political Activism

Service learning can be used as a means for promoting the cause of social justice (Rocha 2001), and combating public apathy, distrust, and contempt toward government and among citizens through student and community involvement (Barber and Battistoni 1993; Kahne and Westheimer 1996; Astin 1997). Service learning asks students to do things *with* others rather than *for* them (Karasik 1993).

Instrumental

Successful service-learning projects from this perspective result in the students' demonstration of specific academic or work-related competencies (Kenworthy-U'ren 1999). Although, by definition a reflective component is required, personal growth or political achievements are by-products of the experience. Students lacking practical experience have opportunities to apply learning outside of the classroom and build a resume that extends beyond academics. Projects enhance and strengthen students' knowledge and skills.

Tips for First Timers:

• Determine which perspective(s) promote your learning objectives.

• Identify the types of activities that are most likely to lead to the achievement of the objectives. Projects should be designed to include these activities.

• A job description should be prepared to ensure understanding among all parties, and expectations regarding dress, behavior, etc., should be outlined.

• Offer several projects so that each student may participate in one that is personally rewarding.

• Be aware of the diversity of students and make efforts to align opportunities appropriately.

. . . an experience of racism, reflected upon in the safety of a classroom, could create optimal conditions for learning. Injustices experienced by fellow students could be introduced to those who would otherwise not know or feel racism directly.

• Design challenging but not overly ambitious projects that fit available time frames.

• Evaluate to determine if the desired learning objectives were met.

Encompassing Service Learning in Non-Traditional Areas of Study

Although courses in public affairs, political science, or education are a natural fit for service learning, other fields also may benefit.

• Computer science majors could co-design a website for a nonprofit or minority-owned business.

• A business major might facilitate strategic planning sessions or create a business plan for a resale shop.

• Chemistry or math majors might serve as mentors for students in underserved schools.

• Physical sciences students could research or test the velocity of crash impacts on children not properly restrained. Such information could be provided to a nonprofit seeking funding for a child restraint program.

Practical Lessons Learned

Regardless of how well designed the service-learning project, there are always surprises (Dicke, Dowden and Torres 2004). In an undergraduate American Government course recently, among the projects was a voter registration drive. The learning objectives for the course were aligned with the instrumental perspective; that is, it was hoped that students would learn more about voting processes through conducting a voter registration drive. What follows, however, is an account taken from student evaluations.

Five students participated in a voter registration drive at a local store. Two students (both Caucasians) arrived early to set-up. During the initial contacts, the manager of the store had been pleasant and even helped the students set up the tables. Shortly thereafter, three other students arrived (all African-American). At that juncture the manager informed the group that they did not represent "the look" the store wanted to portray. As one student reported, "I immediately knew what image we did not exemplify. We were the wrong color . . . and . . . on the wrong side of town."

The subsequent discussion in the classroom raised important Constitutional issues. It also sparked the desire among some to consider staging a boycott. But, one student said "something like this shouldn't happen in a school-based project."

When facilitated correctly, an experience of racism, reflected upon in the safety of a classroom, could create optimal conditions for learning. Injustices experienced by fellow students could be introduced to those who would otherwise not know or feel racism directly. From a political activism perspective it also might result in student activism. However, the learning outcomes were not those that were anticipated. And the question remains, should something like this have happened in a "*school-based project*"?

Conclusion

The more transparent the reasons for using service learning, "the more likely it is that the service and learning outcomes will be successful" (Morton 1996, 278). Community organizations have needs that encompass a broad scope of potential service-learning opportunities. Projects that offer few opportunities for students to interact with others, however, are less likely to result in the achievement of objectives aligned with a moral development perspective since feelings of empathy are not likely to emerge. Likewise, projects that encourage students to challenge injustices may help students achieve learning objectives congruent with the political activ-

ism perspective, but they may also result in conflict and unanticipated consequences.

There is no magic formula that can be used to ensure that students will become actively engaged in their communities. With careful design, however, service learning offers faculty members a means for creating powerful community-based learning opportunities.

References

Astin, A. W. 1997. Liberal education and democracy: The case for pragmatism. *Liberal Education* 83, no. 4:4–15.

Barber, B. R., and R. Battistoni. 1993. A season of service: Introducing service learning into the liberal arts curriculum. *PS: Political Science and Politics* 26:235–240.

Batson, C. D. 1991. *The altruism question: Toward a social-psychological answer.* Hillsdale, N.J.: Lawrence Erlbaum Associates.

Dicke, L. A., S. A. Dowden, and J. L. Torres. 2004. Successful service learning: A matter of ideology? *JPAE: Journal of Public Affairs Education* 10, no. 3:199–208.

Kahne, J., and J. Westheimer. 1996. In the service of what?: The politics of service learning. *Phi Delta Kappan* 77, no. 9:593–599.

Karasik, J. 1993. Not only bowls of delicious soup: Youth service today. In S. Sagawa and S. Halperin, eds., *Visions of service: The future of the national and community service act,* 1–61. Washington, D.C.: National Women's Law Center and American Youth Policy Forum.

Kenworthy-U'ren, A. L. 1999. Management students as consultants: An alternative perspective on the service-learning call to action. *Journal of Management Inquiry* 8, no. 4:379–387.

Morton, K. 1996. Issues related to integrating service-learning into the curriculum. In B. Jacoby, ed. *Service-learning in higher education: Concepts and practices,* 276–296. San Francisco: Jossey-Bass.

Rocha, C. J. 2000. Evaluating experiential teaching methods in a policy practice course: The case for service learning to increase political participation. *Journal of Social Work Education* 36, no. 1:53–63.

CLASSROOM ACTIVITIES

Making Democracy Matter in the Classroom

JOAN MANDLE
COLGATE UNIVERSITY
AND
ADAM WEINBERG
WORLD LEARNING

Democracy Matters is a national organization started by a group of faculty at Colgate University dedicated to engaging students in politics. Our focus is on pro-democracy issues and especially involvement with the movement for a fair and accountable government and campaign finance reform (voter-owned elections, often know as Clean Elections). Over the last four years, we have developed and tested a number of successful service-learning exercises. Each exercise follows a simple four-step model:

Educate: Start by giving students readings and websites that inform them about the democratic process.

Draw Connections: Work with students to draw connections to the larger substantive issues being discussed in the class.

Inform Others: Develop and pilot action campaigns to inform other students on campus and/or people in the community about the issue.

Reflection Exercise: Reflect on the experience as it informs students' own views about politics and political involvement, and the opportunities to get their peers involved.

Example of a Basic Exercise

Our basic exercise is designed to help students explore the issues of money in politics, while also developing their political voice and expanding their available repertoire of political actions.

Part 1: Educating and Drawing Connections

The first part of the exercise is designed to get students to formulate their views about the effect of money as it shapes American politics. Typically, a faculty member will tailor this to a larger course theme (e.g. the environment, race, women's issues, elections).

We suggest to students the following three websites:

1. www.democracymatters.org
2. www.publiccampaign.org
3. www.opensecrets.org

We then ask them to come to class with a 2–4 page essay addressing the following question: *Why do some people believe there is too much money in politics and how does the issue of money in politics affect the larger issues being explored in the class?*

Part 2: Taking an Action

Students with similar views are asked to participate in groups of 3–5. They are then asked to design some form of action campaign that raises awareness about the issues they explored in the essays. Each group should produce a 1–2 page description of their action campaign that includes:

A) *A Goal:* What do they want to accomplish? What is the message they want to inform others about?

B) *A Strategy:* Whom do they want to inform (the audience)? This could be the general student body, a subgroup on campus, or people in the local community, and how do they intend to do this?

C) *Tactic:* How are they going to get the message to the target audience?

Students can go to the Democracy Matters website and follow the "Student Organizing Resources" link to find a large array of projects done by students on other campuses. They find examples of the following:

A faculty member might give the students a week

Table 2.1. Sample Actions for Campus Awareness Projects

PETITION DRIVES: students have set up tables at the student center to hand out flyers and other materials that express their views.

PUBLIC THEATER: students produce a short skit that can be performed on campus (dining hall, campus green) or in community public spaces (local park, recreation center, mall, or street).

TEACH-INS AND DEBATES: including faculty and facilitated by students and/or faculty for other students and/or community members.

LECTURES: done by students in other classes or in local high schools.

OP-ED PIECES: written for the student or local newspaper.

LETTER WRITING CAMPAIGNS: students write to their hometown newspapers or to elected officials.

POSTER CAMPAIGNS: themed and rolled out over a few weeks across campus and the community.

GRASSROOTS CANVASSING: door-to-door canvass in the residential halls and/or in the community where students hand out materials and talk with people about the issue.

LOBBYING ELECTED OFFICIALS: visiting with elected officials and talking to them about the issue.

to design the campaigns. Groups then present the designs to the class. This allows for a robust conversation in class about the trade-offs inherent to different types of campaigns. One way to lead this discussion is to have students comment on each campaign design using the following questions:

1. Is it feasible? (How easy or hard is it to pull off the campaign?)

2. It is desirable? Will it work? What are the pros and cons?

Part 3: Critical Reflection

Students are then asked to draw on the experience of their campaigns to comment on broader issues discussed in the course. How would they develop a broad-based campaign on campus to get students educated and activated around the issues discussed in the course? Or you can have students write more about the actions they took. One idea is to send the students back to the Democracy Matters website. Ask them to read and comment on a paper by Professor Adam Weinberg on the Democracy Matters website entitled, "Creating A Life Long Commitment To Politics." Ask students to use their experience to comment on the article.

Replicating the Model

This exercise can be done in a number of different ways. It can be spread across an entire semester. It also makes a wonderful extra-credit project for 3–5 students in a larger class. It can be done in a brief 2–3 week period.

Regardless of how you use the model, we would offer four observations based on our experiences:

First, the basic model of *educate, draw connections, take an action, and reflect* can be used for any issue. Start with open-ended web-based exploration that gets students to grapple with how change occurs through the democratic process. Then get students to reflect on what this means for the course material. Students always come away from this process with ideas that they want to share with their peers. Give students space to raise those views on campus through an action campaign, and then give them time to reflect on what they have learned.

Second, faculty will find many nonprofit organizations and local community groups excited to partner with you. You don't have to partner, but most faculty find that nonprofits can bring resources to projects in ways that deepens learning.

Third, for many students this will be their first time trying to take a public stand on an issue. From our perspective, taking an action matters if they learn to de-velop an action campaign (goals, strategies, tactics) and they have time to reflect on the experience.

Fourth, our model is purposefully interdisciplinary. The websites and readings pull from sociology, econom-ics, political science, the environmental sciences, and philosophy. Getting students to think across disciplines opens up room for them to develop their own views.

Conclusion

By engaging students in active learning and organizing around deepening democracy, they begin to understand the importance of civic engagement and acquire some of the skills necessary for an engaged citizenry. The issue of money in politics is an excellent hook because it resonates with students and can be connected to a wide variety of subject and class material. By creating action projects to raise awareness, students not only learn to articulate their own positions but also to listen to the views of others—thus engaging in the respectful give and take essential to a functioning democracy.

"Doing" Engagement

Heather Laube
University of Michigan–Flint

I believe that asking students to "do"—and in "do-ing" to make connections between scholarship, their lives, and larger social institutions and social structures—has a significant impact on students' sense of their ability to impact their communities, social policy, and the various organizations and institutions with which they interact. I use a very learning-centered (as opposed to content-centered) approach to course design, which focuses on application and reflection, and on providing students with an opportunity to combine academic learning with practical applications—skills that will be useful to them as active and informed citizens. To me, the goal of a learning-centered approach is not only to provide a piece of work by which to judge a student's knowledge or skills, but also to provide him or her with an opportunity to practice using the knowledge and skills acquired in the course.

A primary civic engagement goal is the expectation that by the end of the course the students should have the skills to articulate concerns to their peers, the media, and decision makers in an intellectually informed and compelling way. I have assigned what I call a "talking paper" in several courses. The goal of this paper is for the student to become an "expert" on an issue by choos-ing a timely topic relevant to the course. Their goal is not to simply state an opinion or restate what others say about the issue, but to take an informed position (that might be presented to peers, colleagues and/or policy makers) based on what they've learned. As a sociologist I believe civic engagement requires structural analysis, so I insist the students engage in sociological (thus in-stitutional/structural/systemic) critique of their chosen issue. They must use strong evidence to support their assertions, taking an informed stance on this issue. I have found it useful to suggest that they consider what they can teach others who may not be familiar with this issue—defining it, explaining what is at stake, and iden-tifying who benefits and who is harmed by the current state of affairs. They must address at least two questions/ critiques they might expect from an individual or group with a different point of view and propose at least one *systemic* change that might remedy the situation. Finally, students include an appendix indicating how one might take further action on this issue. Each of these steps allows students to practice civic engagement, while at the same time providing me the opportunity to assess the degree to which they are successfully connecting their academic knowledge and skills to a contemporary social concern. By framing this assignment as a "talking" paper, as opposed to a research paper, I have found that students embrace the role of expert and feel like they really do have the ability to contribute to the public discourse on their topic.

In my social movements course, students choose a movement and movement organization in which they actively participate. A colleague and I collaborated on developing two similar yet distinct engagement activities as a way to assess whether students achieved the goal of active participation and critical reflection. The first is what we called a "Public Discourse Adventure." One of the biggest challenges for many social movements is getting their issue(s) on the agenda, which often begins by thrusting the issue(s) into public discourse. Students must get their concern into the minds and on the tongues of people outside of their circle of concern, friends and family. In a two-to-three-page reflection, they relate their experience to course material. As you can imagine, this was difficult for some students, but many were quite creative, and the challenge itself was a good way for them to learn about the complexity of this form of active civic engagement (clear articulation of message, legal issues, organization). In a similar vein, students were asked to participate in a significant involvement experience with their movement

Science courses can address issues of the environment; health care/nursing can focus on issues of patient care, public health, and insurance; education can concentrate on student learning, school funding, and teacher education; art and music can explore freedom of expression. The possibilities are endless.

organization. This enabled them to learn about specific strategies and tactics of social movement organizations, practice various forms of engagement, and reflect on their experiences in a written document. As an aside— be sure to remind your students not to do anything illegal! These opportunities do arise and seem exciting, but a student's arrest related to fulfillment of a course requirement is, of course, not going to go over well with the administration.

Not all assessments of civic engagement need to be "active" or focused on "the public." The ability to analyze and employ scholarly concepts is important for any civically engaged person. The awareness of potential costs and benefits of various forms of civic engagement and the ability to discern which tactic is most likely to succeed in a given situation are necessary for those who hope to impact their communities. I have found that asking students to take the role of the expert in a given scenario seems to give them the confidence they need to really get behind and informed about an issue. Writing assignments that integrate course material with empirical observations and ask students to engage in precise and insightful critical analysis are useful for student practice and instructor assessment of civic engagement.

While it is easy to see how civic engagement can be integrated into sociology courses, these assessments can easily be used in a wide range of courses. Science courses can address issues of the environment; health care/nursing can focus on issues of patient care, public health, and insurance; education can concentrate on student learning, school funding, and teacher education; art and music can explore freedom of expression. The possibilities are endless. My overarching goal is that by the end of a course students possess the desire and capacity to be informed, engaged, and ACTIVE citizens, and the assessments I've described provide students with guidelines to follow as they *practice* civic engagement, while at the same time providing me with

material to assess the degree to which they are meeting this goal.

Understanding and Working with Perspectives

Patrick J. Ashton
Indiana University–Purdue University Fort Wayne

The vitality and strength of a democratic society like the United States depends in large part upon the willingness of its citizens to engage in mutual debate of the issues. Colby et al. (2003) argue that it is vital for colleges and universities to provide students with the tools to do so. Having students discuss their deeply held values and beliefs in the college classroom, though, is potentially threatening to both students and teacher. One concern is that the articulation of political or moral positions—especially by the professor—may be seen as either the enforcement of political correctness or indoctrination. Paradoxically, though, the more students have thought about these issues and learned to argue them through, the less susceptible they are to indoctrination. The key is to emphasize that no attempt at any sort of "conversion" is taking place, but rather the goals—in addition to the knowledge of various perspectives—are (1) an appreciation of the intelligence and humanity of those with other perspectives, and (2) a deepened understanding of, and commitment to, one's own perspective.

William Perry (1999) suggests that student intellectual development typically moves through a hierarchy of four stages from dualism, in which meaning and knowledge are clearly divided into two realms and authority is external, to committed relativism, in which authority is internal and difficult decisions and commitments are made in light of, and while sensitive to, the relativistic nature of knowledge. At this penultimate stage, students choose positions that are right for themselves and learn to articulate them.

There are a variety of ways of understanding and classifying perspectives. Below is a typology I have created to help students compare contrasting positions. This typology is not meant to take in all possible perspectives; rather, it attempts to describe and illustrate the dominant ideological positions that underlie much of the political debate in the United States today. Further,

these perspectives have been chosen to clearly illustrate two points vital to functioning in a pluralist democracy: (1) differing policies are often rooted in fundamentally incompatible values and beliefs; and (2) coalitions around specific policy issues are possible, despite the fact that different groups have contradictory values. The key to bridging differences and building political coalitions is finding the language that connects with another group's basic values. Space does not permit me to go into detail here describing each perspective; additional information is available from the author (Ashton 2003).

Discussion of ideological perspectives can and should occur in almost any college class. While social science and humanities courses naturally lend themselves to dissection of issues from differing viewpoints, the natural sciences and professional schools clearly touch on policy issues where reasonable, educated people may disagree. The exercises below are adaptable to a wide variety of disciplines and pedagogical strategies. I have used them in courses from the introductory to the graduate level in a variety of topic areas. My suggestion would be that each of the activities include, if possible, both a writing and a discussion component. Writing assignments can include short in-class discovery writing papers or longer take-home essays. Discussion formats range from pairs of students, to small groups (3 to 5 students), to large groups (6 to 12 students), to the class as a whole.

1. Have students regularly read and analyze the opinion page of your local newspaper or one they access online. Alternatively, they could examine a magazine or scholarly journal with articles on policy issues. Students should attempt to decode the perspective of each writer, showing how their conjectures are based upon the assumptions implicit in each author's argument as well as the actual argument itself. Students can present their

Table 2.2. Contemporary Perspectives on the Social World

	Organic Conservative	Individualist Conservative	Reform Liberal	Socialist Radical
View of Human Nature	Humans are inherently aggressive, competitive, selfish, and hierarchical. Individuals are motivated by potentially uncontrollable biological urges.	Humans are inherently selfish and highly individualistic. They are basically inert or lazy. Individuals are motivated by a rational calculation of self-interest (utilitarianism).	Similar to the Individualist Conservative: humans are generally selfish and individualistic, *but* individuals can be motivated by altruism under certain circumstances.	Human nature is *flexible*. Humans are fundamentally social, but collectively constitute their human nature differently in different forms of society. Individuals are motivated by desire to fulfill human potentials.
Nature of the Social Order	Humans need society to protect themselves from each other and from themselves. Inequality and hierarchy are natural and necessary. Society is a reality *sui generis*; it is like a functionally differentiated living organism in which each part must play its designated role for the overall stability of the whole.	Society exists to protect individual freedom; free market capitalism and private property are the basis of this freedom. Government is the main coercive force. Left to itself, society is a self-regulating mechanism (the "invisible hand"). Society is no more than the sum total of the individuals who make it up and exists only by agreement of those individuals (the "social contract").	Society is the forum in which formal equality among individuals is realized (meritocracy). Because free market capitalism has tendencies toward instability and injustice, the government must intervene to fine-tune the system and keep it running smoothly and fairly.	Society is necessary for human development; it is a system of social relations among individuals who both reproduce and alter these relations. Capitalism is a historically specific mode of production, the basis of which is exploitation and alienation. It is inherently unstable due to class conflict and internal contradictions.
Central Values	Authority, order, and tradition. Freedom *within* bounds prescribed by nature.	Individual liberty and private property (*laissez faire*). Freedom *from* restraint on the individual.	Individual civil rights and equal opportunity. Freedom *of* opportunity.	Equality and solidarity. Freedom *to* actively develop capacities by transcending barriers and creating new options.
Orientation to Social Change	The social system is normally in equilibrium (homeostatic). Change is disruptive and should be minimized. Social change, when it occurs, is episodic.	Change occurs in a naturally slow and incremental way as a result of the buildup of individual actions. Social change is cyclical, like the market.	Humans, through the vehicle of the state, must intervene to make pragmatic modifications in the social system. Social change is evolutionary (progress).	Change is produced by inherent conflict and internal contradictions combined with conscious collective action. Change is transformative (a dialectical process).

Table 2.2. Contemporary Perspectives on the Social World (cont.)

	Organic Conservative	Individualist Conservative	Reform Liberal	Socialist Radical
Ideal System	Paternalistic Capitalism. **Goal:** Stability through elite-controlled growth.	Free Market Capitalism. **Goal:** Increase the production of individual wealth. The least government is the best government.	Meritocratic, Welfare-state Capitalism. **Goal:** Expand and adjust the economic and political pie to provide equal opportunity, formal justice, and stability.	Democratic Socialism. **Goal:** Decentralized, fully democratic decisionmaking in the economic and political realms; distribution of wealth on the basis of need.
Cause of Social Problems	Sudden change which produces a breakdown in social control mechanisms.	Government coercion and disruption of the free market.	An unregulated economy and lack of equal opportunity in the meritocracy.	Exploitation, alienation, inequality, class conflict, and inherent contradictions.
Solution to Social Problems	Recover past traditions which reflect the immutable laws of nature.	Return to the basic principles of freemarket capitalism and rational selfishness.	The government must regulate the economy and the meritocracy to ensure stability and fairness.	Create a mass movement based on socialist principles which will transform both the people and the society.
Philosophers, Economists, and other Proponents	Thomas Aquinas(1225–1274) Edmund Burke (1729–1797) William F. Buckley George Will Rev. Jerry Falwell Rev. James Dobson	John Locke (1632–1704) Adam Smith (1732–1790) Jeremy Bentham (1748–1832) Ayn Rand (1905–1982) Milton Friedman Steve Forbes	John Stuart Mill (1806–1893) John Dewey (1859–1952) J. M. Keynes (1883–1946) John Kenneth Galbraith Paul Samuelson Lester Thurow	Karl Marx (1818–1883) Michl Harrington (1928–1989) Paul Sweezy Cornel West Noam Chomsky Michael Moore
Groups and Think Tanks	Focus on the Family Eagle Forum The Conservative Caucus The Hudson Institute The Heritage Foundation	The Libertarian Party American Conservative Union The Cato Institute American Enterprise Institute	NAACP American Civil Liberties Union (ACLU) People for the American Way Brookings Institution	Democratic Socialists of America (DSA) Midwest Academy Co-Op America Institute for Policy Studies
Periodicals	*National Review* *Conservative Digest* *American Spectator* *American Opinion* *Plain Truth*	*U.S. News & World Report* *Wall Street Journal* *Forbes, The Public Interest* *Human Events* *Commentary*	*Time* *Newsweek* *Harpers* *Atlantic Monthly* *Foreign Affairs*	*Z magazine* *The Progressive* *The Nation, Monthly Review* *Dollars and Sense* *Utne Reader*

analysis in the form of "show and tell" reports or they can be asked to write up their analysis and discuss it in class. Another variation would be to assign the same article or letter to different students, have them write up an analysis, then compare notes with others in class. Have them explore the reasons for any disagreements about authors' perspectives. Yet another variation would be to take the students on a field trip or assign them to go independently to a meeting of a public body where differing perspectives are likely to emerge in the debate (school board, city or county council, state legislature). Have students try to figure out the assumptions behind the views expressed. This exercise might also be accomplished by having students watch C-SPAN or local government meetings that are televised on cable TV.

2. Have students extrapolate the four perspectives to other issues that are relevant to your discipline. Possibilities include crime, poverty, drug abuse, or urban design in the social sciences, or environmental pollution, genetic engineering, alternative energy, or space exploration/colonization in the natural sciences or professional schools. Have students come up with policies to solve the selected problem. Student recommendations might take the form of policy "white papers," op-ed pieces, letters to the editor of a newspaper, or presentations.

3. Have students learn to take the role of the other

When it inspires people to get involved and when it kindles the spirit of volunteerism, persuasion is the stuff of civic engagement.

by arguing for a perspective that is not their own. Assign students a perspective, then pick a contemporary policy problem germane to your discipline. Ask each student or group to propose a solution consistent with their assigned perspective. Reports can be oral or written. Have students make bumper stickers advocating policies consistent with their assigned perspective. Stage a debate or create a series of role plays in which two or more individuals with different perspectives agree to disagree while at the same time attempting to find common ground.

4. Identify people in the community who hold significantly different perspectives. One method to identify these people is by following letters to the editor in your local newspaper. Invite these people in as a series of guest speakers, or bring them all in at once as a panel. Have students develop in advance a series of questions and issues for the guests to respond to. Have students debrief afterwards, orally or in writing.

References

Ashton, P. J. 2003. *Perspectives on contemporary society.* Department of Sociology, Indiana University–Purdue University Fort Wayne. http://users.ipfw.edu/ashton/courseinfo.

Colby, A., T. Ehrlich, E. Beaumont, and J. Stephens. 2003. *Educating citizens: Preparing America's undergraduates for lives of moral and civic responsibility.* San Francisco: Jossey-Bass.

Perry, W. G. 1999. *Forms of intellectual and ethical development in the college years.* San Francisco: Jossey-Bass.

Citizens Talking across the Curriculum

JAMES T KNAUER AND L. SULLIVAN ROSS
LOCK HAVEN UNIVERSITY OF PENNSYLVANIA

An ideal of strong, participatory citizenship informs much involvement in efforts to reform higher education to better educate future citizens. On this view of citizenship, civic education is not simply a job for the

political science department. It requires more than learning how government works. In addition to knowledge, strong citizens need the attitudes and capacities that will equip them for effective citizen discussion across a range of public issues in a deeply pluralistic society. And they need the experience of involvement in community affairs. This recent upsurge of concern for civic education has deep roots in higher education, as revealed in *Greater Expectations: A New Vision for Learning as a Nation Goes to College,* the recent influential study from the Association of American Colleges and Universities.

Greater Expectations advocates liberal learning for "all college aspirants" and across the disciplines, not only in traditional liberal arts disciplines but in professional and pre-professional programs as well. The goal is to help students become "intentional learners" who are "empowered through intellectual and practical skills, informed by knowledge and ways of knowing, responsible for personal actions and civic values." Strong democracy requires "intentional citizens" with interest in and concern for public affairs and with developed capacities for continuing civic learning and engagement (Barber 1984). Even in earlier highly elitist formulations, liberal learning has always had a civic mission. *Greater Expectations* universalizes and reconceptualizes that mission.

Dialogic pedagogy provides a particularly effective strategy for integrating civic education across the curriculum without sacrificing disciplinary content or traditional learning objectives. While research on dialogic pedagogy has focused primarily on k-12 education, its findings are quite relevant in higher education. Peer-to-peer deliberative dialogue has been shown to stimulate engaged learning, especially when students ask each other authentic questions and when they enter into meta-discussions, reflecting, for example, on the nature of disagreements among participants (Simon 2003; Hess and Posselt 2002; Wells 1999). Cognitive tasks of this sort are, of course, widely recognized as at the heart of college education, sometimes taught in special courses focused on critical thinking and frequently incorporated in syllabi across the curriculum. Student-to-student deliberative dialogue on public issues can advance both liberal learning and civic education goals in a wide variety of courses at all levels of instruction.

Dialogic pedagogy can be frustrating. Achieving high-quality learning is not easy. On the one hand, effectiveness requires that student participation be largely autonomous. On the other, left to their own devices students rarely achieve the informed dialogue and depth of reflection desired. Thus genuine student-to-student dialogue is rare in most classrooms, both because it is so difficult for us as instructors to stay out of the way and

because it is difficult for many students to engage each other directly under our watchful eyes. Specially designed dialogue materials and services suitable for use in college courses can help faculty realize the potential of dialogic pedagogy.

National Issues Forums provide a tested and effective approach to deliberative dialogue, and they are receiving increasing attention on college campuses, for both curricular and co-curricular use (www.nifi.org). NIFs use a non-partisan issue framework that identifies a public issue, such as poverty or race relations, and presents three or four perspectives on the issue. Each perspective lays out its own value priorities, assessment of root problems and proposed course of action. These approaches serve as a platform for small-group deliberations.

Democracy Lab is a web-based learning system that fosters civic engagement and the development of intentional learners through deliberative dialogue on public issues (www.teachingdemocracy.org). It offers multiple opportunities for student participation and leadership mentoring, most prominently through its 10-week online forums. Using an adapted NIF model, these forums lead students through an agenda that links dialogue to inquiry and to action. Agenda-setting announcements and instructional modules guide and inform the process, helping students develop the skills of deliberative dialogue, which are the skills of critical and empathic thinking.

Deliberative dialogue takes place in small groups using asynchronous bulletin boards. Since dialogue groups bring together students from several schools and different courses, participants are often called upon to explain material from their course, providing opportunities for learning through teaching. Also, presenting this knowledge in a deliberative setting necessitates more than surface-level assertion—students must dig deeper into the logics and assumptions underlying any knowledge. Such critical thinking is balanced and informed by the oft-underappreciated skill of empathic thinking (Elbow 1986). Indeed, for many students the most challenging and rewarding part of participating in a Democracy Lab forum is the experience of seeing through others' eyes.

All this is not to say that student discussion in Democracy Lab forums always achieves the level of sophistication faculty hope for. One of the concerns sometimes expressed by faculty is that student dialogue groups spend too much time exchanging ignorance. There are two ways of looking at this. One might say that these students are simply not yet ready to participate in productive dialogue because they don't know enough. Alternatively, the opportunity to observe one's students using what you are teaching them can be a powerful formative evaluation tool. Student dialogue groups are a sort of practicum in which students can demonstrate what they have learned (or have not).

Citizens teach and learn from each other all the time, what a colleague calls "public pedagogy." Public pedagogy often fails to engage in critical thinking so citizens spread rumors and misinformation. Public pedagogy often fails to engage in empathic thinking so citizens spread stereotypes and misunderstanding. Democracy Lab offers instructors the opportunity to observe the public pedagogy practices of their students and to take corrective action. Often this involves more knowledge and better understanding. But the need for more knowledge is neither more important nor developmentally prior to the need for a clearer awareness of the limitations of ones own experience and an appreciation of the value of seeing the world from other points of view. Deliberative dialogue on public issues deserves a prominent place in our efforts to revitalize and connect civic education and liberal learning.

References

Barber, B. 1984. *Strong democracy: Participatory politics for a new age.* Berkeley: University of California Press.

Elbow, P. 1986. *Embracing contraries: Explorations in learning and teaching.* New York: Oxford University Press.

Hess, D. and J. Posselt. 2002. How high school students experience and learn from the discussion of controversial public issues. *Journal of Curriculum and Supervision* 17:283–314.

Simon, K. 2003. *Moral questions in the classroom: How to get kids to think deeply about real life and their schoolwork.* New Haven, Conn.: Yale University Press.

Wells, G. 1999. *Dialogic inquiry: Towards a sociocultural practice and theory of education.* Cambridge: Cambridge University Press.

Getting People's Attention

MATTHEW R. AUER
INDIANA UNIVERSITY BLOOMINGTON

"Stop selling. Start helping," urges motivational speaker Zig Ziglar. This is honorable advice for anyone intent on making the world a better place. Nevertheless, there are a lot of sellers out there, and it is important to know what they are selling and to what end. Politicians, journalists, business professionals, religious leaders, teachers, and our own loved ones are consummate sellers of opinions, morals, and received wisdom. Of course, they are often selling us what *they want us* to believe is essential or desirable. Trouble is, our interests and theirs are not always consonant.

Some people are good at getting our attention and persuading us to act. In the democratic arena, the persuasive speaker, writer, or film-maker garners support for policies and political agendas. Public officials and ordinary citizens alike can be swayed, even seduced, by a crisp exhortation, a pithy sound bite, or an inspired essay. When it inspires people to get involved and when it kindles the spirit of volunteerism, persuasion is the stuff of civic engagement.

So it is worthwhile exploring the psychology of making, sending, and receiving persuasive, promotional messages. Students who are wise to the subconscious elements of advocacy and promotion tend to better understand the motives of the messenger. Moreover, the civically engaged student who masters the art of persuasion is better able to convince others to join his/her cause.

The Triple Appeal Principle

Harold Lasswell's classic concept, the "triple appeal principle," is a useful starting point for the study and practice of getting people to listen, buy in, and act. Lasswell, a founder of the policy sciences school of public policy, was fascinated by Sigmund Freud's classic tripartite division of personality: the id, ego, and superego. Lasswell suggested that there were political analogues to these personality types, and that policy ideas and propaganda were processed differently by the different segments of personality. The impulsive side (id) is affected by political messages that arouse infantile responses,

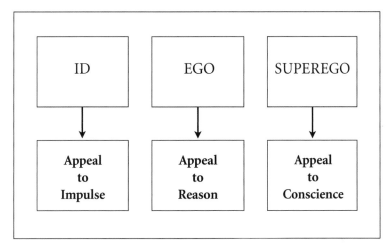

Figure 2.1. Elements of the Triple Appeal Principle

like fear, anger, disgust, or delight. Messages requiring calculation or other forms of higher reasoning affect the rational part of personality (ego). Moral questions and concerns arouse the subject's conscience (superego). Figure 2.1 exhibits the three divisions of personality and their political analogues.

"Persons, institutions, occasions, policies and practices, doctrines, and myths and legends may be examined for the purpose of discerning their appeals to impulse, conscience, and reason," Lasswell declared (1932, 524–525). He went farther still, proclaiming "a principle of triple appeal" as a tool of political management—that is, as a means for managing opinion formation and the conjuring of public support.

The social and behavioral sciences offer ample opportunities to study the triple appeal principle. It has a place in the humanities, too. Consider, for example, the study of great American political speeches such as Lincoln's Second Inaugural. The second paragraph of that speech, less than 100 words in total, targets all three divisions of personality. (Triple appeal elements are embedded in italics, below). Lincoln avowed:

> On the occasion corresponding to this four years ago, all thoughts were anxiously directed to an impending civil war (*impulse*). All dreaded it—all sought to avert it (*impulse*). While the inaugural address was being delivered from this place, devoted altogether to saving the Union without war, insurgent agents were in the city seeking to destroy it without war—seeking to dissolve the Union, and divide effects, by negotiation (*conscience*). Both parties deprecated war; but one of them would make war rather than let the nation survive; and

the other would accept war rather than let it perish (*conscience* and *reason*). And the war came.

Great works of fiction can be illuminated by the triple appeal principle, too. John Steinbeck's *Of Mice and Men,* which many students will have encountered in grammar school, is a case in point. Lennie, the mentally retarded main character, adores rabbits, appealing to our own affection for pet animals (impulse). Lennie's well-being depends on the wits (reason) of his only friend, George. The latter makes a decisive and heartbreaking choice at the story's end (conscience).

Civic Engagement and the Triple Appeal Principle

Civically minded students can test drive the triple appeal principle in the real world. To illustrate, students can critique local advocacy groups' or local government agencies' promotional materials, such as mission statements or speeches of organizational leaders—using the triple appeal principle as the benchmark for effective promotion. Consider a triple appeal critique of promotional efforts by the non-governmental organization, EcoPledge. That organization's web site exhorts readers to "take the pledge" and thereby "join together in a campaign to identify leading companies in all major sectors of the economy and (ask) these companies to take specific, feasible and economically sound actions" (EcoPledge 2005). Students might consider: does this solicitation stimulate readers to do as the organization intends? What part(s) of personality are affected by EcoPledge's call (if any)? How might one change the exhortation to more effectively agitate readers to act? Students can be encouraged to offer a replacement text and to comment on how the new prose more effectively appeals to impulse, reason, and conscience.

Triple Appeal, Student Learning, and the Advancement of Civic Engagement

Civic engagement skills are developed through study and especially through experience, and the triple appeal principle fosters this learning. In particular, it nurtures students' understanding of the concept of citizenship, it is a basis for reflecting on practical experiences, and it is a tool for honing communication skills. Each of these three functions is considered below.

Staff and partners of the University of Minnesota's Center for Democracy and Citizenship (2005) write, "Citizenship is an open, contested idea. It requires discussion, debate, and practice. And, like democracy, it must be created and sustained by us all." Civic engagement is about citizenship, and citizenship is partly a contest of ideas and preferences. Understanding how people persuade others and how the student him/herself can use persuasion is the heart of the triple appeal principle.

Reflection, in the context of civic engagement, is "the means through which people make sense of what they are seeing or experiencing" (Hatcher and Bringle 1997, 153). The triple appeal principle is just such a means for reflection. In the context of promotion and persua-sion, reflection is the difference between being motivated by a persuasive message and understanding *why* a message appeals to and motivates you. The triple appeal principle forces the students to contemplate the latter.

Reflection, then, is a means for shining light on the complex, contingent, and at times, deceptive promotional messages that bombard the civic actor. Coupled with an understanding of the basic intention of civic engagement—to promote human dignity—it is also a powerful tool for helping students craft their own promotional appeals. Students who master the triple appeal principle tend to be conscious of the power of symbols and syntax. The triple appeal principle, then, is a communication skill-builder.

References

Center for Democracy and Citizenship. 2005. *Reinventing citizenship: The practice of public work.* http://www.extension. umn.edu/distribution/citizenship/DH6586.html.

EcoPledge. 2005. *Ecopledge.com.* http://www.ecopledge.com/ecopledge.asp?id2=12790

Hatcher, J. A., and R. G. Bringle. 1997. Reflections: Bridging the gap between service and learning. *Journal of College Teaching* 45:153–158.

Lasswell, H. D. 1932. The triple-appeal principle: A contribution of psychoanalysis to political and social science. *American Journal of Sociology* 37:523–538.

Pedagogy of Collegiality

Vivian Chávez and Ruby Turalba
San Francisco State University

Civic engagement means believing in and acting on one's ability to bring about change. San Francisco State University (2005) believes that through civic engagement, we can be "agent(s) of change in the culture, economy, health, and welfare of the community, the state and the nation." Demographic shifts, coupled with the growing evidence of health disparities among multicultural populations underscore the need to develop contemporary culturally competent pedagogy for civic engagement.

Pedagogy of collegiality is a teaching method that transforms the curriculum to be inclusive of the student voice and to create a balanced environment for learning civic engagement. This essay seeks to engage readers in thinking purposefully about curriculum development and teaching techniques that create dynamic learning processes and strengthen student capacities in reflection, problem solving, community service, and civic engagement. After presenting the theoretical foundations for pedagogy of collegiality, the paper will introduce the *Wheel of Community Organizing* and describe classroom activities that can be applied across disciplines.

Rather than reproducing hierarchical relationships where students understand the teacher as the sole authority figure with all the knowledge, the goal of pedagogy of collegiality is to establish an educational setting that fosters an open and free exchange of ideas. The term pedagogy captures the full experience of learning including the content, methods, student learning styles, and context.

The term collegiality describes a relationship that embodies mutual learning and shifts the center of attention from the teacher to the students—and back to the teacher with the students—so that all may become members of a community of learners. This approach was developed from teaching public health at San Francisco State University (Chávez 2005) and most recently, in community interventions that involve youth media production (Soep and Chávez 2005).

Modeling progressive education since the 1970's, pedagogy of collegiality is rooted in feminist and critical education theories. Freire's (1970, 1973) theory of critical education, also known as "praxis" emphasizes conscientization, the process of developing critical consciousness about oppression and working towards social change (Darder 2003, 2002). Feminist educators' methods are based on assumptions about knowledge, power, consciousness rising, and action learned throughout the women's movement (Naples 2002; Hooks 1994). Feminist pedagogy also focuses on the spatial dynamics in the classroom to physically address power imbalances between teacher and students (Weiler 1991).

Classroom Activities—Participatory Education

"Welcome to Community Organizing! Like every other class, we'll start as individuals. My goal is that by the end of the semester, we'll become a community."

Teaching civic engagement combines personal experience, a passion for social justice, and the historical context of non-violent social action. The course described here aims to promote citizen development and increase competency in critical thinking, language arts, and cross-cultural communication. The class keeps positive with a focus on strengths and assets as opposed to a negative focus on problems and weaknesses. Students complete a mapping exercise of a community of their choice, which later culminates in the development of a Community Action Project where students volunteer and take action to make a difference in that community.

Dialogue and community building are required throughout the semester. Students have ample opportunity to digest, question, discuss, and reflect on course topics and materials. Throughout the semester guest speakers share their community projects in 15-minute

presentations and students are invited to volunteer with these organizations as part of the Community Action Project.

The Wheel of Community Organizing

The wheel of community organizing introduces students to seven principles that build a community of learners, mutually invested in learning from each other. This model provides a three-phase foundation for the course.

Phase I: Weeks 1–4

Listening is a core element of the class. Students identify the ways speaking is privileged over listening and work to be better listeners by engaging in various communication exercises as well as simply reading each other's writing. Students learn to shift from sharing their written perspectives with only the professor, to sharing their opinions with the entire class. Throughout the semester students are gently reminded that the professor will not be the only one to "read their voice" and that democratic education requires their willingness to be vulnerable and share their written work with others.

Building relationships accompanies listening as it creates opportunities for presenting course themes on social justice, community, diversity, oppression, and privilege through creative venues such as video, music, potlucks, and other interactive methods. The goal is to go beyond an introduction to social problems, and move towards identifying solutions that incorporate the human element of community organizing.

Phase II: Weeks 5–12

Challenge and Action are parts of the class where students learn not only about problems, but develop the skills needed to take action. Students practice community mapping and diagnosis, social support and social network analysis, media advocacy, media literacy, and ethics. They learn about globalization, cross-cultural competency and non-violent social action that invites students to reflect beyond an analysis of violence to the application of principles of non-violence in their lives.

The Community Action Project allows students to practice civic engagement for health and social justice in a community of their choice. Examples of past projects are: neighborhood clean-up, community gardening, health education workshops at their church or high school, organizing a campus blood drive, writing letters to the editor, and mobilizing to protest rising student fees and the Iraq war. Specific student projects on civic engagement include:

- A Filipino student organized and conducted an HIV/AIDS workshop for his family and extended kin of approximately 100 people.
- Students volunteered with campus organizations such as the Health Education Student Association (HESA).
- Students took *action* and gained support from the city's Parking and Traffic Department to install a stoplight at a busy and dangerous intersection close to campus. They gathered data for the Traffic Engineering and Operations Division and investigated solutions for improved traffic controls.

Phase III: Weeks 13–15

Evaluation and Reflection enables students to critique and transform their experience in the classroom. While student evaluations are the formal tools used by departments across the university to monitor excellence in teaching, reflection is something done by both students and professor throughout the semester to yield mutually accountability. Opportunities for reflection can be solicited anonymously through personal writing, small group discussions, or with process observers. Before the last class session, reflection can happen by creating a "sacred space" where students bring an object that symbolizes community, sit in a circle, and share its significance.

Celebration of student learning builds self-efficacy and helps to create a sustainable community. The last class is purposefully designed to celebrate students' con-

tributions. In addition to classroom presentations, students bring music, decorate the space, and create time for socializing and building community. It is vital to honor that this will be the last time students and professor are together as a community.

Conclusion

Pedagogy of collegiality asks students and their teacher to collaboratively examine the root causes of health disparities and become inspired to change them. Changing the climate of silence around social injustice requires open debate, honest dialogue, and non-judgmental information.

References

Chávez, V. Forthcoming. *Teaching public health with a pedagogy of collegiality.*
Hooks, B. 1994. *Teaching to transgress.* New York: Routledge.
Freire, P. 1970. *Pedagogy of the oppressed.* New York: Seabury Press.
———. 1973. *Education for critical consciousness.* New York: Seabury Press.
Naples, N. 2002. The dynamics of critical pedagogy, experiential learning and feminist praxis. In N. Naples and K. Bojar, eds., *Teaching feminist activism: Strategies from the field,* 9–21. New York: Routledge.
San Francisco State University. Civic engagement at SFSU. http://www.sfsu.edu/~civic/.
Soep, L. and V. Chavez. Forthcoming. Youth Media and The Pedagogy of Collegiality.
Weiler, K. and P. Freire. 1991. A feminist pedagogy of difference. *Harvard Educational Review,* 1, no. 4:449–474.

Debating Issues through Opinion-Editorials and Letters to the Editor

Laurie Wermuth
California Statue University, Chico

College courses provide an opportunity to engage students in public debate about domestic and foreign policies. Two assignments are described here—writing an op-ed piece and letter to the editor—along with suggestions for adapting these assignments for other courses. The two assignments are from "Sociology of World Affairs," a senior-level capstone course in the sociology major. They are due in the second week of the course

to encourage students to delve into international and national news, and to formulate and discuss opinions. These assignments are framed as participatory democracy and function as a prelude to continuing discussions and in-depth writing projects on national and international events. To facilitate the students' reading, a variety of electronic news sources are linked to the course website, including the BBC, *New York Times, The Econo-*

mist, The Nation, PBS, and others. Peer-reviewed articles, scholarly books, and government documents (from the World Health Organization and UN Development Programme) are also required for a "country report" assigned to each student.

Op-ed and letters-to-the-editor assignments can be designed around a wide variety of issues. For example, courses in the humanities can focus op-eds or letters to the editor on civic issues related to works of art and popular culture. Philosophy or history courses may wish to debate such issues as the death penalty, the ethics of first-strike war policies, or the risks vs. benefits of resurrecting nuclear power as a solution to increasing demand and tightening supplies of oil. In the natural sciences, students can evaluate and speak out on other issues, such as global warming, renewable energy technologies, forest management policies, or loss of species and habitats. They may want to debate preservation of the Hubble Telescope or the future of the U.S. space program. The social sciences can engage a full range of issues, from those listed above to, for example, the need for universal health care insurance, childcare for working parents, or the problem of too few jobs that pay a living wage. Issues of government regulation vs. "laissez-faire" policies can be debated, along with "fair markets" vs. "free markets."

Collective Op-Ed Articles

In this assignment, students write a two-page Opinion-Editorial essay. In Fall 2004, the topic was the Iraq War. The class agreed that if there was significant agreement of opinions, I would attempt to combine parts of the essays into one op-ed article. If there were a wide variety of opinions, students would be grouped to combine their articles into several op-ed pieces. Our campus's student newspaper, *The Orion,* was our choice for submitting these essays. The issues were discussed in class and students were encouraged to post their essays on the course's electronic bulletin board.

Because the resultant essays were overwhelmingly against various aspects of the war, I proceeded to develop a collectively authored op-ed piece, which was handed out and posted on the course website for discussion. Students were asked to make suggestions and to make sure there was nothing in the letter they were uncomfortable with as an author. They could make revisions anonymously if they wished. Based on this process, minor revisions were made, including removing one

controversial sentence. The revision was handed out in class and posted online for a second round of editing. Several more minor editorial changes were made, and then all agreed that the article could be sent to *The Orion.* The article was published on the op-ed page a couple weeks later, and a copy was posted at the entrance to the sociology department office.

The op-ed assignment generated discussion beyond the class, prompting participants to discuss the war with other students. The process helped students articulate their views and take them more seriously. Knowing their statements would be in print and that they would have a public audience generated heightened interest and motivation. It was also stimulating to hear and debate various observations and arguments regarding the war. The article is too lengthy to reproduce in full, but here is an excerpt:

The War on Iraq: Our Opinions
*By Students in Sociology of World Affairs,
Fall 2004:*

. . . Some of us know soldiers who have been in Iraq or are still there. Some of those soldiers believe taking out Saddam Hussein was a meaningful objective. We read the newspaper about local soldiers killed in battle and wonder sadly why they had to die. We note that children of our country's most privileged are not found among the troops. Many soldiers entering the military did so in hopes of being able to fund a college education that would otherwise be unattainable. Is it fair that they die in greater numbers than those whose parents can afford to help pay for college? And what about the value of Iraqi lives being lost? The war promised "operation Iraqi freedom" but the turmoil has destabilized the country and brought destruction, chaos and death. Iraq has become a land of opportunity for terrorists to recruit angry young people into a radical Islamist movement against the American infidels. It's important that we participate in our own democracy if we are to attempt to spread democracy to other parts of the world. We encourage other students to speak out on their views and to vote in the upcoming election.

Letters to the Editor

A second assignment encourages attention to local, state, national, and world events by having students write a letter to the editor. In the World Affairs class, students wrote on some aspect of American foreign policy. They were encouraged to plan ahead where to send their letters. If they read articles about foreign policy that provoked their responses, they could send their letters to those publications. Students posted their letters on the course website for others to read and comment on, and they received written feedback from me that they could incorporate if they wished. The letters covered a variety of topics, such as the need for the U.S. to increase financial aid for AIDS drugs in poor countries, sign the Kyoto Protocol on global warming, generously fund tsunami relief, and listen to our European allies in foreign affairs decision-making.

Pedagogical Benefits

Both of these assignments got students reading in-depth news reports. Instead of getting the usual snippets of news from television networks, they read stories from the BBC, *New York Times,* or *The Economist.* Students were also exposed to critical news sources, some for the first time. These included *The Nation, Mother Jones,* and the *Utne Reader.* An additional goal was met in that students began to take their own ideas and opinions more seriously. Student feedback indicated that they also enjoyed hearing other students' opinions, especially in classroom discussion.

Moderating discussion about controversial issues requires care, so that no one gets attacked for expressing

> *Students are concerned about domestic and foreign affairs, and writing opinion pieces creates opportunities for both learning about the issues and linking students to public debate.*

minority opinions. Starting the discussion, I find it helpful to remind the group that there is a wide range of opinion in just about any group in our society, and that we should expect to hear and consider a variety of views. I emphasize that we can all learn from one another by bringing *information* to the discussion, as opposed to just trying to win an argument. We all gain by patiently working through the issues with evidence, feeling, and analysis.

Students are concerned about domestic and foreign affairs, and writing opinion pieces creates opportunities for both learning about the issues and linking students to public debate. The classroom discussion is our primary forum, where a variety of evidence and opinions can be considered. Secondly, the course's electronic bulletin board provides a stable and growing written dialogue of threaded thoughts and reactions. Thirdly, publication in a newspaper, newsletter, or magazine provides a wider audience. Participation allows students to discuss their agreements and disagreements civilly, a process that is perhaps as important to civic engagement as learning about the issues. Extending the dialogue beyond the classroom to bulletin boards (electronic or cork), newspapers, and other periodicals further enhances this process.

Building Skills for Social Action

KATHARINE BYERS AND SABRINA WILLIAMSON
INDIANA UNIVERSITY SCHOOL OF SOCIAL WORK

S352, Social Welfare Delivery Systems, is the second class in the policy sequence taken by social work majors. In this class we examine how policies are developed, implemented, and evaluated in social service agencies as well as in local, state, and federal government contexts. Here we describe the major activities that encourage

civic engagement and discuss how these activities can be modified for use in other disciplines. This series of activities is designed to build skills progressively throughout the course so that, after graduating, students possess a repertoire of skills that enable them to continue their civic engagement.

Classroom Activities Related to Civic Engagement

Raising Community Awareness: The Homeward Bound Walk

Each spring in Bloomington there is a walk to raise money for local agencies that provide services to persons experiencing homelessness. Though social work students have often participated as "walkers," we desired increased student involvement in planning the event and in addressing a secondary goal of the walk: raising community awareness about the issue of homelessness. To this end, we created a new assignment in the spring of 2005.

In this assignment, students rank their preferences for working in one of the following groups: elementary school students, junior and senior high students, college age students, faith communities, and civic groups. Together, students develop a presentation about the issue of homelessness and affordable housing that was appropriate for their assigned audience. The deadline for the assignment is early in the semester and students gave their presentations to each other before submitting them to the walk's steering committee for use in the community. The benefit of structuring the assignment in this manner is that steering committee members have access to all the presentation materials for their use and students are able to engage with the material in a way that makes it "come alive" for community members of various ages.

Seeking Funding: Developing Grant Proposals for Community Agencies

Social service agencies, faced with increasing budget constraints, are frequently looking for additional funding for programs to address ongoing needs. Each of the last five years, we have incorporated a grant-writing project into this class that 1) helps students develop grant writing skills, 2) engages students with community agencies to address local needs, and 3) frequently results in actual funding of new projects that benefit the community. Again in groups, students identify a community need and a partner agency. Sometimes, the instructor is aware of agencies needing assistance through networking with the social service community. In other instances, students in practicum or volunteer experiences with local agencies are knowledgeable about a particular need.

In their groups, students research the need and identify potential funding sources. To complete their as-signment, students follow the application directions for the funding source that they choose. In most cases, the grant application includes a needs assessment, a discussion of program objectives, an evaluation component, and a program budget. In collaboration with their agency and in consultation with the course instructor, the student groups develop and revise the proposal, submitting it by the funding source deadline. The direct benefits to the social service community are clear when grant proposals written by students are actually funded. Also, students develop skills that empower them for future grant writing, either when they serve on agency boards or when they work in agencies as professionals.

Increasing Political Participation: Compiling a Portfolio

Throughout the semester, students follow legislation that is of interest to them at both the state and federal level. Bi-weekly a portion of class is devoted to a segment we call "policy in the news." During this time, students discuss the bills they are tracking. Near the end of the semester, students submit a portfolio with the following items: a copy of an advocacy letter he or she wrote to an elected official, a copy of a letter to the editor he or she submitted, a summary of a phone conversation he or she had with an elected official or staff member, and an original policy brief. The legislation that students have tracked throughout the semester serves as a context for completing the items in the portfolio. At the completion of this assignment, students report an increase in their confidence in communicating with elected officials and in their ability to track bills through the legislative process.

"But I Teach in the School of Business": Modifications for Other Disciplines

The assignments described here can easily be modified for other disciplines. A first step in incorporating civic engagement is to determine which organizations and non-profit causes are supported by faculty members in your department. Next, identify "real world" skills that your students need, and brainstorm ways they can put these skills to use in local agencies and organizations.

For example, many local groups have fundraising "walks" or "runs" similar to Homeward Bound. These events are time consuming to organize and assistance from students would certainly be valued. Accounting students may be involved in data entry and cash flow elements of major fundraising events. Students can design spreadsheets, online payment options, etc and can be on-site consultants when the programs are used and when the event takes place. Theatre, drama, and music students can develop creative pieces that are relevant to the topic of the event and provide entertainment on the walk route. Students in food and nutrition programs can prepare healthy snacks and recipe booklets to sell at the walk, and proceeds can be donated to the event.

Similarly, the development of grant writing skills could be incorporated into many disciplines. Courses that focus on nonprofit management, organizations, community leadership, educational leadership, nursing community practice, and others are natural settings to incorporate a grant writing project with a civic engagement focus. Additionally, instructors in other courses could think creatively about how their expertise might be useful in partnering with community agencies to develop grant proposals. For example, an art class might partner with a local school to write a proposal to support a school-based arts project. A Spanish language class might work with a local community agency serving the growing Hispanic population to write a grant proposal for more interpreters to assist people in accessing community services. The community needs in social services, the arts, education, health care, and other fields are increasing as funding from public sources is increasingly restricted. Students developing grant proposals can learn essential grant writing skills that they can use in future civic engagement activities while providing concrete help to local agencies during their college course work.

Finally, the ability to track legislation and communicate with elected officials is important to professionals in many disciplines, in addition to being a valuable skill for citizens. Students in every professional school and most academic disciplines can benefit from assignments that require them to be critically aware of what is going on in local and national politics and to communicate their position on current or proposed legislation.

Conclusion

At the end of each semester we hear from students that these assignments have been meaningful learning experiences. Additionally, agencies are appreciative of the enthusiasm and creativity that students bring to their projects. Leading by example in civic engagement is a win-win strategy for both students and the community.

Using Readers' Theater

Gerald Lee Ratliff
SUNY Potsdam

Searching for inventive approaches to promote classroom engagement has more tra ditionally been viewed in terms of students presenting oral reports or working in small groups engaged in research projects that are subsequently shared as part of a panel or question-and-answer response with other classmates. Although well intentioned, these instructional strategies may not sufficiently provide the element of "creativity" that is an essential ingredient in sustaining student engagement.

Using basic Reader's Theatre classroom presentation techniques, however, is an inventive instructional design that provides both a visual and oral stimulus for students who may be unaccustomed to using imagination in the analysis, interpretation, and performance of printed texts (Ratliff 1999). Although Reader's Theatre is part of the traditional theatre movement that seeks to dramatize individual character actions or attitudes, there are a number of Reader's Theatre conventions that are useful to promote a more trans-disciplinary approach to the classroom study of texts in the sciences, history, business, women's studies, psychology, politics, sociology, or philosophy, to mention just a few examples (Gustafson 2002; Sloyer 2003).

The following Reader's Theatre exercise was designed for an introductory course in the humanities to address contemporary issues. It featured a compiled script of familiar texts across the curriculum and focused on promoting collaborative and problem-based learning skills. Each instructor, of course, should approach the exercise in a manner that is comfortable for an individual style of teaching. Liberties should also be taken to adjust or extend the exercise to meet the special needs of individual classroom assignments or discipline specific student learning objectives. Creative expression and originality are key ingredients in determining the role that selected Reader's Theatre techniques may play in promoting student engagement in a classroom setting.

A class of twenty-two non-theatre, undergraduate students spent three weeks discussing the broad theme of civic and political engagement. During that time period, each student was responsible for identifying brief excerpts from a variety of printed texts—historical documents, short stories, essays, public addresses, song lyrics, journal articles, poems, and pamphlets—that exemplified the common theme. Another week was spent in the analysis and investigation of the recommended texts. Special attention was given to the arrangement and integration of the informative data, current events, and historical incidents that would frame a compiled, thirty-minute classroom script. A final script and individual performance roles were determined by two student directors.

A two-week rehearsal polished the sequential order of edited episodes and more visual elements like music, video, and suggestive costumes were added to enhance the presentation. Finally, during the rehearsal period the students' artistic response to the thirty-minute program theme emerged as a production metaphor: "life is living in desolate, blank space" when there is an apparent lack of moral and civic education. Each excerpt included in the compiled script subsequently reflected the ethical, historical, political, moral, or social nuances of the production metaphor.

The student's creative approach to visualizing the production metaphor for an invited audience was to stage the program in a vacant campus science laboratory, performing in an empty space surrounded by discarded scientific equipment and enclosed by a series of iron bars taped on the laboratory floor. Fragmented windows, oversized padlocks, and placards that read "No Trespassing" or "Reduce Speed Ahead" were suspended from the ceiling. Students wore white hospital gowns with black armbands and went shoeless. Tape-recorded excerpts from historical speeches; slide projections of public demonstrations; and occasional sound effects like a gun shot, funereal music, or the clang of church bells periodically punctuated the production.

The Reader's Theatre exercise served as an instructional tool to pursue composite, trans-disciplinary textual portraits of contemporary issues, social movements, historical eras, and political climates. Students were actively engaged in the selection, analysis, and adaptation of complex texts, and they pursued new supplemental reading or research adventures that enhanced their aesthetic understanding, critical thinking, social analysis, and language skills. The production toured local high schools, civic centers, public forums, and state agencies as part of a community engagement service-learning initiative. Students also conducted a question-and-answer session on the program theme following each performance, and actively engaged the audience in a discussion of civic and public policy responsibilities. Subsequent student evaluations of the classroom exercise indicated an increased understanding of the role that Reader's Theatre can play in articulating substantive civic, moral, and social concerns; and also indicated a heightened understanding of how classroom exercises can be translated into a public dialogue that promotes a more persuasive strategy to address contemporary issues.

References

Gustafson, C. 2002. *Acting out: Reader's theatre across the curriculum,* Worthington, Ohio: Linworth Publishing.

Ratliff, G. 1999. *An introduction to reader's theatre.* Colorado Springs, Colo.: Meriwether Publishing, Limited.

Sloyer, S. 2003. *From the page to the stage: The educator's complete guide to reader's theatre.* Portsmouth, N. H.: Teacher Ideas Press.

Public Achievement and Teacher Education

MICHAEL C. KUHNE
MINNEAPOLIS COMMUNITY AND TECHNICAL COLLEGE

One form of civic engagement that works well is Public Achievement. This article highlights three different civic engagement activities that work well in the Urban Teacher Program (UTP) at Minneapolis Community and Technical College (MCTC).

According to the Public Achievement web site (2004), Public Achievement "is a youth civic engagement initiative focused on the most basic concepts of citizenship, democracy and public work. Public Achievement draws on the talents and desires of ordinary people to build a better world and to create a different kind of politics." The simplest way to understand Public Achievement is as an ongoing, action- and project-oriented team activity designed to allow participants to reflect on and name the democracy skills that they learn.

MCTC's Urban Teacher Program incorporates Public Achievement to help the program meet its mission (2003), which professes to instruct students "to practice and model advocacy and activism," while instructing students to "understand methods of conflict resolution . . . pose and solve problems; promote change . . . [and s]erve as role model[s] in education and politics." These objectives are met through the students' participation in two Public Achievement-focused seminars.

In one seminar, students participate on Public Achievement teams and select critical issues in their communities, identify specific problems within the issues, and create public work projects that respond to those problems in nonviolent ways that contribute to the commonwealth. In the subsequent seminar, the students go through the same process, this time as coaches of teams whose members come from three different Minneapolis K-12 schools.

To describe Public Achievement classroom practices, I have sorted the practices into three stages to match the process that Public Achievement teams experience: issue development, problem clarification, and public project.

The first stage is issue development. While there are a number of different classroom practices one could use at this stage, we have found relational meetings to be effective. According to Edward Chambers, the rela-

tional meeting is "an encounter that is face to face . . . for the purpose of exploring the development of a public relationship" wherein one "search[es] for talent, energy, insight, and relationships" (2004, 44–45). In our setting, the goals include increasing self-awareness about one's own interests while learning the importance of building public relationships.

We ask students to do two relational meetings. One is with a classmate. Once they have conducted a relational meeting with a classmate, we ask that they conduct another relational meeting with someone in their community. Typically, this relational meeting will grow out of the first meeting (in fact, we ask classmates to make suggestions to one another). These meetings are usually more tension-filled than the classmate relational meeting. Many students struggle with this activity, likening it to a cold call in sales. However, those who are able to deal with their discomfort benefit from the experience. One student, writing anonymously, argues that, "[t]he most important lesson I learned about relationships is that I do not need to have everyone like me. What I need to do is build relationships that are mutually respected by both parties in order to create successful accomplishments in public work." Through these relational meetings, students become clearer about not only their partner's interests but also their own. Incorporating relational meetings into the curriculum has helped our students learn a method of conflict resolution based on relationships.

Once students have formed issued-based teams, the next step is for the teams to clarify particular problems within the issue. A classroom activity we use is power mapping. Students use large sheets of paper and write the issue in the middle. From there, branches are drawn to indicate specific aspects of the issue. For instance, a team might form around the issue of racism. The branches from this issue might include the racial profiling of African American males, recent events on campus involving racist remarks directed at Muslim students, tensions between immigrant communities, and so on. Each new branch promotes discussions, helping teams move from general issues to specific problems.

Once the team clarifies a specific problem, a new

power map is created. This time, the specific problem is named in the middle, and the branches now lead to organizations and the names of specific people. This activity helps teams identify their particular problem's stake holders. Once these stake holders are identified, team members research the problem. This might entail traditional research methods, but it often involves another series of relational meetings with people identified in the exercise. Some teams periodically return to power mapping, refining both the problem and the stakeholder list in the process. This activity helps students understand how to pose and solve problems as they analyze the power dynamics of any issue and problem.

Once teams clarify a specific problem, they produce a public project. Unlike traditional small-group projects, public projects must identify and work with an audience that resides outside of the classroom. The type of public project depends on the specific problem being addressed. In addition to projects that focus on internal campus matters, other teams have reached into communities for their public projects. One team formed September 12, 2001, less than 24 hours after the Twin Towers collapsed: their project—to create a series of forums wherein discussion about discrimination against Muslims could occur. This group presented their forum in eight different Minneapolis schools. They also presented at a public work celebration to over 120 stake holders. I appreciate the way that this public dimension of their work elides the students' notions of academic learning as separate from "the real world." Asking our students to make their work public teaches them how to promote positive change. It also gives them a taste for what it might mean to be a role model as a citizen teacher.

Public Achievement is the vehicle for UTP to meet its civic engagement goals. *At the same time, Public Achievement provides an action-based learning environment for teaching candidates to explore the important public dimensions of their work.*

References

Center for Democracy and Citizenship. 2004. Overview. http://publicwork.org.
———. 2004. Public achievement: Do the extraordinary. http://publicachievement.org.
———. 2004. Practice—Teachers: Democracy in the classroom. http://publicachievement.org/2_1_2_practice_teach.html.
———. 2004. Teacher's guide—The core concepts of public achievement. http://publicachievement.org/TeacherGuide/CoreConcepts.html.
———. n. d. Public achievement teacher's guide: Mind mapping and power mapping. http://publicachievement.org/TeacherGuide/pdfs/MindMapping.pdf.
Chambers, E. with M. Cowan. 2004. *Roots for radicals: Organizing for power, action, and justice.* New York and London: Continuum.
Urban Teacher Program—Minneapolis Community and Technical College. 2003. Urban teacher program mission and vision statement.

Expanding Civic Involvement and the Learning Landscape through Courtroom Observations

BRENDA E. KNOWLES
INDIANA UNIVERSITY SOUTH BEND

For 27 years, I have required the students in my introductory business law classes to attend a state or federal court of general jurisdiction. Each then writes a two-to-three page, single-spaced report of this experience. This assignment requires the class members to stay a minimum of 45 minutes; they can view any court case, even those unrelated to business. I announce this court observation on the first day and note that the report is due the last week of the semester. Although some students initially dread this exercise, no one has ever argued for its discontinuance. Rather, all have found the report extremely valuable, both educationally and personally. Indeed, the thoughtfulness of their responses often moves me to tears.

One of the most venerable institutions in our country, the court system consequently is familiar to all students. Still, misconceptions about its essential nature abound. In particular, media depictions of court proceedings color student attitudes. Dispelling these faulty impressions therefore becomes a primary objective of the assignment. The seriousness of the litigation and the high stakes for the people involved contrast starkly with the often trivial cases decided on afternoon television. Thus, the class members quickly apprehend that the packed galleries shown in the media represent only a plot-development device. Indeed, beyond the families, the students frequently are the only non-court personnel in the room.

Yet, courts bristle with activity. Attorneys and clients noisily taking their respective places on the daily docket pose distractions for the other litigants and the public. Courtrooms also powerfully depict the human condition—criminal defendants are in shackles; family members become demonstrative at the reading of verdicts; testimony centers on such unpalatable topics as incest and child molestation. Conversely, dry subjects—antitrust law, zoning variances, and probate matters—command the judge's and jury's attention as well.

Whatever the topic of interest, courtrooms are fraught places. Sometimes the proceedings involve good theatre; sometimes they involve intense pain; and sometimes they are downright boring. But even the students' bemoaning the tedium of the proceedings allows me to re-emphasize the significance of due process and fundamental fairness. In short, teaching moments are plentiful.

The mirror of society reflected in these proceedings points up the socio-economic and demographic variables the students have studied in this and other courses. Now, however, these heretofore theoretical constructs take on a human face. For example, the students can link our in-class coverage of *voir dire*, or the process of questioning potential jurors, to the actual persons sitting in the jury box. Understanding the "back story" of how these persons were selected leads to a heightened respect for their role in the proceedings. This knowledge sometimes elicits student criticisms of the panel's lack of racial and ethnic diversity as well. The prosecution of a local attorney charged with embezzlement leads to a re-evaluation of both the students' views of those most likely to perpetrate crimes and the importance of the ethical theories considered during the course. Personal injury cases feature expert witnesses armed with projections of lost wages and medical expenses, thereby reinforcing the in-class discussion of risk management and foreseeability. Such litigation also brings home the fact that, theory and policy notions aside, tort law at base consists of injured people whose lives have been inexorably altered by another person's conduct.

The immediacy of observing actual applications of the course concepts can kindle deep introspection.

For example, the class members may know the defendants from high school or employment. These situations lead the students to ponder the choices they have made; they also recognize that the power of the law's focus on an individual is not to be dismissed lightly. The testimony sometimes embarrasses them; they frequently feel like voyeurs and do not enjoy hearing about others' misfortunes. Expressions of such sentiments provide an opportunity to contemplate the tension between personal privacy and the constitutional underpinnings that require transparency in order to preserve people's rights. On reflection, the class members acknowledge the moral bankruptcy of star-chamber types of "justice." They see over-worked (and sometimes under prepared) attorneys, as well as brilliant advocates. They admire most judges but disparage a few as seemingly diffident and uncaring.

The students' first interaction with the public sector beyond traffic stops by the police or applying for a driver's license surprises them: they did not expect the rigorous security procedures, and the abundance of technology—including computers on the judge's bench—amazes them. They are grateful for the exchanges (usually unsolicited) initiated by the judge and/or the attorneys at the close of the proceedings. The architectural touches in the courtroom further enhance their respect for the content and procedures they have witnessed.

In a mere 45 minutes—although many choose to stay longer—the class members have gained an appreciation of this well-functioning system. Courts now represent a public good that they value more highly. Because their experience base is small (they don't routinely see themselves as part of societal workings), they begin to savor their role in ensuring the preservation of this vital link to citizenship. Beforehand, they may have viewed courts primarily as forums for dispute resolution; but they take away from this observation heightened esteem for the role of courts in mediating broader societal issues (child custody, the need for translators for litigants for whom English is a new language, and immigration) and for the law itself.

Given these positive outcomes, this exercise would translate very effectively to a variety of disciplines—obviously to law, criminal justice, and public policy, but also to social work, psychology, economics (risk allocation and the cost of resources), sociology (inequality), gender studies (discrimination), philosophy (ethics and jurisprudence), English (universal stories), art (the influence of place), and speech/communication (argumentation and presentation skills). Hence, I encourage anyone to adapt this easily implemented lesson to his or her particular pedagogical style and academic field.

For me, few aspects of my teaching praxis have yielded such high payoffs in intellectual development. First and foremost, this assignment allows the students to recognize the verbal precision and doctrinal complexities that underlie law. Hearing the attorneys' and judges' straightforward use of such Latinate phrases as the *prima facie* case or seeing their reliance on commerce clause or copyright infringement precedents adds legitimacy to the classroom learning objectives. Students' narratives furthermore bespeak their pride in the rule of law represented by these proceedings and their renewed understanding of their civic obligations in this

context. The overwhelming majority assert that, as a result of this exercise, they look forward to jury duty, whereas they previously would have tried to avoid this responsibility. Most also declare that they plan to return for another observation on a voluntary basis. They emphasize that they now are motivated to educate themselves about judges who are up for re-election. Simply put, they perceive their connectedness to the quality of justice meted out in their locale and the importance of their discharging their civic obligations in this regard.

An old proverb states that teachers merely open the doors, the students enter by themselves. This assignment has become the portal by which many students realize the value of civic engagement and become inspired to participate in the everyday workings of this cherished linchpin of the American experience.

Connecting Scholarship and Social Responsibility

RONALD J. DUCHOVIC
INDIANA UNIVERSITY–PURDUE UNIVERSITY FORT WAYNE

As both an educator and a scholar, the contemporary university faculty member struggles with a vexing dichotomy. On the one hand, each sub-discipline of human knowledge represents a highly integrated body of information whose breadth and depth at the dawn of the 21st century are both awe inspiring and intimidating. How is it possible to present a coherent, intelligible, and reasonably complete understanding of any given discipline within the confines of a traditional college course? On the other hand, faculty members are charged with the responsibility "to lead," but to lead in the sense of "rearing" or "bringing up" or "to raise." Each faculty member bears the formidable responsibility of guiding fresh, inquisitive minds to become active contributors to and creative fashioners of their social milieu. This educative process far transcends the mere transmission of expert knowledge, the simple communication of specialized technologies, or the inculcation of arcane mysteries. It is a process that must exemplify the defining characteristics of humankind and, by this example, empower students to assume the demanding roles of intellectual, personal, and civic commitment.

An intellectually committed human being pursues

with rigorous attention to honesty, integrity, and completeness not simply the knowledge associated with a compendium of facts, but rather the wisdom and the interconnected understanding that are the defining characteristics of human intellectual history. While expertise in a discipline is necessary, it certainly is not sufficient; command of a body of knowledge goes far beyond the basic level of technical competence. Personal commitment is the bedrock of an individual's daily person-to-person interactions and, over the course of a lifetime, it characterizes and defines a human being, making a person a truly humane individual. This dimension requires an unyielding dedication to an individual's innermost circle of associates, an unflinching adherence to a set of ethical principles, and the temerity to act in the face of criticism or derision. Finally, civic commitment requires a wider perspective, demanding that an individual assume a personal responsibility for the broader sweep of humanity. It is an imperative that forces an individual human being to recognize that John Donne's bell does indeed toll for everyone. The ultimate challenge of civic commitment is the internalization of the principle that an individual's self-interest is meaningful only to the extent the individual creatively and actively contributes to the common well-being of humankind.

At this point, faculty members who are sensitive to this modern dichotomy in higher education will be ready to exclaim in exasperation, "How can I do it all"? From the perspective of many educators and scholars, this is a perfectly reasonable response. However, I respectfully submit that a closer examination of our craft offers an alternative to a visceral outburst of helplessness, and to some extent, hopelessness. As a chemical educator I have found that it is possible, even in an information dense and highly technical field like Chemistry, to raise issues that require my students to make the connections required by the values of intellectual, personal, and civic commitment. Building on the specialized content of a Chemistry course, it is possible for an instructor to raise questions that address a whole series of issues:

1. The widespread advertisements promoting anti-bacterial soaps leave unasked the question of their benefit. Are such agents necessarily beneficial?

2. Should the indiscriminant use of antibiotics in the food industry to accelerate weight-gain go unchallenged?

3. Should the production of electricity using fossil fuels be encouraged even though the resulting production of acid rain and greenhouse gases has serious negative environmental effects?

4. How should our society balance the competition between reasonably-priced pharmaceuticals and the requirement to fund continuing pharmaceutical research?

5. What is the appropriate role of government in the regulatory review of the pharmaceutical industry?

6. How should we balance the benefits of nuclear energy with the radiological and chemical hazards accompanying nuclear waste?

7. What is the effect of routine vaccination programs on the human immune system? Vaccination programs have positive and negative effects on the human population. How are these competing effects evaluated?

8. While DNA/stem cell research holds the promise of cures for many genetic diseases, what is its impact on societal norms?

The conscious decision to introduce these issues in the context of a Chemistry course immediately takes the course beyond the level of mere technical expertise. Rather, by raising these issues for students who now possess the technical expertise to evaluate, explore, and judge critically each issue, students are engaged at the level of the intellectual, personal, and civic dimensions outlined above. The cost in time required to introduce these questions is more than compensated by the increased diversity and rich dimensionality that is added to the course.

It is crucial to the success of this approach that no particular ideology or point-of-view be preferred or advocated. On the contrary, students are challenged to examine critically their own attitudes and behaviors utilizing the technical expertise they have gained in the course, and then, to determine how their personal and civic actions should change in the light of this analysis. Specifically, students are asked to link the learned content of the course to the intellectual, personal, and civic dimensions of their lives, becoming individually committed to specific actions, and civically responsible for decisions at the societal level.

By engaging students in conversations about technical issues that require personal and civic decisions, it becomes clear that each individual can contribute to and participate in a societal decision process. In effect, potentially oligarchic determinations are democratized

> *By engaging students in conversations about technical issues that require personal and civic decisions, it becomes clear that each individual can contribute to and participate in a societal decision process.*

and a course in Chemistry becomes an essential component of the American experiment in participatory democracy. The study of Chemistry is not simply an academic requirement, is no longer a purely intellectual exercise, but has become a crucial instrument in the preservation of political liberty.

This approach need not be limited to discussions within the classroom. The preparation of a short research paper (3–5 typewritten pages) focused on a particular chemical concept and its societal impact again requires students to interconnect technical expertise with the broader intellectual, personal, and civic dimensions of human knowledge. This can be extended in several additional directions: the analysis of current events in the popular media (print, radio, television, or motion pictures) and the production of public forums open to the entire university community.

Finally, this exercise is not limited to fields whose technical expertise underpins our technological society. The same approach can be used in courses focused on the social sciences, the arts, and the humanities if the instructor carefully selects points of contact between the course content and the intellectual, personal, and civic dimensions of human knowledge. The keys to success are the engagement of students in a critical analysis based on the core knowledge of a specific course, and then, the determination of changes in personal and civic behavior as a result of this analysis.

Motivating Mathematical Concepts with Politics

R. B. CAMPBELL
UNIVERSITY OF NORTHERN IOWA

Many universities require students to take a mathematics course which is described as general education mathematics, survey of mathematics, mathematics for the liberal arts, or quantitative literacy. Many texts for such courses have recently added chapters on election procedures and apportionment. Teaching this material can enhance understanding of mathematics as well as provide specific information on various methods for determining the winners of elections or allocating delegates to constituencies.

Students will have to conduct elections in social, fraternal, religious, and other organizations to which they belong; hence they should be familiar with the commonly employed methods for determining the winner. These include plurality (the candidate with the most votes wins), a run-off between the two candidates who received the most votes, a sequence of run-offs where the candidate with the fewest votes is eliminated from subsequent elections (the Hare method), and the Borda count (each voter ranks all the candidates, and a point total for each candidate is calculated based on those rankings). Students should find these election procedures interesting because different procedures will produce different winners for a given set of voter preferences, and withdrawing a candidate who does not win can affect the outcome of an election under all of the above procedures.

It is not possible or appropriate to prove Arrow's impossibility theorem in a course at this level, but it is important for students to be aware of its consequences: there is no method of conducting an election which satisfies all the properties which an election procedure should satisfy. For politics and civic engagement, this bears the message that the Utopian goal is not always attainable, and one should be satisfied with what is possible. For mathematics, this bears the important message that mathematics does not always produce one right answer; one must use more than mathematics to make a decision.

Students are not likely to use any of the apportionment methods that have been proposed for the House of Representatives. Having students mindlessly plug numbers into algorithms does not build interest in mathematics. However, it may be possible to generate interest from the fact that each of the methods either allows violation of quota or manifests the Alabama paradox. (The quota for a state is the number of seats in the House times the population of that state divided by the total population of the U.S.; a state with a quota of 21.4 representatives violates quota when it is assigned a number of representatives other than 21 or 22 [e.g., 23]. The Alabama paradox occurs when increasing the number of seats in the House results in a state losing one of its representatives.) Interest in violation of quota and the Alabama paradox must be maintained to the causes of these problems: the methods of greatest divisors used from 1791–1850, major fractions used from 1911–1940, and equal proportions used from 1941–present all use a ratio to measure distance from the quota and hence allow violation of quota; largest fractions used from 1850–1910 uses a difference as the measure of distance from the quota and hence allows the Alabama paradox. Students should calculate a few distances from the quota, as both differences and ratios, to discover that which state is farthest from its quota depends on which measure of distance is being used. This will better serve students than applying the apportionment algorithms.

For politics and civic engagement the apportion-ment methods illustrate that by using alternative reasonable definitions of fairness someone can often claim to be treated unfairly, hence there is no fair apportionment. For mathematics, this provides an excellent opportunity to illustrate the alternatives of ratios and differences as measures of distance, as well as the fact that mathematics alone cannot provide one correct answer.

In introductory general education mathematics courses one should provide both applications of mathematics which the student might use, and mathematical concepts which lay a foundation for future reasoning. The election procedures provide an application which students are likely to use, but also illustrate the concept that mathematics alone cannot provide a unique correct answer to any questions. Students are not likely to apply any apportionment algorithm, but the alternatives of difference versus ratio for measuring discrepancies is a concept which will arise in many contexts.

The Do-It-Yourself Interest Group

Chapman Rackaway
Fort Hays State University

Simulation is a well-established form of curricular instruction utilized to expand and activate student interest in fields of classroom study (Endersby 1995; Jones 1980; Smith 1996; Twelker 1973; Vile 1994). While students are engaged in a simulated activity rather than in pure lecture and discussion, there is no reason why the simulation could not be replaced by real-life interaction, inspiring students to greater participation and action (Jefferson 1999; Hardy and Rackaway forthcoming).

I wanted to take my students beyond the classroom and into a new environment of participatory learning. In our community the city commission regularly reviews issues and passes ordinances that affect our students, such as shifting tax burdens from property taxes over to sales taxes and the use of collected tax money. With significant issues at stake, it became apparent that students could actually lobby elected officials as part of the class.

I tasked the students with creating their own organized interest: a group built around the concept of lobbying the local government for issues that are impor-tant to students. Students have subsequently learned the paperwork in creating an organization by filing as an on-campus student group, developed an organizational mission, surveyed the student body to better understand their "constituency," attended and spoken at city commission meetings, and lobbied local officials one-on-one. Participation in the group is mandatory, with course points allocated to students based on their level of participation.

Six main areas constitute organized interest participation: 1) in-class meetings for the group, no more than one fifteen-minute section of a twice weekly 75-minute class; 2) out-of-class meetings, at least once per week; 3) research on issues and voting history; 4) development of campus survey questions and administration of the survey through our internal Docking Institute of Public Affairs; 5) attending city commission meetings, and 6) taking a leadership role in the group. Since city commission meetings occurred outside of school hours, I gave students regular class time to prepare strategies they could then present to the commission. The group should have instructor guidance but student leadership, so I required students to meet outside of class as well. I assigned students to cull voting records from the local newspaper, and the group even polled our students on issues of importance to them to make their case stronger, as research and information are some of the lobbyist's best strengths. The students then had to attend the meetings of the commission to prepare for presenting their case. Students created a structure of leadership and applied for recognition as a legitimate campus organization. One student is the "president" of the group for bookkeeping and accountability purposes. A secretary/communications director is another vital role, and a treasurer is necessary for student group recognition. The leaders take attendance at each event and report back to the professor for grading.

At the end of the semester, students reflect on the experience and write a three-page paper summarizing their part in and learning from their participation. I also encourage my students to plan for possible future efforts. If students are so inclined, they may continue on with the group's efforts well after their class work is done. My intention in creating the course was to begin a life-long process of direct political engagement among students, and hopefully they will continue to be involved well after the class credit ends.

At first blush one might think that this program would only be applicable in a political science class, but any course with an experiential-learning component could establish its own interest group using a similar model. For instance, a business class could lobby on local economic development issues or sales taxes. Nursing students could create an organized interest that would present issues to the hospital board or other governing body. Local school boards would be logical targets of education classes that could lobby on funding, policies, and the diversity of issues about which school boards decide. The biological sciences could find opportunities to lobby on behalf of biotechnology issues, research support money, the Parks and Recreation Commission about water conservation, use of pesticides, etc. Any subject area that can be regulated or funded by a governmental entity can elect to develop a lobbying group.

Students spend the first class period brainstorming issues that are either currently before the commission or should be, in their opinion. The faculty member may either want to choose the governmental entity to lobby or allow the students to explore their options and come to conclusions on their own. As an example, my pilot group discussed the possibility of limiting the group to campus issues versus local, and then local versus state. The important factor is to pick the area or types of policy to lobby on and then choose the appropriate governmental entity with which to address those concerns. In subsequent classes, the students research and prioritize issues and prepare to lobby by attending commission meetings and by informal contact with commissioners. Another class period consists of brainstorming survey questions and refining them for administration. The survey is optional, but having hard data such as "78% of students believe the city commission should create a 'Renter's Bill of Rights,'" makes the lobbying activity that much more professional and realistic.

As part of the program, students develop a variety of skills that are vital in their future careers and efforts as engaged citizens. Issue background and voting histories are important pieces of information to know before beginning to lobby, so the group reinforces research skills and the ability to synthesize that information as well as analyze it for use in lobbying presentations. After tasking the students early on with the research assignments, I later noticed improved research paper quality across of the board. Team building and presentation skills are natural extensions of the publicly visible practice of lobbying and help students grow in those areas. Oral research paper presentations in class were more polished and professional after having delivered a fact file personally to a sitting member of the commission. Finally, lobbying provides the students with a better understanding of the diversity of issues that affect them in the communities they live in, even if for a short period of time.

References

Endersby, J. W. and D. J. Webber. 1995. Iron triangle simulation: A role-playing game for undergraduates in congress, interest groups, and public policy classes. *PS: Political Science and Politics* 28:520–523.

Hardy, R. J., C. B. Rackaway, and L. Sonnier. 2005. In the robes of the supreme court justices: Critical thinking through the use of hypothetical case law, analyses and interactive simulations. *PS: Political Science and Politics* 38:411–415.

Jefferson, K. W. 1999. The Bosnian war crimes trial simulation: Teaching students about the fuzziness of world politics and international law. *PS: Political Science and Politics* 32:589–592.

Jones, K. 1980. *Simulations: A handbook for teachers.* London: Kogan Page.

Smith, E. T. and M. Boyer. 1996. Designing in-class simulations. *PS: Political Science and Politics* 2:690–694.

Twelker, P. 1973. A basic reference shelf on simulation and gaming. In *The guide to simulations/games for education and training.* Lexington, Mass.: Information Services.

Vile, J. R. and T. R. Van Dervort. 1994. Revitalizing undergraduate programs through intercollegiate mock trial competition. *PS: Political Science and Politics* 27:711–717.

An Exercise in Community Transformation

NATHAN HAND
UNIVERSITY OF IDAHO
AND
KATHARINE KRAVETZ
AMERICAN UNIVERSITY

This essay describes an activity that offers young people the opportunity to integrate learning, civic engagement, and career planning. This simple, powerful, student-created and student-led exercise relates community transformation and civic participation to the aspirations of young people who are embarking on careers involving civil society.

Scholars and practitioners have written about the importance of youth civic engagement from the perspective of integrating the civic world into the classroom (Eble 1983, 146; Hollander and Hartley 2000), and about students actively engaging in their own learning through problem-solving (Whitfield 1999, 109). The goal of teaching students about—while involving them in—community issues is to produce adults who are active participants in their communities and have some understanding of the challenges in communities and the strategies to meet these challenges.

At the same time, young people often face difficult career choices. Should they pursue a life of community or government service? Are they more suited to community organizing? Do they want to create innovative private sector initiatives? Will civic work be the focus of, or a sidelight to, their careers? In order to help people make sound career decisions, we should encourage them to reflect on how their own experience and aspirations fit into the larger issues of civic life and how communities change.

The Transforming Communities Semester is an undergraduate program designed to integrate community-based learning with young people's current and future aspirations. It includes a seminar designed to link public policy to community issues and to study different methods of changing communities, including volunteerism and direct service, community development, advocacy and litigation, education and research, the political process, and community organizing. Participants also study the role of government, business, nonprofits, and leadership in communities. It is a goal of Transforming Communities to help its participants discover the means and institutions that bring hope and change to communities, in order to create in them the confidence that they can both pursue a satisfying career path and make a difference in communities. It is therefore critical to link the students' community and academic experiences with the larger question of how communities transform. Participants should also understand the choices that are available to them if they want to become actively engaged in community transformation. All of these goals should be interrelated, and the final exercise of the semester provides the integration students need.

To begin the exercise, the discussion leaders tape signs representing the means of community transformation around the room. In Transforming Communities, the signs included: service/volunteerism, community development, community organizing, research/teaching, advocacy, litigation, politics/government, and the private sector. Participants are then asked to place themselves near the sign which most closely approximates the career path they are likely to choose. Most members of the group immediately place themselves near a sign. A few ponder the choice, and some place themselves between signs. The leaders then tell the group: "It's your world. Tell us why you chose this path." Tossing a small globe to each student, one by one, they make sure everyone speaks. Many speak about their internship, another community experience, or an interaction with a particular seminar speaker that has instilled in them a passion for a particular career choice. They also find themselves sharing what was once their internal dialogue and conflict.

In the second part of the exercise, the leaders ask participants to place themselves near the sign which they believe represents the most effective path to community change. What happens? Some students remain where they were, some move to other locations, and some again place themselves between signs. Some individuals place themselves in the middle of the room! Now when the globe is passed, students not only explain the reason for their selection, but also their reasons for moving or not moving away from their career choice. At this stage the complexity of community change became apparent. In particular, participants began to recognize and digest their own strengths and weaknesses and how these might impact their careers. Also, many students recognize that, in order to change communities, they might need to integrate the work they do with the work of others.

This simple exercise has proved effective in many contexts, because it fosters recognition of basic concepts and principles of community change, communication of these concepts and the choices to be made, integration of the participants' own plans with the larger issues in civil society, and adaptability to one's own changing ideas and the ideas of others. This culminating activity points out the many strategies and institutions available to those embarking in this work of community transformation, and the ways they can integrate strategies and themselves to effect positive change. Issues which at times appear insurmountable can now be approached with new optimism.

We have found this exercise applicable to a wide range of groups and situations. While the Transforming Communities participants have been together and forged close bonds over several months before this exercise takes place, several groups with little or no prior experience together have engaged in it with energy and enthusiasm and, anecdotal evidence suggests, positive outcomes. The activity works particularly well with groups in which the participants know each other, but can also be used to bring strangers together. It seems to work well with young people who are embarking on ca-

reers, as well as people who are already established, either to help them in career change or to evaluate how to make their current work more rewarding, both in general and to them personally.

The exercise is also applicable to the following settings: (1) other conferences in such areas as higher education, service learning, national service, advocacy, community development, and community organizing; (2) college, including orientations, upper class seminars, classes involving civic education, and community-centered and leadership groups such as student government, and career planning seminars; (3) graduate courses in such fields as public administration, public affairs, and non-profit management; and (4) comparisons of the public, private and non-profit sectors' approaches to community change.

It is of course important to conduct the exercise in a way that does not pass judgment on any career choice. To that end, the leader can begin the exercise by making some introductory comments to make participants comfortable, assuring them that there are no right or wrong choices, and stressing the larger civic issues.

We are interested in further exploring the difference in creating the norms/signs for exercise participants, and having the participants create them on their own, without preconceived notions. Each method appears to have its advantages and disadvantages. Perhaps such exploration would lead to some combination of the two approaches, where the participants begin the process and the leader suggests alternatives which the participants have not explored. These and other innovations may further enhance its ability to raise awareness of community change and stimulate personal growth in our youth.

References

Eble, K. E. 1983. *The aims of college teaching.* San Francisco: Jossey-Bass.

Hollander, E. and M. Hartley. 2000. Civic renewal in higher education: The state of the movement and the need for a national network. In Ehrlich, T., ed., *Civic responsibility and higher education.* Phoenix, Ariz.: Oryx Press.

Whitfield, T. S. 1999. Connecting service- and classroom-based learning: The use of problem-based learning. *Michigan Journal of Community Service-Leaning* 6:106–11.

Using Political Activism to Teach Critical Thinking

Mary Ange Cooksey
Indiana University East

Logic is one of the most difficult areas of philosophy in which to get students interested. New ways of teaching critical thinking can jumpstart student enthusiasm and increase levels of learning. One innovative approach to teaching logic is to apply its principles and concepts to a study of the American political process. By integrating the traditional curriculum of logic into hands-on research into civic engagement and political involvement, students become more active learners, and take more away with them in the end. This instructional strategy can work in teaching a traditional logic class, or in teaching critical-thinking skills in other academic areas as well. With some moderate revisions to a standard syllabus, teaching critical thinking through an examination of political citizenship can engage students in a more meaningful learning experience and encourage their development as informed and participatory citizens.

The Political Activism Project is a curriculum infusion project wherein elements of political activism are layered over the traditional components of logic rather than taught in their place. Students are introduced to the elements of logical inquiry, while at the same time they are introduced to the elements of political activism and voter participation. They become familiar with the language of logic and its formal methodology by applying them to the systems and structures of the American political process. The political activism project begins with a study of the uses of language and the elements of logic and critical thinking. Meanings and connotations of words are discussed in relationship to their impact on arguments, and the elements of premises and conclusions are described and discussed. Once students begin to grasp the concept of logical argumentation, they begin to apply what they have learned to the first component of political activism—an examination of published arguments for and against voting.

Students locate arguments for and against voting in electronic or periodical literature. They then work to extract premises and conclusions from the narratives in order to evaluate their strength or weakness. Students sort out the trustable elements of the arguments from those that are not by determining what elements suffer from a volatility of language or lack of clarity of meaning. Students then exchange their findings in class discussion, and compose an essay describing their results. They are then ready to move on to the next phase in the study of logic—argument analysis for validity, cogency, and truth. The political activism project proceeds with its next component—an investigation of voter education and registration procedures in their state and local communities.

Students conduct internet or field research to discover how potential voters become registered in their hometowns, and if they themselves are not registered to vote, they are required to do so or provide a compelling argument for their choosing not to do so at this time. Students investigate electronic resources that are available to voters, such as the website of the office of the secretary of state, and they are required to access and read the Voter's Bill of Rights. They then set out on foot to discover whether or not there are adequate resources in their communities for voters to accomplish the third component of political activism—an exploration of resources available for voters to learn about political parties, candidates, and the offices for which they are running.

Students accomplish this third phase in the political activism project by visiting the local headquarters of the major political parties and procuring whatever information is available about upcoming races, the candidates, and the political parties themselves. Students critically evaluate the political party platforms and analyze the arguments embedded in their ideologies for feasibility and fairness. Students then invite candidates from local races to come to class and present their arguments for election or re-election. Students craft questions for candidates, then critically evaluate their responses for truth and cogency in relation to political party platform and local conditions and needs. Critical evaluation of the candidates continues with students' explication of campaign literature and signage. Students analyze the language and messages embedded in candidates' printed materials, examining the arguments by checking for validity, strength, cogency, and truth.

Students continue their work in political activism

by conducting literature-based research into voter trends in their states and local communities. After securing data from the city, county, or state offices, students analyze historical voting information such as voter turn out and demographic trends in preparation for comparison to upcoming election results. If the course is taught in the fall, the opportunity for analysis would occur with the general election in November; if the course is taught in spring, with the primary in May.

Students' study of formal logic continues with a discussion of fallacies and invalid forms, while their field research continues with an analysis of the voting process on Election Day. An examination of election results and local views on the value of voting follows. After Election Day, students poll their friends and family to determine their attitudes toward political activism, then critically evaluate responses for fallacies and inconsistencies in the perceived relationship between activism, voting, and good government. Students submit an analysis of their findings and write a reflection essay on their own views of voting and their experiences at the polls that year.

The semester culminates in students' submission of a portfolio of their written work. This includes a blend of assignments in formal logic as well as field notes and narratives from the experiences in political activism noted above. Perhaps the most important component of the portfolio is the list of recommendations students are asked to make that would improve the American political process and encourage higher turn out at the polls.

The contents of the portfolio could include:

The political activism project . . . is effective because it allows for instructors to be creative while still preserving the traditional content in their fields.

1. Field notes/narratives about: a) trip to the courthouse; b) trip to parties' headquarters; c) attempts at locating information about political parties, local races, and current candidates (include list of races and candidates); and d) attempts at contacting candidates

2. Analysis of arguments for and against voting

3. Analysis of major party platforms

4. Analysis of in-class candidates plus two questions developed for each

5. Analysis of political signage/pamphlets/flyers (at least 1 of each if possible); react to content *and* presentation (colors, photos, graphics)

6. Field notes/narrative about Election Day voting experience

7. Election results—national, state, and local races

8. Voter activism polling results (at least 10 respondents)

9. Reaction to SOS website and voter's bill of rights

10. Recommendations to improve political process and voter turn out

The political activism project enables students to explore the concepts of logic while learning about civic engagement and political activism. This type of curriculum infusion project is effective because it allows for instructors to be creative while still preserving the traditional content in their fields. Projects such as these are valuable teaching tools for they not only infuse new life into old subjects, but they provide new skills with which students can become more politically active and productive citizens.

A Compelling Reason to Study Cities

Janet Cherrington
Minnesota State University, Mankato

In a general education course, Introduction to the City, students find compelling reasons to study cities. They visit city streets that provide living examples of shops selling all sorts of goods where one can pass every imaginable kind of person—the up and coming as well as the down and out, the young and the old as well as the rich and the poor. Students see, feel, and articulate not only a change in their urban perspective, but apply this changed perspective through concept maps, a field-based walking tour, and community-oriented research.

Concept Maps

Angelo and Cross (1993) define concept maps "as drawings or diagrams showing the mental connections that students make between a major concept the instructor focuses on and other concepts they have learned" (197). One of the most intriguing aspects of the Introduction to the City class is discovering how students (going to the same university and living in the same city) construct very different mental images of the urban environment. Initially concept maps are used to discover what preconceptions and prior knowledge structures students bring to these areas. With this information, the instructor develops a road map for deciding when and how to introduce new topics, as well as to identify misconceptions that may cause later difficulties.

Ten minutes before the end of the first class, the instructor distributes a sheet of paper with a concept map framework consisting of three prompts: the title "Training Your Mind to Go Visiting," brief instructions, and some graphical illustrations that include a cityscape pencil sketch, the Minnesota State University insignia, and the city of Mankato's logo. Students are asked to construct a personalized concept map using words, drawings, and images. Above all, students are assured there are no *right or wrong* answers. Afterward the maps are collected, retained by the instructor, and used for class discussion. Throughout subsequent lectures, ideas from the concept maps are interjected. At the close of the semester, students are given a blank sheet of paper and asked to construct a concept map anew. Afterward they compare their original concept map to the newer one and collectively assess the changes. Initial concept

maps are primarily constructed on the basis of personal experience, interests, and rudimentary knowledge. In the final concept maps, however, these primary associations move on to add secondary and even tertiary levels of association about the urban perspective and how it applies to the university and to Mankato, Minnesota.

Field-Based Walking Tour

Students build on their historical and geographical awareness of urban life by studying the origin and development of world cities, patterns of global urbanization, and the processes of planning an urban environment. One of the course readings, Kevin Lynch's *The Image of the City,* encourages students to pay attention to their mental interpretation of the city (Lynch 1960). Lynch asks, "How do people perceive the built environment?" and "What are the underlying elements common to human perception of the city?" His premise is that armed with a better understanding of how people perceive the city image, urban planners can actually design better cities. Reading Lynch's work encourages students to develop an individualized appreciation of the imagery and physical surroundings of the city. An Internet-based "virtual" tour assignment provides students with a historical overview of Minnesota State University and Mankato, Minnesota (Cherrington 2000).

A two-hour, instructor-narrated walking tour takes learning outside the classroom as students venture down the streets of their host city. The tour is at once several things. As a map, the tour serves as an orientation to help new students navigate their way around town. As a history lesson, it provides students with a historical overview of their school and how Minnesota State University, Mankato, evolved from the valley campus of Mankato Normal School (1866), Mankato State Teachers College (1921), and Mankato State University (1975) to the present highland campus. As a wide-angle lens, it allows students to see that Mankato is a unique city with many examples of adaptive reuse, ranging from different time periods. Together the map, the history, and the lens evoke a new mental image of the city (Cherrington 2002).

Intro to the City Walking Tour Paper Evaluation Rubric

	Poor	Fair	Average	Good	Excellent	Total Points	Total Earned
Major Points							
Is there an introductory paragraph that states what the paper will cover?	6	7	8	9	10	10	
Is the paper free of typos and spelling errors? {# or less}	[7], (0-4)	[6], (5-8)	[5], (9-11)	[4], (12-13)	[3], (14-15)	15	
Are there quotes and references in the paper, relating to the articles and text readings [with appropriate citations]?	[0,1], (0-4)	[2], (5-8)	[3], (9-11)	[4], (12-13)	[5+], (14-15)	15	
Does the paper address the subject matter? Are there examples of critical thinking?	(0-5)	(6-10)	(11-13)	(14-16)	(17-20)	20	
One or two photos, sketch, old newspaper clippings included with captions & text wrap.	(0-5)	(6-10)	(11-13)	(14-16)	(17-20)	20	
Attention has been given to a specific research topic or concept.	(0-5)	(6-10)	(11-13)	(14-16)	(17-20)	20	
Other							
Is there a Bibliography and is it appropriate (yes or no)?	4	5	6	7	8	8	
Is the paper well organized and developed?	4	5	6	7	8	8	
Is the paper clear and easy to read?	4	5	6	7	8	8	
Is the grammar of high quality?	4	5	6	7	8	8	
What are the number of pages (not counting title page and bibliography)?	1-2(6)	3(7)	3+(8)	4(9)	4+(10)	10	
Is there a summary paragraph that brings the paper together?	4	5	6	7	8	8	
Total Points						150	
Comments:							

Rubric by: Janet Cherrington–Minnesota State University, Mankato

Figure 2.2. Intro to the City Walking Tour Paper Evaluation Rubric

Along the route, students also witness how the university's host city has responded to significant urban changes such as decentralization and the accompanying decline of the central business district (CBD), with programs of adaptive reuse and an entertainment district. A designated "rest stop" on the walking tour is the Mankato Intergovernmental Building, where students see the rooms in which the city council and planning commission meet. The latter serves to encourage a better understanding of the local governing/planning process by having students attend, orally report on, and write about a public meeting later in the semester.

Community-Oriented Research

After the tour, students engage in a creative writing assignment: to describe their impressions of the city historically, culturally, and socially before and after the walking tour. As part of this assignment, students also research and write about a particular site of interest to them within the city. Completed essays are peer reviewed using an instructor-generated rubric with guidelines on introductory/ending paragraphs, paper organization, and development (see fig. 2.2). Working in these small groups builds individual writing skills and broadens the students' overall knowledge of Mankato. After the peer reviews, students are given an additional week to incorporate suggestions and/or stylistic changes before the essays are graded. With permission, student research is used to build additional links to the Internet-based walking tour (Cherrington 2005).

Conclusion

After walking the environs of Mankato and completing their community-oriented essays, students report feeling less isolated, interacting in genuine ways beyond the campus and work. Uploading essays to the existing Internet-based walking tour of Mankato recognizes the meaningfulness and usefulness of student research that is, in turn, publicly disseminated. Familiarity with city council and planning commission meetings provides students with the confidence to observe, reflect on, and write about how citizens participate in the local government model. Introduction to the City joins higher order thinking and analysis, and synthesizes these with community-oriented research to encourage civic engagement.

References

Angelo, T., and K. Cross. 1993. *Classroom assessment techniques.* San Francisco: Jossey-Bass.

Cherrington, J. 2000. Mankato walking tour. http://www. intech.mnsu.edu/cherrington/Tour/TourPages/Mankato TourCover.htm.

———. 2002. An urban studies model of applied learning integrating internet-based visualization and multimedia technology. In M. Roccetti and M. Syed, eds., *International conference on simulation and multimedia in engineering education,* 63–67. San Diego, Calif.: Society for Modeling and Simulation International.

———. 2005. Student essay index. http://www.intech.mnsu. edu/cherrington/papers/list.htm.

Lynch, K. 1960. *The Image of the city.* Cambridge, Mass.: MIT Press.

Student Philanthropy as a Vehicle for Teaching the Subject Matter

JOAN FERRANTE
NORTHERN KENTUCKY UNIVERSITY

The Mayerson Student Philanthropy Project at Northern Kentucky University (NKU) encourages students to identify a community need, search for nonprofits with projects to address that need, and then invite those nonprofits with 501(c) (3) designations to apply for small grants between $1,000 and $4,000. This philanthropy project seeks to make a difference in the civic life of the community through learning, scholarship, community involvement, and mutually beneficial partnerships with nonprofits. Mayerson students develop the civic literacy skills needed to conceptualize community need, to appreciate and consider diverse viewpoints, and to make informed deliberations and decisions about how to address the identified need.[1]

Faculty from all disciplines are eligible to participate in the Mayerson Student Philanthropy Project as no discipline or course has a monopoly on preparing students for civic participation. Examples of courses that have integrated the philanthropy component include Drawing I, Applied Anthropology, College Writing, Managing Organizational Change, Sales Management, Sports Marketing, Nursing in the Community, Sociology of the Environment, and Strategies of Persuasion. Participating students in all classes complete the following tasks:

- Identify a community need

- Form community boards (small work groups)

- Select nonprofits that meet community needs

- Interact with people in the nonprofit sector (interviews, site visits, in-class presentations by nonprofits)

- Answer seven reflective questions

- Issue and evaluate RFPs (Requests for Funding Proposals)

- Engage in a deliberative group decision-making process to select successful applicants and award $4,000

Depending on the individual course goals, faculty may require students to:

- Write a funding proposal to submit to the class on behalf of a 501(c)(3) organization

- Volunteer at a 501(c)(3) nonprofit organization

- Learn about the history of philanthropy and nonprofits

- Explore careers in the nonprofit sector

- Raise additional funds

Faculty use the student philanthropy project as a vehicle for teaching the subject matter, not as an add-on. This way, students come to realize that an academic discipline offers tools and concepts for identifying community needs and thinking about solutions. For example, one professor teaching a Sociology of the Environment course (focusing on the human causes of and solutions to environmental degradation) found that students' in-depth examinations of nonprofits helped them understand the many things individuals and local organizations can do to address environmental problems that otherwise seem overwhelming. Students in the class claimed that the face-to-face interactions with nonprofit leaders helped them to realize it is possible to take action. Furthermore, the competitive aspect of awarding small grants led to highly constructive discussions about establishing funding priorities in light of limited resources.

Likewise the philanthropy component enriched the MGT 410 (Managing Change) class. Each of four student groups chose one local non-profit agency and collaborated with it to develop a RFP. The RFP described a project that will bring about change in the community. Students not only gained experience in developing change plans, but also saw first-hand how nonprofits work for change in the community. In addition they were able to analyze changes within the participating nonprofit organizations and they reflected upon the ways that philanthropists and volunteers create change in the community. Some students experienced personal change as a result of participating in the project. Most importantly, MGT 410 students learned more about their community and how they might impact it.

How do participating students come to identify a community need, learn about nonprofits in a position to address that need, and select projects worthy of funding? First, they make a commitment to pay attention to things going on around them in their communities, talk with community leaders, and then share their observations with classmates. The academic discipline and course theme shape those observations.

Once students settle on a need, they search the internet and local newspaper archives to learn about nonprofits with missions tied to that need. More importantly, they use their eyes to observe previously unnoticed signs and buildings associated with nonprofit agencies in their community. Eventually students generate a list of relevant nonprofits and contact them to determine interest and solicit proposals. Students review the proposals, visit the nonprofits, share observations, argue, debate, and eventually come to an agreement about which proposals to fund.

Some examples of funded projects include

- A $1,000 investment to Licking River Watershed Watch supports the ongoing collection, interpretation, and presentation of data as it relates to the river's water quality. The data system needs to be in place to ensure that the Licking River meets the vision of swimmable and fishable waters as defined by the 1972 Clean Water Act.

- A $2,000 investment in Athletes.com to pay for the production of three public service announcements to market a no-cost web-based service connecting high school athletes seeking scholarships with Division II and III-level college recruiters with small recruiting budgets.

Thanks to the generosity of the Manuel D. and Rhoda Mayerson Foundation, NKU students have awarded more than $280,000 in 173 projects involving 131 nonprofit agencies over five years. It is important to point out that students have raised $30,000 of that total. Recall that fundraising is not something we require of participating students. It is something they decide to do. NKU classes have raised money by holding a comedy night fund raiser at a local café, gathering (with the permission of the owner) coins thrown into a fountain by passers-by, and holding bake sales. On several occasions students have successfully approached their employers for funds. Students in a Sales Management class applied sales techniques to raise $3,525. The students formed teams; one team, which included a musician, volunteered his band to hold a benefit concert. Another team asked local businesses to donate items (pizza, gift certificates, etc.) and held a raffle. Several other teams called on local businesses, friends, and relatives to make donations. A Strategies of Persuasion class routinely raises $5,000 by sending fundraising letters to relatives, friends, and acquaintances persuading them to contribute to their effort. The success of these student-driven fund-raising initiatives at NKU, a low-tuition, primarily commuter school, suggests that a philanthropy component need not depend on foundation or other grant making sources. Students can raise the money. Of course a philanthropy component requires there be money to invest in the community. But the amount of money need not be large—it can be as small as $100 or $200. No matter the amount, students still have to determine a need and decide the best way to invest available dollars.

Note

1. For more information on the Mayerson Student Philanthropy Project's history, mission and guidelines go to civicengagement.nku.edu.

SERVICE LEARNING AND EDUCATING CITIZENS

3

A Service-Learning Checklist

LINDA CHRISTIANSEN AND KATY WIGLEY
INDIANA UNIVERSITY SOUTHEAST

The Service-Learning Project Checklist

Campus Support

1. Visit your campus teaching and learning center.

Teaching learning centers are a wonderful resource for faculty starting service-learning projects. Not only are you likely to find information and pedagogical resources on ways to incorporate service learning into the curriculum, you will receive lots of support and encouragement as you work through the process of beginning your project. Because the staff of these centers has the opportunity to interact with faculty and staff from across campus, they can also help you brainstorm about potential campus collaboration opportunities and identify colleagues also interested in service learning. To help support faculty engaged in service learning and civic engagement, some universities even offer Faculty Learning Communities in these areas.

Staff of the teaching and learning centers often have a broader knowledge of additional campus support opportunities. They can help point you to, and will sometimes assist in the preparation of, grants and partnerships as well as identify other campus offices where you will likely find additional informational regarding potential community partnerships.

2. Apply for campus funding.

Nothing makes your project seem as important as the financial support of the campus. Seek out and apply for grants supporting new teaching methodologies, student-faculty interaction, community involvement, and Scholarship of Teaching and Learning. If you are after larger, state-wide or national grants, first securing a campus grant (and the official support of your project implied therein) will often be helpful—if for no other reason than having already done some of the grant preparation work!

3. Visit campus outreach offices.

Identify and work with campus outreach offices (such as volunteer centers) to look for (additional) community partners. These offices are wonderful resources because their primary goal is to reach out to community partners and agencies. We suggest availing yourself of this service regardless of whether or not you have already identified a community group—you may well find possibilities and needs you never knew existed.

Community Support

4. Visit community centers and support agencies.

If you already have an idea for your service-learning project, visit an office or a program agency familiar with the topic or theme of your project. In our case, agencies and organizations working with disadvantaged and minority groups were the first stop in our quest to find out what *we* could do to help *them* and their clients.

If you have not identified a target audience, general community agencies are always happy to work with you to see how your project and ideas can fit one of their needs or address their service mission. Think big in these exploratory meetings because once your project is a success, you will likely seek to expand its scope and breadth.

5. Identify community grant opportunities.

Just as you want to have the support of your campus, you also want to have the support of the community. If your project directly addresses an area of community need, you might find support in local philanthropic agencies. And, don't stop at just your community—look for state grants. Indiana Campus Compact awards grants to faculty for various service-learning and civic engagement projects and has the added benefit of being affiliated with national service-learning initiatives as well as programs for the member institutions.

Awareness

6. Know your community.

Always stay current with the needs of your community and think how you can provide assistance. We all know how important it is for graduates of our colleges and universities to be good citizens and good community members. As faculty and staff, we must support our students by providing them with hands-on community experience.

7. Publicize.

Don't forget to let people know about the good work you and your students are doing. Publicity includes having your colleagues see your work, as well as letting your target audiences know you are reaching out to them. It is not enough to post flyers around campus and place the occasional advertisement in the campus paper. You must put promotional material in areas where the people who need your help will see your information. Be mindful of language and access barriers by working to produce materials in other languages and informing various media outlets of your service dates and locations.

8. Reflect.

Always close your project with an opportunity for reflection. Ask any agency or organization with whom you have worked to provide feedback regarding the effectiveness and benefits of your project. Have your students keep a journal or submit a formal paper detailing their experiences. Close the loop . . . use all the feedback and your experiences to make changes and improvements in the project for the next time.

A Service-Learning Checklist Reflection

We developed this three-part checklist for faculty who are starting or expanding a service-learning project. The inspiration for this checklist was the result of our redoubled efforts to revitalize the IRS Volunteer Income Tax Assistance (VITA) on our campus. While the pri-

mary service-learning component of this project was clear—training students in tax preparation in order to work with poor, elderly, and non–English speaking community members—the secondary service-learning components expanded and improved the program by including the involvement of students and faculty from other disciplines working in support of the project, as well as connecting service learning and civic engagement by involving community agencies.

To illustrate a successful use of this checklist, see how the foundations of our program relate to the items on the checklist (the numbers listed parenthetically correspond to specific items on the checklist):

A collaborative partnership with the professor coordinating VITA and the campus teaching learning center led to expanding the IU Southeast VITA program (#1). Paramount among the changes was to actively target additional community members who were in need of tax preparation assistance (#3, 4), develop partnerships with other departments on campus (#1, 3), and seek support by securing local and state-wide grants (#2, 5). In the first year of revamping the program we saw: students in the graphics arts program design new VITA posters, including ones in Spanish (#7); students and the coordinator from the Spanish program serve as translators for the Spanish sessions; and students in taxation and accounting classes prepare tax returns. The students involved in the program reflected via paper, reports, discussions, or journaling their experiences in the program and the faculty members involved related the benefit to their student's learning (#8). Afterward, you should interview community agencies to determine the benefits and identify any additional needs that can be addressed through future service-learning and civic engagement collaborations (#6).

Some disciplines may find it difficult to find a way to become involved in civic engagement though service-learning. These disciplines should consider partnering with another area to support an already-established program. We have accomplished this by including professors from sociology, graphic arts, web design, nursing, education, and Spanish, along with business students.

Using this checklist and our applications as a model will help non-traditional disciplines to reconsider their civic content. Just as each community is unique, so is each service-learning project. Make it your own and make it work best for your community and for the learning of your students.

Building the Right Relationship: Collaboration as a Key to Successful Civic Engagement

Elizabeth M. Goering
Indiana University–Purdue University Indianapolis

Service learning, when executed well, can potentially benefit individual learners as well as the larger community. On the individual level, service learning increases self-esteem, fosters problem-solving and leadership skills, enhances social and emotional development, and improves academic performance. On the community level, service learning promotes a sense of civic responsibility and transforms students' creativity and energy into resources for redressing social problems. Unfortunately, the experience of service learning often falls short of its potential, as service learning can actually reinforce preexisting prejudices, replicate power inequities, and become paternalistic or patronizing. A challenge for any teacher hoping to provide meaningful civic engagement opportunities for students is maximizing the aforementioned benefits while minimizing the risks.

Since 2002, I have engaged students enrolled in Advanced Topics in Group Communication in service-learning activities. Over the years, students have completed a variety of projects, including planning events, assessing programs, and conducting communication workshops, for a wide range of community organizations. As is the case with any classroom activity, some of these projects have been more successful than others. As I have reflected upon them, I have discovered three different approaches to service learning that may provide a useful framework for understanding their varying success. The three approaches (provision, prescription, and collaboration), borrowed from the field of organizational consulting, make different assumptions about the responsibilities of the agency being served and the service provider, thereby creating different power relationships. While each of these approaches

Because collaboration balances the power between students and the community organizations they serve, it creates a more symbiotic relationship . . . the kind of relationship that can sustain service-learning endeavors over time.

has the potential to benefit students and the community, I have discovered that the third approach—collaboration—is the optimal approach. Because collaboration balances the power between students and the community organizations they serve, it creates a more symbiotic relationship than either of the other two models and creates the kind of relationship that can sustain service-learning endeavors over time.

In the first consulting model, provision, an organization "contracts with" a service provider for a particular service. For example, an elementary school principal might identify playground fights as a problem and invite college students enrolled in a "Conflict Communication" class to provide conflict management training for the elementary school students. The client identifies the problem *and* the solution, then contracts with the college students to implement her solution. This model has been utilized frequently in my class. Students volunteer the required number of hours with an organization, providing whatever service the organization requests.

The "prescription" consulting model is another common approach student groups take to service learning. In this model, the service *provider* assumes responsibility for diagnosing the problem and prescribing a cure. When applied to service learning, the students or instructor select a project they think will benefit the organization or community. For example, students may choose to plan a benefit concert and simply select an organization that will receive the contributions generated through their event.

While service-learning projects that operate within the provision or prescription paradigms may be successful, they run a greater risk of encountering the afore-mentioned problems associated with service learning. Because the inherent power inequities in these two models create a relatively wide space between "server" and "served," these approaches can reinforce existing prejudices and foster paternalism.

Collaboration offers an alternative approach to service learning that reduces these potential risks because it establishes a more equitable balance of power. In collaboration, the focus is on joint participation between client and service provider. All relevant parties participate actively in defining the problem and generating possible courses of action. Because true collaboration calls for equal participation from all stakeholders in all stages of problem solving, service-learning opportunities informed by this model minimize some of the previously identified concerns.

Hence, establishing effective collaboration is a good—if challenging—goal of civic engagement. But, how does one establish collaborations that can serve as a solid foundation for service learning? Keyton and Stallworth (2003) identify four criterial attributes of collaborative relationships, noting that for collaborations to succeed, the parties involved must have: shared decision making, shared goals, equal input, and interdependent relationships. Keyton and Stallworth argue, in fact, that "if one or more of these elements is weak or missing, collaboration is jeopardized" (240).

In addition, I have found that the likelihood of success is greatly enhanced if micro-level collaborations are embedded within the context of macro-level Collaborations. Most successful civic engagement activities are the result of collaborations at the micro-level that take place within Collaborations that are established, even institutionalized, at the macro-level. In other words, the department or university has an ongoing collaborative relationship with community organizations, and the students collaborate with individuals from those organizations to design appropriate, mutually beneficial service-learning projects. For these dual-level collaborations to be successful, both levels must be characterized by all four of the criterial attributed identified by Keyton and Stallworth.

Establishing productive dual-level collaborations is beneficial for a variety of reasons. The first justification is primarily pragmatic, in that embedding micro-level collaboration within macro-level Collaboration is compatible with time constraints of the academic semester. True collaboration is a time-intensive process,

and if students can join existing partnerships, they can accomplish much more in limited time than they could if they had to forge new relationships with community organizations each semester.

A second convincing argument for situating collaboration at the dual levels is that with this structure the success of the civic engagement effort does not rely on the success of an individual student project. In a recent semester, students in my Advanced Group Communication class partnered with the Indianapolis Public Schools (IPS) and the Peace Learning Center (PLC) to design and implement service-learning projects. On a macro-level, the project was the result of Collaboration between the Department, IPS, and PLC, but on a micro-level, the individual student groups collaborated with representatives from IPS and PLC to design and implement their specific projects. The communication that characterized the micro-level collaborations varied considerably in terms of the level of equality and the degree to which decision making truly involved all participants. Not all students were equally committed to their projects, and not all PLC liaisons were equally motivated. Still, in spite of some less effective interaction at the micro-level, the macro-level Collaboration was a success.

A final justification for establishing dual-level collaborations is that this structure maximizes the benefits of history, by allowing civic engagement endeavors to build on previous successes. The civic engagement experiment referred to above was built on the previous success of Collaboration between IPS and PLC, and the success of this experiment became the "history" upon which subsequent collaborations could be built.

In conclusion, my past experiences with service learning suggest that while there are many approaches one can take to service learning, the approach with the greatest capacity for fulfilling the potential of civic engagement while simultaneously avoiding some of its pitfalls is collaboration. Furthermore, if the individual service-learning projects can be collaborative relationships that are embedded within macro-level Collaborations, the promise of civic engagement is even greater.

References

Keyton, J., and V. Stallworth. 2003. On the verge of collaboration: Interaction processes versus group outcomes. In L. R. Frey, ed., *Group communication in context: Studies of bona fide groups*, 235–262. 2nd ed. Mahwah, N.J.: Erlbaum.

Maximizing the Power of Reflection

CYNTHIA ROBERTS AND SCOTT SMITHSON
PURDUE UNIVERSITY NORTH CENTRAL

Service learning is a form of experiential education which enables students to actively apply classroom material to work with a community organization. Learning occurs through the process of action and subsequent reflection upon the experience, and can result not only in academic and cognitive development but in personal and social development as well (Eyler 2002). Kolb (1984) suggests that learning occurs as part of a cycle in which students experience something, reflect on that experience, then draw the reflections together into a cohesive theory, subsequently impacting future action. However, student involvement in a service-learning project does not ensure that they will make the connection between their experience and the content of their academic studies (Eyler 2002).

Reflection, defined by Hatcher and Bringle as the "intentional consideration of an experience in light of particular learning objectives" (1997, 153), is the key component that facilitates making that connection. Reflection is considered "the glue that holds service and learning together . . . " (Eyler, Giles, and Schmeide 1996, 16). Effective reflection empowers participants to take ownership of their learning, stimulates critical thinking, and enhances effective teamwork.

However, the quality and depth of learning can vary tremendously from student to student if assignments are left too open-ended. Well structured reflection activities can help to minimize variation and facilitate the connection. Based on work by Gainen and Locatelli (1995) and Rama, Ravencroft, Wolcott, and Zlotkowski (2000), the following planning questions might be considered when designing reflection activities:

- "What type of course is the project being incorporated in?"
- "What knowledge is required for completing project tasks?"
- "What skills are required for completing project tasks (investigative, presentation, teamwork)?"
- "What is the grading weight assigned to the project?"

Thinking about these questions in advance can help to determine the appropriateness of the reflection device, connect it to coursework, plan relevant training, and decide on an appropriate weighting strategy.

To achieve optimal learning, reflection activities should occur throughout the course of the engagement rather than merely appearing at the end as a final paper requirement. Activities established before the experience help students gain a preliminary understanding of the community partner, anticipate possible challenges, develop project implementation plans, create personal learning goals, and begin building competencies needed for successful project execution. Activities structured during the engagement can facilitate the connection of coursework to experience, ensure that service is being performed competently, or focus on resolving challenges, developmental issues, or team difficulties. Reflection upon project completion challenges the students to think critically about the entire experience and its relevance to course content and their future endeavors. This is also when they can be challenged to consider the important intersection of knowledge and social accountability.

Journaling is one of the most common approaches to reflection due to the ease of implementation and potential depth of response received. And there are many options for how it can be structured from free writing to a structured analysis of critical incidents (Hatcher and Bringle 1997). Students can be asked to integrate key terms from the course into their writing. An equally effective method involves the creation of the three-part journal in which students identify an experience on the top third of the page (*what happened?*), analyze the relevance of course content to understanding that experience in the middle (*so what does this mean?*), and apply the learning to their personal or professional lives in the final third of the page (*now what will I do differently?*). Sometimes, more formal strategies may be used in which students are given several essay questions at the beginning of the term and asked to complete a certain number of these throughout the term. A series of prompts given before, during, and after the service-learning experience can be beneficial as well. To improve journaling quality, faculty members are encouraged to:

Table 3.1. Questions to Stimulate Reflection
(Compiled from Eyler 2002; Hatcher and Bringle 1997; Watson 2001)

	Before	During	After
Individual	What do I intend to learn? What skills do I want to develop? What do I already know? How do I feel about my project and colleagues? What difficulties might I encounter? Why? What will make this a good experience for me? How will I make sure it is?	What happened? How did it affect me? What was exciting, puzzling, inspiring, frustrating, impressive, upsetting, challenging? How can I use *this material* in my work? How has this experience changed my thoughts, values, or opinions so far? What will I do differently next time based on what I've learned?	Did I learn what I had intended to learn? Why or why not? How will I think, act, or behave differently in the future because of this? In what ways have my sense of self, values, and self-confidence been changed because of this experience? Do I have more/less understanding or empathy than I did before? Why? Would I do something like this again or recommend this to others? Why or why not?
Group	How will we work together on this project? What will make this a good team experience? What does acceptable performance look like?	How well is everyone contributing to our discussion/work? What is going well/not so well in our team? What should we try to do differently next time we meet? How does our work together relate to *what we are discussing* in class?	How well did we work together? How did our work benefit our client? What issues did it address? Did we impact anything? What contributed to our success? What more needs to be done? What could have been improved during this semester?
Community	What do I know about this client? What does our client expect from us? What other situations influence this problem?	What have I learned about this agency so far? How is this agency impacted by what is going on in the larger political/ social sphere? How is the community impacted by this agency? How does our work/this agency illustrate the subject we are covering in class?	What did my client think of our product/presentation? What have I learned about this agency, these people, or the community? How does it correspond to what I learned in the book/article? Similarities? Differences?

- Provide clear written instructions to students at the beginning.

- Provide plenty of written question prompts to guide students through desired levels of analysis. Questions regarding key issues, potential/existing problems and possible solutions, and critical incidents occurring during the experience can be useful in guiding students to deeper levels of insight.

- Provide a sample entry or two that will serve as a model for writers.

- Establish and disseminate grading rubrics prior to the exercise to provide direction and performance expectations.

Although one typically thinks of reflection in terms of the assignment of written exercises such as journaling, it may be helpful to include other activities that provide alternative routes for sharing experiences and insights. Discussion in class, between teammates, and with community partners should be encouraged to introduce students to alternative viewpoints and to challenge them to think critically. As technology becomes more accessible, dialogue can be facilitated electronically using email, websites, discussion boards, or chat rooms. Instructors can trigger the discussion by posting a specific question related to the experience and requiring students to share responses with the group, in turn stimulating further exploration. Postings do not have to be limited to text, they can include graphic depictions of significant issues or events. Reflection can be also encouraged using more creative means such as the development of final presentations, posters, skits, or videos. Regardless of the media chosen, students should make contributions at regular intervals about their reading and its relationship to their observations, interactions, and experiences, ultimately developing new ways of thinking about an issue or strategies for self-improvement (Mabry 1998). The method chosen to stimulate reflection should be challenging enough to stretch the students beyond their comfort levels to think in new ways.

Reflection can also occur at multiple levels when applicable, ranging from individual introspection to group discussion and organizational analysis. Reflection at the group level, utilized when work is being performed by teams, has an added benefit of enhancing learning about interpersonal and team effectiveness. Reflection at the agency level can address societal, political or organizational issues and place the learning in a larger context. Table 3.1, compiled from the work of

Eyler (2002), Hatcher and Bringle (1997), and Watson (2001), provides a strategy for developing questions that ensures a comprehensive reflective process. For further precision, questions containing italicized text can be customized to explicitly address key concepts.

Grading rubrics shared with the students can provide additional direction to writing efforts, assist with enhancing depth of discussion, and finally, outline performance expectations. Based on the type of assignment, grading criteria might include depth and clarity of discussion, application of course content to experiences, personal insight and learning, logic of conclusions, quality of examples, technical aspects (format, grammar, etc), creativity, and overall instructor reaction. Surbeck, Han, and Moyer (1991) suggest a way to classify depth of discussion for grading purposes:

- **Reacting:** discussing feelings, emotions, impressions of the experience

- **Elaborating:** making a connection or comparison with other experiences, theories, or positions

- **Contemplating:** considering alternative personal insights or future action based on the experience

Regardless of the mechanism chosen to stimulate reflection, its incorporation into the service-learning process in a well-defined systematic way is crucial for ensuring that students make the connection between experience and course content, ultimately contributing to a deeper level of learning. Although "journaling" readily comes to mind, other methods can be as effective at magnifying the power of reflection.

References

Eyler, J., D. E. Giles, and A. A. Schmiede. 1996. *Practitioners guide to reflection in service learning: Student voices and reflection.* Nashville, Tenn.: Vanderbilt University.

Eyler, J. 2002. Reflection: Linking service and learning—linking students and communities. *Journal of Social Issues* 58, no. 3:517–534.

Gainen, J., and P. Locatelli. 1995. *Assessment for the new curriculum: A guide for professional accounting programs.* Accounting Education Series 11. Sarasota, Fla.: Accounting Education Change Commission and American Accounting Association.

Hatcher, J., and R. Bringle. 1997. Reflection: Bridging the gap between service and learning. *Journal of College Teaching* 45, no. 4:153–158.

Kolb, D. 1984. *Experiential learning: Experience as the source of learning and development.* Englewood Cliffs, N.J.: Prentice-Hall.

Mabry, J. B. 1998. Pedagogical variations in service-learning and student outcomes: How time, contact and reflection matter. *Michigan Journal of Community Service* 5:32–47.

Rama, D. V., S. Ravencroft, S. Wolcott, and E. Zlotkowski. 2000.

Service learning outcomes: Guidelines for educators and researchers. *Issues in Accounting Education* 15, no. 4:656–689.

Surbeck, E., E. P. Han, and J. Moyer. 1991. Assessing reflective responses in journals. *Educational Leadership* (March):25–27.

Watson, S. 2001. Reflection toolkit. Northwest Service Academy Web site. http://www.northwestserviceacademy.org.

Moving from Service to Justice

Linda S. Maule and Nancy Brattain Rogers
Indiana State University

This article describes two service-learning courses that address the priorities of engaging students in the community, preparing students for participation in a democracy, and teaching students about critical social issues. These experiences were developed in response to concern that while service learning is an effective method for engaging students in the community and providing exposure to important social issues, it often does not empower students to take action beyond the voluntary service that they have provided. To help students develop civic engagement capacities that will empower them to participate in formal and informal political processes and work for long term change, we constructed the following five-stage strategy.

In the first stage, students develop the research skills required to address complex social problems. Particular focus is paid to fact, rather than instinct, as a basis of developing a position. Students research the social problem they will address in their project, identifying theoretical approaches that explain and offer solutions to the problem. Students then assess the weaknesses and strengths of the theoretical approaches and determine which are most compelling.

The second stage focuses on development of communication skills to effectively participate in democratic dialogue. Students do not learn the skills of "adversarial" debate but rather, they learn how to speak to one another civilly with emphasis placed on the critique of unsubstantiated positions, not people. These skills are practiced through structured discussion. Students also select their service project at this stage. The third stage is implementation of the service project.

Critical reflection is the fourth stage. Multiple opportunities are provided for structured reflection in which students analyze the unintended consequences of the service-learning project (i.e., what are the ways in which the project is merely a quick fix and may perpetuate, instead of resolve, the social issue.).

In the final stage, students develop long-term strategies for solving the problem. This stage is critical so students do not leave these courses thinking that a service-learning project is the most effective way to resolve a social problem. Students write a final paper describing the ways in which they are going to take the "path of most resistance" at the personal, community, national, and global levels. They go beyond focusing solely on changes in their attitudes and behavior to write about strategies for making systemic changes. Students may choose to advocate keeping the status quo but they have to defend their position, explaining why existing public policy is satisfactory.

Student Activism in Theory and Practice

Women's Studies 450, Student Activism in Theory and Practice, is a General Education capstone course, where students study the theoretical foundations of activism and the practical skills required for successful activism. A central component of the course is the organization of the Take Back the Night March and Rally. The purpose of Take Back the Night (TBN) is to educate the community about violence against women and to raise funds for Terre Haute community-service agencies that work with the survivors of violence.

Stage 1—Through readings and presentations, students learn how to plan an effective rally and use art activism to disseminate their socio-political message. Students explore various strategies for bringing about social change and determine the strategies they wish to employ. They assess the weaknesses and strengths of each approach in the abstract, as well as the context in which they wish to bring about the change.

Stage 2—Students present their ideas to the class and, by consensus, determine which projects they will undertake and themes for the annual events.

Stage 3—Leading up to the TBN march and rally, the students run a number of activities in conjunction with the Vigo County School Corporation. The first is a K-12 TBN Art and Essay Contest, where the students determine the theme of the contest and its guidelines, write letters inviting kids to participate, judge the entries and post them at the mall, and seek out donations from sponsors to award to the winners. The final event is the TBN march and rally.

Stages 4 and 5—After completion of each activity, students reflect upon their experience, identifying how their liberal arts education and disciplinary background helped them to contribute to the planning and implementation of the activity and how what they learned would help them in their professional lives and in their roles as citizens. In addition to these post-activity reflection papers, students produce a 15–20 page macro reflection paper that includes the following:

- What I Bring to the Table
- The Problem of Violence Against Women
- Activism: In Theory and Practice
- My Contributions to TBN
- My Suggestions for the Improvement of Future TBNs
- What I Learned from the Experience and How I Will Apply These Lessons in the Future
- Educational Lesson
- Policy Action Steps

Hull House Service-Learning Trip

The second initiative, the Hull House service-learning trip, includes two courses, RCSM 150, Philanthropy and Society, and WS 200, Introduction to Women's Studies.

Stage 1—Students read articles on Jane Addams and/or the settlement movement and write a paper that connects the readings to class discussions on poverty. In addition, students watch a film—*Hull House: The House that Jane Built.* Together these introduce the students to the multiple ways in which Jane Addams, among others, manipulated the socio-economic and political system of Chicago to cultivate a powerful social reform movement.

Stage 2—Both classes participate in structured discussions regarding the causes and best means of alleviating poverty.

Stage 3—In October, students travel to Chicago to complete a service-learning project with a Hull House community center.

Stages 4 and 5—Students complete a less intensive service project with a local community center and complete a paper that includes a discussion of the specific actions students plan to take to impact the lives of people living in poverty and how they plan to navigate both the informal and formal aspects of the political process.

Faculty can integrate the model of investigate, evaluate, articulate, actuate, and contemplate into disciplines and courses not traditionally viewed as vehicles for service-learning experiences with little effort. Moreover, this model works with both intensive and less intensive service-learning activities:

- A science teacher could ask students to investigate issues relating to environmental quality. Students could monitor their community's environmental quality, participate in a roadside trash pick-up or recycling effort, and write a policy paper.
- Students enrolled in an American History course that covers the Great Depression, the Progressive Era, and the New Deal could conduct oral histories to assess the impact of critical events and policy (i.e. Medicaid, Social Security) on individuals and communities.

Faculty will value this approach because it views service learning as but one piece of an effort to develop students' skills at analysis, communication, and application. Additionally, it helps students to think systemically and systematically. Lastly, it provides students with the opportunity to connect what they are learning in class to the world in which they live; and, it gives them a chance to practice working towards meaningful change through activism and the promulgation of policy.

Developing the Attitudes and Practices of Civic Engagement with Service-Learning Course Development

KATHLEEN M. FOSTER, MOLLIE WHALEN, R. TODD BENSON, AND JOHN W. KRAYBILL-GREGGO
EAST STROUDSBURG UNIVERSITY OF PENNSYLVANIA

Development of the attitudes and practices of civic engagement by undergraduate students is dependent, in part, on the climate and expectations of the campus community. That is, for any affective or cognitive development as related to civic behaviors to occur, what is needed is the opportunity for students to participate in a guided journey of awareness, exploration, and application. Opportunities can be provided for students in both formal and informal learning models. Examples of informal learning experiences are found primarily in co-curricular activities offered through college and university volunteer and fraternal organizations. A formalized learning experience is one in which students are guided through a discovery process that helps them focus on issues of social justice and leads them through the development of an action plan and finally to a level of implementation. One approach taken at East Stroudsburg University of Pennsylvania was the development of an interdisciplinary course with a focus on service learning.

As the faculty representing a variety of programs met, the kinds of initiatives many of us were including in our curricular and co-curricular work with students began to be discussed. We discovered common interests and themes around the issue of promoting student participation as citizens working for social change and social justice. Several faculty and professional staff, from various disciplines, decided to develop a course that would provide the theoretical grounding and practical experience for service-learning activities that would focus on the analysis and advocacy end of the continuum proposed by Fourre (2003). Although the course is designed with interdisciplinarity in mind, we determined that the best "home" for it is in the Department of Sociology.

The course, Practicing Social Justice & Social Change Through Civic Engagement, is designed to help students learn to identify meaningful social and political issues; to then envision a "just society" relative to the identified issues; and to develop social change strategies to work toward achieving that vision. The course requires stu-

dents to take the necessary steps to implement some of those strategies. Ultimately the goal of the course is to demonstrate how, through civic engagement, students can contribute to social, political, and institutional change.

The learning goals described above are achieved through a series of steps covering a 15-week semester. Assigned readings help the students review several theories of social justice. The students are then supported in developing a values-based personal theory of social justice. The instructors, from a variety of disciplines, facilitate class discussion about social and political issues that are of concern to the students. Students are asked to research and define the scope, dimensions, and manifestation of specific social issues, analyzing the social, historical, and political forces that influence the issues, and identifying previous approaches to addressing the problem. They are required to develop a personal vision of a community, society, or world in which the identified issue(s) no longer exist. In a critical next step the students review and discuss a variety of strategies for working toward that vision and develop an action plan for social change. Students are required to take concrete steps to implement one or more of those strategies. Each student contracts with the instructor and provides evidence of working a minimum of 10 hours out-of-class time on these steps.

Students are required to write an ongoing journal reflecting on class content, identified values, and affective responses to opposing value positions. A final paper, based on these reflections, analyzes the student's development of a more informed and complex social conscience and commitment to citizenship participation. Students are required to develop a formal presentation or poster suitable for an academic conference to summarize their civic engagement around their particular issue.

Three significant objectives embedded within the course transcend the role of student and embrace the broader role of civically engaged citizen. Viewed developmentally, each student is encouraged throughout the course to: (a) enhance recognition of self as a member of a larger community that is experiencing a variety of social issues and problems, one of which they may have a particular passion about analyzing and addressing with social change strategies; (b) adopt an evolving perception of self as a potential agent of change; and (c) realize the commitment necessary for socially responsible citizen professionals seeking systemic change.

An essential ingredient in the process of fostering student development and commitment to citizen participation centers on exploring the initial attitudes, beliefs, and predispositions students possess entering the course. The process of enhancing self-awareness is ongoing through class and small group dialogue as well via the reflection methods previously discussed. Primarily, students are invited to explore any attitudes that may support a more "cynical" view that no matter what is tried, "nothing will change." Students are also encouraged to identify any beliefs they possess related to the notion that change efforts should contribute to "immediate" changes. Both of these perspectives may contribute to truncated efforts at civic engagement when change is not rapidly forthcoming. By identifying and grappling with these attitudes and beliefs from the beginning, students can work through some of their own unrealistic expectations in order to develop a predisposition toward a more sustained practice of citizenship.

The value of this model lies in the ability to adapt it to any number of academic disciplines. The course is organized in a way that allows students to self-direct their learning, eliminating the need for the instructor to be an expert in a specific content area. Instead, the instructor guides students as they research their chosen issue and helps them build alliances and develop strategic relationships with individuals who are experts and activists in their respective disciplines. Researching the issues and developing strategic alliances are two fundamental skills of civic engagement that students develop and internalize through participating in this course. As they build these skills, students develop a constructivist framework of purpose for their discipline-specific content.

Another benefit to this course design is the potential outreach it can provide to disciplines that are not typically associated with service learning. The students have the opportunity to become ambassadors for service learning and civic engagement, by reaching out to other departments. The students' commitment to the issues combined with their exposure to service learning as a pedagogical approach may encourage faculty who do not teach in traditional service-learning disciplines to consider the possibility of using service learning as a teaching tool.

The process we engaged in while developing this course models the type of behaviors we hope to see in our students. As a group, we envisioned a campus where our students have the attitudes, dispositions, and practices of active, engaged citizens. As a result, an action plan was developed and implemented that impacts the students, the campus, and the surrounding community.

References

Fourre, C. 2003. *Journey to justice.* St. Paul, Minn.: Good Ground Press.

Improving Literacy through Service Learning

CHRISTOPHER WILKEY
NORTHERN KENTUCKY UNIVERSITY

A major goal of many composition instructors is to teach students how to view writing as a way of making a difference in the world. As a composition instructor, I take seriously the call to encourage students to engage in writing that has direct social consequences beyond the classroom. I have developed a first-year composition service-learning course that focuses on the theme of "freedom" and the Underground Railroad. A primary task of my students is to assist 7th graders at a local "inner-city" middle school in their course work, while mentoring them and helping them to formulate and develop their own freedom-themed projects. This involves helping the 7th graders use reading, writing, and class discussion to critically engage issues related to the Underground Railroad. Students are expected to complete at least 15 hours of service work with the 7th graders. These hours are fulfilled primarily by mentoring the students at the middle school during their class periods. At the end of the course, the freedom-themed projects are presented during the "Freedom-Focused Service-Learning Celebration Day" at the university.

This service-learning composition course encourages college students to explore how education might be utilized for the purpose of promoting a more "just" and "free" society. Subsequently, students engage in reading and writing practices that encourage them to critically reflect on how their service experiences at the middle school can work on the behalf of the broader social good. In order to facilitate discussion of what might constitute an education that works for social justice, throughout the course students are asked to generate multiple perceptions of "what justice is." In building a classroom environment where social justice issues remain front and center, students learn to position educational issues they identify at the middle school within the more general context of national debates over the role of public education in our lives as citizens.

I have designed a sequence of writing projects that begins by asking students to explore their own personal experiences with literacy and progresses toward asking them to consider how learning can be used to develop a sense of civic responsibility. As many composition scholars have argued, service-learning courses that effectively promote civic responsibility will enable students to make a transition "from the personal and the intersubjective toward analyses of larger political, ideological, and institutional forces and processes that shape the social conditions governing personal experience and interaction" (Adler-Kassner et al. 1997, 5). In my own initial efforts to encourage students to move from the personal to the political, my first major writing project invites students to reflect on their personal experiences with learning to read and write in relation to social problems they identify with public education. Students write their own "literacy autobiography" in order to clarify some of their own attitudes toward literacy education in general. As the students begin to prepare for their work with the 7th graders, it is essential that they are given the opportunity to consider the role reading and writing have played in their individual lives. Thus,

students write a personal essay that narrates a "turning point, a key event, or an encounter that reveals some aspect" of themselves as readers and writers (Deans 2003, 27). By coming to terms with some of their own experiences with social issues related to literacy education, my hope is that students will be in a better position to thoughtfully consider how they might productively mentor and collaborate with the 7th graders.

The next two writing projects focus on the ethics of service, particularly as it relates to the service work my students engage in with the 7th graders. Students write critical accounts of their own work at the middle school by exploring the tension between their desire to help these students and the "service" they actually engage in. The writing assignment revolves around the central question of how best to promote ethical relationships between college students and those they seek to serve at the middle school. Through class discussion and collaboration with each other, my students generate additional questions to help them compose individual essays that address ethical concerns that they identify through their work at the middle school.

For example, an especially valuable question that my students have addressed involves considering how matters of wealth and privilege make it difficult for them to fully identify with the learning struggles many of the 7th graders experience in the classroom. Responding to these questions in class and in their essays allows students to critically reflect on their service work as efforts to establish reciprocal interactions with the 7th graders, where both college students and middle school students learn something from each other on more equal terms. In doing so, my students and the 7th graders alike can become more conscious of how to engage in inquiries into the idea of freedom by enacting inter-personal relationships of respect and dignity.

Subsequently, students engage in reading and writing practices that encourage them to critically reflect on how their service experiences at the middle school can work on the behalf of the broader social good. I bring in critical readings focusing on the ethics of service learning that highlight some of the dangers involved in assuming that inner-city students, or those students labeled "at risk," lack the literacy skills for being successful in school. My goal is to have my students identify the writing strengths exhibited by the 7th graders and to learn to utilize that knowledge to tutor them more effectively. At the same time, my students improve their own writing skills by learning how giving good feedback through the tutoring process can help them critically reflect on their own writing in general.

The final writing project of the course asks students to reflect on their own efforts to work with the 7th graders to develop their own project related to the theme of "freedom." Projects can take on a variety of forms—everything from written texts to visual images. The projects are displayed on the university campus during "Celebration Day" at the end of the course. In order to help students prepare and implement their work with the 7th graders, this writing project proposes the kind of freedom-focused project they hope to produce with the 7th graders.

My experience in teaching this course is that students can engage in reading and writing practices that encourage them to critically reflect on how their service work does and does not enact genuine civic engagement with a local community. The service-learning pedagogy I have described in this essay can be extended to any service-learning course in which reading and writing are used as foundations for developing critical reflection on service work, especially if that service seeks to develop a more socially conscious citizenry in our public schools.

References

Adler-Kassner, L., R. Crooks, and A. Watters. 1997. Service-learning and composition at the crossroads. In L. Adler-Kassner, R. Crooks, and A. Watters, eds., *Writing the community: Concepts and models for service-learning composition*, 1–17. Urbana, Ill.: NCTE.

Deans, T. 2003. *Writing and community action: A service-learning rhetoric with readings.* New York: Longman.

Texts and Contexts: Performance, Community, and Service Learning

Joanne R. Gilbert
Alma College

I view service learning as a way for students both to *value* difference and *make* a difference. By integrating service learning into the curriculum, students can become civically engaged as a part of their education rather than as an extra-curricular activity.

Through service-learning pedagogy, I hope to help students overcome the tendency to stereotype others, and to give their time and energy to those who need it most. For the past nine years, I have achieved these objectives and more through nine service-learning projects, several of which have been repeated a number of times, as I offer at least one service-learning course per term. This essay focuses on two specific pedagogical techniques that both students and community members have found empowering and even transformative: 1) Everyday Life Performance and 2) the creation of a memoir portfolio.

Everyday Life Performance

Most of my service-learning courses have involved performance and require students in my performance courses to work one-on-one with community partners throughout an entire academic term. Because I focus on advocacy as part of the service in service learning, students have worked successfully on projects with populations such as senior citizens, juveniles on probation, and survivors of domestic violence. These opportunities for civic engagement entail the collection and either solo or group performance of community members' oral histories. In all cases, students spend considerable time interviewing community members in order to get to know them and record their life stories. Students audiotape these interviews and transcribe them in order to produce a script. In the context of group performance, in which the production conveys a single theme (e.g., advocacy for mentoring youth), students weave portions of their transcripts together, along with statistical background data, literature, and other assorted texts, ultimately producing a collage script. For solo performances, students transcribe and perform a brief section of their collected interviews. In all of my performance-based service-learning projects, community partners attend the students' solo or group performances and a reception afterwards—an extremely rewarding experience for both students and partners.

In both solo and group performance projects, the technique I use is called "Everyday Life Performance" (ELP). Developed by Bryan Crow (1988), Nathan Stucky (1988), Robert Hopper (1993), and others, this technique involves a three-step process of 1) listening to an audiotape of naturally occurring speech, 2) speaking the words of a transcript along with the tape, and 3) performing this "text" without the use of tape or transcript. By asking students to match another person's vocal (and by extension, physical and psychological) mannerisms, I am able to facilitate a "total immersion" experience for them. This intense performance of difference helps students transcend the tendency to stereotype and (for many of them, for the first time) truly understand a perspective vastly divergent from their own. This innovative service-learning pedagogy provides a useful model for others interested in teaching students to understand and value difference.

Creating a Memoir Portfolio

Equally challenging and gratifying is the service-learning project I have assigned to my Interpersonal Communication classes each fall since 1999: the creation of a professional quality memoir for individuals who have lost a spouse or family member, using transcribed oral histories and family photos. Students practice their reflective-listening and perspective-taking skills by meeting their community partners weekly, and learning their life stories through intensive interviews. After recording and transcribing the story, each student, in consultation with her/his interviewee, creates a comprehensive memoir (a document featuring text and photos, produced using Microsoft Word software) to present to her/his partner and partner's family. The recipients of these memoirs are extremely grateful for the artifacts which will remain in their families as tangible representations of

In all of my performance-based service-learning projects, community partners attend the students' solo or group performances and a reception afterwards—an extremely rewarding experience for both students and partners.

cherished memories. The students, too, are deeply affected by this experience, and often maintain relationships with their partners after the completion of the project. Indeed, service learning is a powerful way to teach perspective taking. When critically reflecting on their experience in their assigned papers, students consistently label this experience as profound, even life changing, offering comments like, "I have learned more about myself this past month than I have the past 18 years."

Undoubtedly, service-learning projects can accomplish a great deal both by developing students' abilities and in serving various community members. These projects affect the students and the community in powerful and potentially transformative ways. Populations such as senior citizens, juvenile offenders, survivors of domestic violence and grieving families gain companionship, advocacy, and increased self-esteem. Students learn that compassion and respect for others is key to understanding multiple perspectives. Most important, students realize the commonalities that exist among all of us. No longer do they default to cynical reactions and stereotypes of certain populations; now they appreciate the unique individuals who comprise these populations. No longer are they focused solely on their own gains; they are gratified and excited by giving to others. It is difficult to measure the impact of such experiences, but it is apparent that both the service and the learning continue for all involved.

References

Crow, B. 1988. Conversational performance and the performance of conversation. *The Drama Review* 32:23–54.

Hopper, R. 1993. Conversational dramatism and everyday life performance. *Text and Performance Quarterly* 13:181–183.

Stucky, N. 1988. Unnatural acts: Performing natural conversation. *Literature in Performance* 8, no. 2:28–39.

Using Community-Based Learning Modules to Introduce Languages and Culture

Arcea Zapata de Aston
University of Evansville

This article presents a definition of service learning, concepts involving a specific project at the University of Evansville, examples of specific modules, and results. In keeping with the most current strategies for student-centered learning and the fundamental values of service learning and civic engagement, the approach described in this essay proposes credit-bearing, experience-based modules that place students in their community. The main idea is to develop course modules that are linked to specific civic engagement and/or disciplinary learning objectives.

Service learning is conceived of as a process of combining the learning that takes place in a classroom with community activities. Some of the skills developed in the service-learning modules described below include linguistic competence, critical thinking, and personal responsibility. Specifically, in service-learning modules, language students acquire skills and knowledge of the complex relationship between languages and culture. Language exposure in a cultural context through community activism serves not only a linguistic purpose but also creates a natural learning environment that enhances appreciation of the local, national, and international cultural arena.

Unlike typical classroom credits, service-learning credits are earned through a combination of community service and classroom activities. Whereas typical classroom training focuses in a variety of communicative activities with little to no exposure to real societal interaction, service learning pays central attention to community involvement, all of which has a direct impact on linguistic ability while expanding critical thinking, live communication, and civic engagement.

To earn academic credit for these community modules, students need to complete both in-class and fieldwork hours. To receive one semester credit hour, students meet for 11 one-hour sessions of in-class training and application exercises and complete 30 hours on their community activity. To receive an additional credit hour, they complete 60 hours of community activity. (These hours do not include transportation and preparation time.) The classroom activities will be structured around the five Cs (communication, cultures, connections, comparisons, and communities—called standards) as stipulated by the American Council on the Teaching of Foreign Languages (ACTFL) throughout all activities, lessons, and surveys, written papers, oral presentations, and evaluations.

In the module for the first C, Communication, all students become involved in a large variety of communicative, interesting activities. They practice the standard in one session, apply it in their fieldwork, and report back in the next class session with written and verbal reports. The same structure of lesson, application, and feedback applies to each of the other four standards. The Cultures module allows students to acquire the sociolinguistic component of language. Connections with other fields of knowledge will be established across all activities to allow the students to use language as a vehicle to obtain information as well as a communication tool. Comparisons with other fields of knowledge and with other cultures widen the students' cultural horizons and promote diversity and tolerance of the other, which in turn enhances understanding of the student's own culture.

The aspect of Communities is presented in an innovative way through the incorporation of service-learning and civic engagement activities. Students actively participate in community projects that work in two directions: first to provide a context where the students learn by getting in touch with communities by means of active service; and second to become a good background to solidify language knowledge, widen cultural horizons, solidify civic engagement, and promote diversity and tolerance of the other by helping their own cultural formation.

This modular approach provides a win-win situation that can be utilized in classes of many different disciplines. In Spanish language courses, for example, the students might work with K-12 students from different schools around town. They could get involved with programs such as clubs; after schools programs; summer activities; local, national, and international celebrations; as well as activities with different cultural, social, and political organizations. Students interested in practicing and learning more about Spanish and Latino/Hispanic communities might work with local Hispanic-based organizations to facilitate some of these connections. A module at my institution would serve as a liaison for the student to get connected to the social, cultural, and community world outside the University and participate in something that is pertinent to the subject of their field of study. In this way, there will be different programs outlining both the needs of the Hispanic community in large, and the critical need of the students for building their language and culture capacity.

Similarly, students in political science will work to promote civic engagement in Hispanic communities, outlining topics such as the process of elections, how to vote, political decision-making processes, etc. In this context, some of the upper-level classes have conducted surveys in the Hispanic community for a local organization that needed the survey data to present to the mayor of the city to assess the needs of the Hispanic community.

There are a variety of other ways in which this approach can be implemented. It could take several shapes beginning with an outreach program to bring awareness of diversity in the school population. Also, celebrations of major local, national, and international events will serve as a way to awaken the university community to the concept of diversity and the need to become part of the new, changing globalization that is impacting every part of our lives. It is a way to start a system of interdisciplinary collaboration—involving language, culture, and the community—that will lead to a better compre-

hension and application of the diverse and dynamic world that we are living in today.

The synergies for community and the academic institutions are tremendous as students assist with special teaching projects and other activities that are too often neglected due to demands for the basics. The students will be better prepared for their careers through practical experience and a structured learning process. This project links activities across the university, community, and indeed the globe, as participants carry their experiences to their careers. The incorporation of hands-on activities of service learning and the learning of diversity and tolerance that immerse the students in the reality of learning-by-doing will become tools that enhance active learning in and outside the classroom. In this way, the students will become participant members of the community by rendering a service but also by learning language and culture in the process of the service involved.

It is expected that through the service learning program, students will feel motivated to work with the community, and that this work, in turn, will help them understand what civic responsibility entails. I found that the students exhibited better awareness of civic responsibility during their in class discussions through the remainder of the course. They also wrote papers about Hispanic culture and presented the papers at a panel during the Hispanic Heritage Event. They also continued teaching English classes to several Hispanic groups in the community after all the community service activities were complete.

Developing Citizenship through a Service-Learning Capstone Experience

CHARMAINE E. WILSON
UNIVERSITY OF SOUTH CAROLINA AIKEN

Several years ago, our department sought a means by which our senior-level students could know they were well equipped to make significant differences in their communities. We wanted them to gain hands-on understanding of the way their knowledge, skills, and abilities could be applied to improve life for others. To achieve our goal, we developed a service-learning capstone experience course for majors. Students provide 75 hours of community service for charitable organizations such as

the Boys and Girls Club, Habitat for Humanity, the abused person's shelter, Girl Scouts, and the Council on Aging. Students have raised thousands of dollars, organized events, helped construct homes, improved marketing, and more. In this article, I discuss our capstone and suggest ways our approach might be used by other disciplines.

Service learning provides students with the opportunity to understand and demonstrate that they have more than a college degree in a specific discipline; they also possess "civic competence." Students become engaged citizens by gaining an understanding of civic needs and the means by which those needs are addressed. For example, one student assisted a healthcare organization with its major fundraiser, an auction. She persuaded local businesses to donate items for the auction, sold advertising in and produced the program, and participated in the event. The auction raised thousands of dollars to provide free indigent care. The student had been unaware of the large number of local citizens unable to pay for needed services. She learned about community needs and ways to address them. So powerful was the experience that the student continues to volunteer with the organization, which welcomes her assistance. Other students have continued with the agencies beyond the required hours, returned in subsequent years to work on projects, and a few have changed goals to work in social service careers.

The first step in developing a discipline-based service-learning capstone course is to establish learning objectives. The primary objective for our students is to understand and demonstrate their ability to apply communication principles and theories to community needs or problems. Students must integrate learning from their college experience, including problem solving, decision making, and persuasive skills to address local issues. They should also be able to demonstrate communication competence, which involves integrating and applying learning from several courses, as well as engaging in careful and critical self-reflection of communication behavior.

After determining objectives, faculty must identify possible sites and determine the nature of work that is consonant with course objectives. To emphasize civic responsibility, our students generally volunteer with nonprofit service organizations, schools, or government agencies, depending on the nature of the work. The work at the service-learning site must provide numerous opportunities for interaction and draw on skills and abilities learned in major course work. Accordingly, students

Service learning provides students with the opportunity to understand and demonstrate that they have more than a college degree in a specific discipline; they also possess "civic competence."

assist with fund raising, develop or revise newsletters or other documents, or provide tutoring.

Other disciplines would have other expectations; for example, math or business majors could work with senior citizens on tax preparation, assist young parents with budgeting, or help agencies improve recordkeeping strategies. English majors could work with literacy groups. Theatre students could assist with story hours or an after-school drama club. Computer science students might help agencies establish systems for maintaining lists of donors or assist in a networking project. Engineering students could assist a group like Habitat for Humanity with building projects, work with youngsters on science projects, or aid city agencies with planning efforts.

For our capstone, one faculty member supervises the 10–15 students enrolled per semester. Students consult with the faculty supervisor to discuss interests and possible sites the semester before participating in the capstone, then contact agency personnel directly to define work parameters. This empowers students to find experiences that are most compatible with their interests and goals.

Once a good match is established, the student completes a one-page contract specifying the nature of the volunteer work. The agency representative and faculty supervisor both sign the contract. We find fewer problems occur when the agreement is specific and in place before the first class day.

In addition to setting objectives and defining work sites and tasks, departments must define and link the academic components of the capstone to program objectives. We require a reflective journal because reflection is a way to ensure that the service results in learning and a greater sense of civic responsibility (Zlotkowski 2005). Students describe their experiences and then reflect on and analyze them in the journal. The faculty supervisor must stress that the journal is analytical, because the reflective journal should "bridge the theory-practice divide" (Soukup 1999); students must apply to the volunteer experience theories and principles learned in the classroom (especially communication classes).

We have found that reviewing and evaluating drafts is essential to the learning process, so students submit drafts after 15 and 45 hours.[1] In addition, our students must do a research paper or substantive project related to their volunteer efforts, and make a final presentation to the department faculty. These assignments help us meet our program objectives for researching, writing, and presenting results. Other departments may have other objectives, and thus other assignments.

An additional aspect of the capstone that we have found essential is having regular meetings with the students. Four or five group meetings during the semester allow the faculty supervisor to communicate efficiently with the capstone students. The first meeting of the semester (held the first week) allows time to review the syllabus, clarify expectations and assignments, and establish meeting times and due dates. The second meeting (held the second week) focuses exclusively on the journal writing process. The third meeting (held the fifth or sixth week of the term) focuses again on journal writing, with time to discuss accomplishments, concerns, or problems. Fourth and fifth meetings allow the faculty supervisor to discuss other academic elements of the enterprise, the leave-taking process, and any concerns the student may have.

We also require individual meetings between the faculty supervisor and the students. The number depends on the overall time frame and the number of group meetings, but three works well for us. The faculty member can review journals, help the student deal with challenges, answer questions, and provide encouragement.

In sum, the service-learning capstone experience provides an outstanding opportunity to both develop civic competence and become more engaged in the community by applying the skills and abilities learned during the college experience.

Note

1. For more on promoting reflective writing, see Hatcher and Bringle, 1997 and Gibson, Kostecki, and Lucas, 2001.

References

Gibson, M. K., E. M. Kostecki, and M. K. Lucas. 2001. Instituting principles of best practice for service-learning in the communication curriculum. *Southern Communication Journal* 66, 187–200.

Hatcher, T. A., and R. G. Bringle. 1997. Reflection: Bridging the gap between service and learning. *College Teaching* 45, 153–158.

Soukup, P. A. 1999. Service-learning in communication: Why? In D. Droge and B. O. Murphy, eds., *Voices of strong democracy: Concepts and models for service-learning in communication studies,* 7–11. Washington, D.C.: American Association for Higher Education.

Zlotkowski, E. 2005. Service-learning and the first-year student. In M. L. Upcraft, J. N. Gardner, and B. O. Barefoot, eds., *Challenging and supporting the first-year student: A handbook for improving the first year of college,* 356–370. San Francisco: Jossey-Bass.

ASSESSING STUDENT LEARNING 4

Using the National Survey of Student Engagement to Assess and Enhance Civic Engagement in the Classroom

John C. Hayek and Michelle Salinas Holmes
Indiana University Bloomington

To what extent are your students engaged in civic-related activities? How would you know? What types of questions could you ask to determine the breadth of their civic and moral development? How could you use this information to induce students to be more civically engaged?

The National Survey of Student Engagement (NSSE), an ongoing research initiative based at Indiana University Bloomington, was designed to help answer questions like these. About 1,000 different colleges and universities have collected information from thousands of students since 2000. The survey measures the extent to which college students engage in educational practices empirically linked to high levels of learning and development. NSSE also includes a number of questions well suited to measure aspects of civic and moral development such as service learning, community service, and exposure to diversity.

This article highlights a number of ways faculty members can use NSSE items and results to make good choices on how to assess and enhance civic engagement in the classroom. More specifically, it demonstrates how NSSE can serve as a useful tool in three key course areas: 1) planning, 2) delivery, and 3) assessment. Although these examples focus on NSSE, a similar approach could be taken with other sources of civic engagement information on campus.

Course Planning:
Using NSSE as a Civic Engagement Checklist

Many faculty members spend hours of preparation fine tuning their content and pedagogy but fail to realize the potential positive influence of their courses on students' civic awareness through intentionality in their planning. For instance, according to NSSE data,

college students report that their institutions are as influential as family or friends in serving as the primary source of information on volunteering and social or political issues. In addition, students report varying levels of interest in issues related to health, education, religion, and security (National Survey of Student Engagement 2004). Discovering important social causes and playing off these interests when designing new curricular elements can be an effective way to engage students in civic-related activities. When this information and influence are channeled into course planning activities, it can have a meaningful impact on students' behavior both inside and outside the classroom. For instance, faculty members could use the following questions from NSSE to help think about the extent to which their courses engage students in various civic-related activities.

✓ Do I include service-learning or community-based projects in my course?

✓ Are there opportunities and resources for students to learn from one another in the form of peer tutoring?

✓ Do course activities stimulate student involvement that will contribute to the welfare of the community?

✓ Will students leave my course understanding the importance of voting?

✓ Do I include diverse perspectives in class discussions or writing assignments?

✓ Will students leave my course with a better understanding of people from different backgrounds and beliefs?

Using a checklist of civic engagement activities during course planning increases the likelihood that this type of student involvement occurs purposefully and is not left to chance.

Course Delivery:
Incorporating NSSE into Mid-Semester and End-of-Semester Evaluations

Asking civic-related questions during course planning is a good first step to enhance engagement in the classroom. However, faculty and student perceptions of the learning experience can be very different. For instance, results from NSSE indicate that about 70% of first-year students believe that their coursework emphasizes memorization; whereas, only 31% of faculty believe this to be the case (NSSE 2004). By incorporating various NSSE items into both mid-semester and end-of-semester student evaluations, faculty members can monitor the extent to which core skills and abilities needed to engage effectively in civic activities are being both espoused and enacted by faculty members and students inside and outside the classroom. A number of NSSE items that could be used in student evaluations are included below.

✓ Does this course emphasize analyzing and synthesizing, making judgments, and applying information to real-world problems?

✓ Does this course help you communicate effectively, think critically, and behave ethically?

✓ Does my teaching style and class learning environment promote high quality relationships with me and other students in the class?

✓ To what extent are you encouraged to work effectively with classmates during and outside of class?

Many faculty members . . . fail to realize the potential positive influence of their courses on students' civic awareness . . . According to NSSE data, college students report that their institutions are as influential as family or friends in serving as the primary source of information on volunteering and social or political issues.

✓ How much time do you spend per week preparing for my class?

✓ How often are you encouraged to attend campus events and activities?

Including a greater proportion of engagement items in course evaluations will help reinforce the importance of certain activities that are fundamental to student and civic development. Another advantage is that many of these activities can be worked on and improved almost immediately and require minimal resources to address. Thus, in order to enhance course delivery related to civic engagement, it is not only important to ask good questions, it is critical that these questions are actionable.

Course Assessment:
Using NSSE for Benchmarking and Focusing on "Nevers"

Course assessment asks questions related to student learning and makes appropriate adjustments to improve student success (Angelo and Cross 1993). The NSSE items highlighted above can also be used effectively to assess and benchmark classroom performance at institutional and national levels. For example, imagine that you discover through NSSE or other sources on campus that only two out of ten seniors in your class participate in community service or volunteer work—a number that is significantly below both your institutional and the national average. By using NSSE as an internal and external benchmarking tool, faculty members can confirm the strengths or weaknesses of various civic-related activities. This improves their ability to focus attention and resources on key targets of opportunity.

Another strategy is to focus on NSSE items where

students respond "never" when asked how often they participate in a given civic-related activity. For example, on average, approximately 60 percent of all seniors have never participated in a service-learning class and 44 percent have never tutored or taught other students (NSSE 2004). Setting the goal of moving all the "never" students in your class to at least "sometimes" in several key areas would be a major accomplishment and would substantially raise the bar if you could convince other faculty members to do the same. Getting students started in the civic engagement race is sometimes as equally important as making sure other students are running at full speed. Focusing attention on "nevers" is a great way for faculty members to quickly raise the level of civic engagement on campus.

Conclusion

Many faculty members are making great strides in promoting civic engagement on campus by using NSSE and other related data and information sources. Faculty members can be more intentional and purposeful in their efforts by including civic engagement activities in course planning, by incorporating student and civic engagement items into course evaluations, and by making sure to systematically assess their efforts and target key areas to help promote civic responsibility in their classrooms. For more information about The National Survey of Student Engagement, see http://www.nsse.iub.edu.

References

Angelo, T. A., and K. P. Cross. 1993. *Classroom assessment techniques: A handbook for college teachers.* 2nd ed. San Francisco: Jossey-Bass.

National Survey of Student Engagement. 2004. *Student engagement: Pathways to collegiate success.* Bloomington: Indiana Center for Postsecondary Research.

Assessing the Multiple Dimensions of Student Civic Engagement: A Preliminary Test of an ADP Survey Instrument

JUAN CARLOS HUERTA, DANIEL J. JORGENSEN, AND JOSEPH JOZWIAK
TEXAS A&M UNIVERSITY–CORPUS CHRISTI

This essay reports an effort to assess civic engagement among undergraduates at Texas A&M University–Corpus Christi (TAMUCC). At this early stage in the development of our project, the goals are two-fold. One is to develop a common set of workable measures for civic engagement. Another is to assess the impact of American Democracy Project (ADP) activities in contributing to civic engagement. To do this, we have developed an extensive survey of student civic engagement. The goal of the survey is to effectively merge the two literatures of organizational commitment and civic engagement. Following Reinke (2003), the survey asks students to rate their levels of engagement in the classroom, school-related non-academic activities, and non-school related volunteer activities (political, social, religious, and cultural). The survey also queries students as to their motivations behind civic engagement practice using the affective, obligatory and instrumental framework developed by Meyer and Allen (1997).

Instrument and Method

A pre-test/post-test research design was utilized on a non-probability sample of three introductory political science classes. Two course sections implemented an explicit ADP curriculum that included service learning and adoption of the *New York Times,* and one section did not alter the typical curriculum.

The instrument used to assess citizenship outcomes evolved from two literatures, that of civic engagement and organizational commitment. To address the civic engagement aspect of the literature, we utilized an instrument developed by Reinke (2003). This instrument captures the status of citizenship in a single scale and four facets of engagement in four sub-scales of political, religious, social, and cultural engagement. To capture the practice dimension we utilized the organizational commitment questionnaire developed by Meyer and Allen (1997), however, we revised the wording from organization to community. This allowed us to capture

Table 4.1. Frequency distribution by ADP participation Survey Version						
ADP Participation			Frequency	Percent	Valid Percent	Cumulative Percent
No	Valid	Baseline	120	56.9	56.9	56.9
		Post-test	91	43.1	43.1	100.0
		Total	211	100.0	100.0	
Yes	Valid	Baseline	118	41.4	41.4	41.4
		Post-test	167	58.6	58.6	100.0
		Total	285	100.0	100.0	

the facets of affective, obligatory, and instrumental practice of civic engagement. Together, these two scales are added together to form the dependant variable civic engagement. Exposure to ADP was captured through recording the course section in which the respondent was enrolled and asking the respondent to self-report attendance at ADP project events.

The instrument also included three sets of variables shown by the literature to explain levels of citizen engagement. These include questions focusing on demographic, socialization and environmental variables that may account for levels of civic participation and engagement (Laurian 2004). Appendix A contains the complete survey instrument utilized in this research.

Although the method limits generalizability to other populations, the research does provide an opportunity to test the scales created in the instrument for reliability, and allows a preliminary glimpse of effects from this short-term exposure to ADP.

Findings

In all, 496 pre- and post-tests were completed by students. Table 4.1 shows the frequency tabulation of students taking each survey by participation in the ADP project.

Using the SPSS syntax for the Cronbach model of internal consistency, reliability was assessed based on the average inter-item correlation (Alpha). Table 4.2 shows the results of the reliability tests on the scales used to determine status of civic engagement while Table 6 shows the scales of affective, obligatory and instrumental practice.

The results demonstrate that with the exception of instrumental practice, the scales utilized by the questionnaire have alpha coefficients above .70, which are considered highly reliable. Instrumental practice did not reach the .70 threshold, with an alpha of .43 the reader is cautioned in drawing any conclusions using this scale. Reliability diagnostics from the SPSS program suggest that reliability of this scale is increased to .68 when the question "It costs too much time and money to be involved in the community" is removed from the scale.

The preliminary survey results in Table 4.3 show outcomes for the single semester over which the survey was given. These results indicate that those students who participated in the courses with the ADP-enhanced curriculum already tended to have higher scores in civic engagement than those in the non-ADP course. This could be a result of the on-going learning communities program in which the ADP courses already participate. The data does suggest that ADP courses appear to encourage greater participation in civic engagement seminars outside of class, and an increase in the affective and obligatory practices of civic engagement.

Lessons Learned

The goal of this paper is to establish a "quick hit" in the assessment of the status of student civic engagement and student motivations to practice civic engagement. By establishing the reliability of the various scales employed in the instrument we accomplished a key objective of our research.

This was not without some pitfalls. The first planning issue is to allow enough time for Institutional Review Board (IRB) approval. Depending on the university, this can be a quick or time consuming process. The

Table 4.2. Reliability Coefficients for ADP Status and Practice Scales

Status
- Political — .80
- Social — .77
- Religious — .87
- Cultural/educational — .67

Practice
- Affective — .74
- Obligatory — .73
- Instrumental — .43

Table 4.3. Preliminary Results of ADP Survey

	Non-ADP Curriculum		ADP Curriculum	
	Pre	Post	Pre	Post
Participated in a Service-Learning/ Community-Service Project in a Class	32%	26%	33%	30%
Participated in a Civic Engagement Seminar Outside of a Class	31%	42%	39%	46%
Total Status (mean)	32.17	33.57	33.97	34.19
Affective Practice (mean)	**10.98**	**10.83**	**11.01**	**11.35**
Obligatory Practice (mean)	**13.85**	**13.49**	**14.01**	**14.05**
Instrumental Practice (mean)	12.23	11.57	12.57	12.33
Total Practice	**37.00**	**35.97**	**37.59**	**37.80**
Total Civic Score	69.09	69.67	71.570	71.793

second hurdle we encountered was the selection of media and production of the survey instrument. Physical production is costly in terms of time and money, regardless of the technology you use. It is in the physical product process that data entry concerns should be addressed too. Optical Character Recognition (OCR) forms, which are expensive and require specific media, printing, and reading technology can appear to be a large upfront cost, but can reduce the costs, and perhaps errors that manual data entry can bring about. In our research the develop-

ment of the sampling procedure and sampling frame also became a concern. While most colleges and universities have a willing institutional research department to help with these issues, entry into the classroom can be an issue. We found it was easy to enter our colleagues' classes within our own college, but it became much more difficult when seeking entry into classes in other colleges within the university, particularly with a pretest/post-test model that required two interruptions during the semester. Finally, while rigor can be gained

SURVEY ADMINISTRATOR:
TO SAFEGUARD THE PARTICIPANT'S CONFIDENTIALITY, PLEASE REMOVE
THIS COVER SHEET ONCE THE PARTICIPANT HAS COMPLETED IT AND
RETAIN IT FOR OUR RECORDS.

NAME: _____

(First Name & Last Name)

Course # _____   Section _____   Participant ID _____

Date of Administration _____

Survey Version: 1.   Baseline

2.   Post-test

Course # _____   Section _____   Participant ID _____

Date of Administration _____

Survey Version: 1.   Baseline

2.   Post-test

Figure 4.1. American Democracy Project Student Survey

with a pre-test/post-test model, in practice such a model can be difficult when concerned with matching subjects in a case-wise manner, particularly over longitudinal studies. Although more students took the post-test then the pre-test, relatively few of the cases took both the pre-test and the post-test.

While we believe that further use of this instrument in other populations with various research methods will yield effective results to assess the outcomes of the American Democracy Project in achieving civic engagement among students, we suggest that the revised scale for instrumental practice be used to increase the reliability of the instrument.

Appendix A: Survey Instrument

AMERICAN DEMOCRACY PROJECT STUDENT SURVEY

Your class will be **participating in a research project** being conducted by faculty of the Social Science Department at Texas A & M University–Corpus Christi. **The purpose of the research is to determine particular effects of a course curriculum**

on students. At the beginning of the semester you will be given a questionnaire which will examine your attitudes and beliefs toward various dimensions of your life. At the end of the semester you will be given a second questionnaire that explores the effects of the program and re-examines the same attitudes and beliefs.

Your responses will remain confidential and will be released only as summaries of all responses so that no individual's answers can be identified. No reports about the study will contain your name. We will not release any information about you.

Your participation in this program is important. This research project provides the opportunity for you to assist the researchers in assessing and improving the curriculum they use. Data collected from this research will be combined with grade data from the course to determine the efficacy of the program in question.

Taking part is voluntary. Although the survey is voluntary, your participation will help ensure that the study results truly represent the outcomes of students at Texas A&M University–Corpus Christi. All students who participate in the program will complete two questionnaires. If you do not wish your child to participate in this study, which will mean that we won't include your results in the data, please turn this survey in the individual administering the survey. If you wish to participate please complete the information on the next page.

AMERICAN DEMOCRACY PROJECT
STUDENT SURVEY

This survey is designed to measure general attitudes and perceptions of college students towards their communities, education and future. This information will be used in conjunction with the American Democracy Project and enhancing service-learning programs on campus. Please respond as honestly as possible, relying on your current feelings regarding your community. Your responses will be kept confidential. All parts of the survey should be completed.

SECTION I

1. Write your birthdate in numbers in the space : _____ / _____ / _____
                                                   month   day   year

2. Your gender: ☐ Male ☐ Female

3. Your ethnicity (please check all those that apply): [Optional]

    ☐ African American   ☐ Hispanic

    ☐ Asian American/Pacific Islander   ☐ Native American/Alaskan Native

    ☐ Caucasian (non-Hispanic)   ☐ Other (Specify) _____

4. Year in School (1st, 2nd, 3rd, 4th, etc.) : _____

5. Major(s): _____

6. The primary wage earner in my immediate family is a

    ☐ Professional/manager   ☐ Skilled laborer

    ☐ Clerical/sales person   ☐ Semi/unskilled laborer

    ☐ Foreman/supervisor

7. I would consider myself or members of my immediate family to be politically active.

    ☐ Yes   ☐ No

8. I, or a member of my immediate family, have worked in a community service organization or for the government (National/State/Local). ☐ Yes ☐ No

9. Community involvement is important to other members of my family. ☐ Yes ☐ No

Figure 4.1. American Democracy Project Student Survey (cont.)

References

Laurian, L. 2004. Public participation in environmental decision making. *Journal of the American Planning Association* 70, no. 1:53–67.

Meyer, J. and N. Allen. 1997. *Commitment in the workplace: Theory research and application.* Thousand Oaks, Calif: Sage Publishers.

Reinke, S. 2003. Making a difference: Does service learning promote civic engagement among students? *Journal of Public Affairs Education* 9, no. 2:129–138.

Sax, L. 2004. Research on the assessment of civic engagement. http://www.aascu.org/programs/adp/about/default.htm.

Sax, L. and A. Astin. 1997. The benefits of service: Evidence from undergraduates. *Educational Record* 78, no. 3/4:25–33.

Stivers, C. 1990. The public agency as polis: Active citizenship in the administrative state. *Administration and Society* 22, no. 1:86–105.

SECTION II

Please indicate how strongly you agree or disagree with each statement at this point in time. Circle the number that best describes your response (1=strongly disagree, 2=disagree, 3=agree, 4=strongly agree).
It is important that you respond to all of the questions.

	Strongly Disagree	Disagree	Agree	Strongly Agree
1. I keep up with local, state, or national political news.	1	2	3	4
2. I am knowledgeable about local socioeconomic issues and problems.	1	2	3	4
3. I vote in local, state, or national elections.	1	2	3	4
4. I have petitioned the government or participated in a petitioning campaign.	1	2	3	4
5. I donate money to political candidates.	1	2	3	4
6. I have volunteered time to support a political candidate.	1	2	3	4
7. I am currently a member of a group involved in politics.	1	2	3	4
8. I donate money to group(s) working to solve social problems in my community (other than a religious organization).	1	2	3	4
9. I am a member or supporter of a group(s) working to solve social problems in my community (other than a religious organization).	1	2	3	4
10. I volunteer time to group(s) working to solve social problems in my community (other than a religious organization).	1	2	3	4
11. I volunteer time to a religious organization.	1	2	3	4
12. I donate money to a religious organization.	1	2	3	4
13. I have volunteered time to support arts, cultural, or educational programs in my community.	1	2	3	4
14. I donate money to support arts, cultural, or educational programs in my community.	1	2	3	4
15. I have written to a political official or to the editor of the local paper on a political or social issue.	1	2	3	4
16. I really feel that my community's problems are my own.	1	2	3	4
17. Being a "citizen" of my community has a great deal of personal meaning for me.	1	2	3	4
18. I take pride in my community.	1	2	3	4
19. I do not feel emotionally attached to my community.	1	2	3	4

Figure 4.1. American Democracy Project Student Survey (cont.)

	Strongly Disagree	Disagree	Agree	Strongly Agree
20. I do not feel like "I belong" in my community.	1	2	3	4
21. I owe a great deal to my community.	1	2	3	4
22. It is my responsibility as a member of my community to improve it.	1	2	3	4
23. As a member of my community there are some things that I *must* do.	1	2	3	4
24. My community does not deserve my loyalty.	1	2	3	4
25. I do not have any obligation to other people in my community.	1	2	3	4
26. Being involved in my community makes me "better off" financially.	1	2	3	4
27. Community involvement is an important means of meeting people.	1	2	3	4
28. It costs too much time and money to be involved in the community.	1	2	3	4
29. Being involved in my community helps me get the things I want.	1	2	3	4
30. Being involved in the community is as much a matter of necessity as desire.	1	2	3	4
31. I do not find courses in school relevant to my life outside of school.	1	2	3	4
32. I intend to work in a career that will make contributions to society.	1	2	3	4
32. I have a realistic understanding of the daily responsibilities involved in the jobs (careers) in which I am interested.	1	2	3	4
33. Being involved in a program to improve my community is important.	1	2	3	4
34. I learn more when courses contain hands-on activities.	1	2	3	4
35. The things I learn in school are useful in my life.	1	2	3	4
36. Courses in school make me think about real-life in new ways.	1	2	3	4

Figure 4.1. American Democracy Project Student Survey (cont.)

SECTION III

Now tell us a little about your experiences here at Texas A&M Corpus Christi (TAMUCC)

37. In the past year I have participated in a service-learning or community service project related to coursework at TAMUCC.   ☐ Yes   ☐ No

If yes to 37 please complete 38 & 39
In No please go to 40.

38. The service-learning or community service project was a voluntary part of the course's curriculum.   ☐ Yes   ☐ No

39. I received a grade or extra credit for participating in the service-learning or community service project.   ☐ Yes   ☐ No

40. In the past year I have attended a seminar or participated in an activity other than a class at TAMUCC that was related to civic engagement or community service.   ☐ Yes   ☐ No

If yes to 40 please complete 41
In No please go to 42.

41. I received a grade or extra credit for attending a seminar or participating in an activity other than a class at TAMUCC that was related to civic engagement or community service in the past year.   ☐ Yes   ☐ No

	Strongly Disagree	Disagree	Agree	Strongly Agree
42. Attending TAMUCC has positively changed my views toward community service and/or civic engagement.	1	2	3	4

Thank you for your time completing this survey.

Figure 4.1. American Democracy Project Student Survey (cont.)

Assessing Student Learning in Service-Learning Internships

DAVID BOYNS AND MICHAEL DECESARE
CALIFORNIA STATE UNIVERSITY, NORTHRIDGE

Civic engagement is an idea whose time has come in higher education. National higher education associations, college and university administrators, and individual faculty have all begun to recognize the importance of developing students' civic capacities. As a result, an increasing number of university programs require their students to participate in some form of civic engagement—typically a service-learning course or an internship—before graduation. Though the emphasis on civic engagement cuts across disciplinary boundaries, it appears strongest in the social and behavioral sciences. Sociologists, specifically, have made several recent

Table 4.4. Participation in Service-Learning Internships and Commitment to Civic Engagement	With Internship		Without Internship		
Question	Mean	N	Mean	N	Difference
I plan to go to graduate school in social work.	2.90	71	2.08	27	0.82
I plan to go to graduate school in sociology.	3.32	71	2.70	27	0.62
I plan to begin working in a field unrelated to sociology.	2.27	71	1.76	27	0.50
I think studying sociology prepares me for a job helping people.	4.34	71	4.31	27	0.03
Studying sociology will help me to be able to change society.	3.75	71	3.88	27	-0.13
I am interested in studying people.	4.33	71	4.59	27	-0.26
I plan to work in a field related to sociology.	3.94	71	4.21	27	-0.27

attempts to disseminate syllabi, instructional materials, and model courses in service learning and civic engagement (e.g., Kowaleski, Ender, and DiFiore 2001; Ostrow, Hesser, and Enos 1999).

Regardless of the academic disciplines to which they are connected, however, most assessments of civic engagement projects have focused on students' actual levels of *engagement*. Less attention has been paid, however, to assessing the nature and extent of students' *learning* during the course of their civic engagement projects. It has often been taken for granted that students learn from their civic involvement. But the questions of what and how much they learn have been largely left unanswered. This article addresses these questions by assessing the nature and extent of students' learning in a required service-learning internship (SLI) course taken in the Department of Sociology at California State University, Northridge (CSUN).

All of our majors are required to participate in a SLI, under the supervision of a faculty member, for a minimum of one semester. They typically perform their work in police stations, probation departments, homeless shelters, youth centers, and halfway houses. Interns are required to work at their site for a minimum of 75 hours, and may work up to 100 hours, over the course of the semester. Though the formal requirements vary somewhat, students are typically required to keep field notes and journals documenting their experiences, to solicit a formal evaluation from their site supervisor, and to develop and complete a research paper.

Method

We administered questionnaires during the Fall 2004 semester to 101 graduating seniors to determine their assessment of, and satisfaction with, various aspects of programmatic effectiveness in the Department of Sociology. The questionnaire included a series of items about different components of the sociology program that are directly related to civic engagement. These questions focused on:

- the reasons why an orientation toward civic engagement compelled students to choose sociology as a major;
- the extent of students' participation in a SLI;
- students' satisfaction with their SLI; and
- the degree to which students had cultivated a commitment to civic engagement as a consequence of their experiences in studying sociology.

Results

Our analysis reveals some important relationships among students' service-learning orientations, their participation in community-based internships, and their commitment to civic engagement. It also offers some insights into the means by which service-learning programs might be assessed.

Table 4.4 presents students' reports of their commitment to civic engagement, and the differences in commitment levels between students who have, and have not, participated in SLIs. The results indicate that the 71 students who have completed SLIs report stronger intentions to pursue future civic-engagement opportunities (e.g., attending graduate school in social work, obtaining a job helping people) than the 27 students who have not yet completed their internships. Overall, the data suggest that SLIs promote an orientation toward civic engagement among many students; and, as we discuss below, they can serve as an important "reality-check" for other students who are interested in pursuing occupations oriented toward civic engagement.

The data indicate that participation in SLIs is especially likely to increase students' motivation toward pursuing graduate studies in social work. Strikingly, however, some students report that their participation in our program's SLIs *increase* their commitment to working in an area that is *unrelated* to sociology. In other words, SLIs appear to provide practical experiences that actually decrease some students' motivation toward specific forms of civic engagement. Our data suggest that participation in service learning motivates students to acquire further education in the social sciences. At the same time, however, it provides a practical "reality-check" about the difficulties inherent in civic engagement activities. As a result of their internship experience, and most likely as a consequence of the difficulties of community work, students are less likely to believe that they will be able to effect change in society as a result of studying sociology and that they require more education to effectively do so.

Table 4.5 summarizes students' satisfaction with their SLIs and the degree to which their experiences enhance their commitment to civic engagement. In every

Participation in service learning motivates students to acquire further education in the social sciences. At the same time, however, it provides a practical "reality-check" about the difficulties inherent in civic engagement activities.

area, students who have participated in a SLI are more likely to provide higher evaluations of their commitment to civic-engagement activities if they were more satisfied with their internship experience. Thus, the more satisfied students are with their internship, the more likely they are to be interested in continuing to study people, to feel prepared for a job helping people, to plan to work in a field related to sociology, to believe they are more able to effect change in society, and to attend graduate school.

Finally, our data point to the gendered nature of service-learning activities. Women (mean = 3.73) are much more likely than men (mean = 3.25) to report satisfaction with their SLIs. This suggests *not* simply that women may be more inclined toward service learning, but that service-learning activities should be properly gauged in order to promote participation by different student populations.

Conclusion

Our study compares students who have completed a SLI with those who have not, and it reveals clear differences in their respective civic engagement orientations. This particular result points to the usefulness of a comparative research design in developing an effective assessment of service-learning activities, and in evaluating student learning that occurs as a consequence of participation in SLIs.

Proposed modifications to existing service-learning programs should be based on reliable and valid data. We believe that our instrument provides such data. In addition, it is not limited in its application to sociology. The questionnaire can be easily and fruitfully adapted to the evaluation of service-learning components in other disciplines as well. As the service-learning movement continues in higher education, it will become increasingly important to assess the nature and extent not only of students' civic *engagement,* but of their *learning.* The research summarized here presents the results of our department's ongoing attempt to do so.

Table 4.5. Satisfaction with Service-Learning Internships and Commitment to Civic Engagement	Dissatisfied With Internship		Neutral		Satisfied with Internship	
Question	Mean	N	Mean	N	Mean	N
I am interested in studying people.	3.70	11	4.21	24	4.85	21
I think sociology will prepare me for a job helping people.	3.90	11	4.29	24	4.62	21
I plan to work in a field related to sociology.	3.30	11	4.05	24	4.45	21
Studying sociology will help me to be able to change society.	3.40	11	3.58	24	4.25	21
I plan to go to graduate school in sociology.	3.00	11	3.25	24	3.76	21
I plan to go to graduate school in social work.	2.00	11	3.19	24	3.41	21
I plan to begin working in a field unrelated to sociology.	2.10	11	2.19	24	2.32	21

References

Kowalewski, B. M., M. G. Ender, and J. DeFiore, eds.. 2001. *Service-learning and undergraduate sociology: Syllabi and instructional materials.* 2nd ed. Washington, D.C.: American Sociological Association.

Ostrow, J., G. Hesser, and S. Enos, eds. 1999. *Cultivating the sociological imagination: Concepts and models for service-learning in sociology.* Washington, D.C.: American Association for Higher Education and American Sociological Association.

DEPARTMENTAL AND DISCIPLINARY APPROACHES TO EDUCATING CITIZENS

5

Department-Wide Engagement: Creating and Supporting Durable Structures for Campus and Community Change

KEVIN KECSKES
PORTLAND STATE UNIVERSITY

Committed faculty at my home institution, Portland State University (PSU), are energized by their professional experiences with community-based pedagogies. However, they are also concerned that many students will be exposed to community too late in the curriculum. Thus, we have learned that for students to more fully reap the benefits of these rich learning environments we need to intentionally sequence community activities. This coordination can happen effectively at the departmental level, especially within the requirements for the major.

Faculty Culture and Civic Education Disconnected?

So, why doesn't this coordination happen more frequently? In addition to general time constraints, the traditions of a largely individualistic faculty culture can also impede collective work. Service- or community-based civic learning techniques require collaboration among faculty, students, and community partners, yet traditional faculty cultural norms do not generally place a high value on these activities, nor recognize the need for faculty training and support. This inconsistency between collective strategies and an individualized faculty culture can limit the effectiveness of engaged pedagogies. Because individualism anchors most faculty work life, community-based civic education programs and students' community experiences often remain uncoordinated and disconnected (Sax, et al. 2000; Sigmon 1998). Unless this disconnection between the individu-

alized norms of faculty and university culture and the collective needs of students and community members involved in community-based civic education and service settings is bridged with innovative approaches, these promising community-embedded techniques will continue to be of only modest benefit.

Increasing Departmental Coherence —How and Where to Start?

Over three years ago, PSU was the first institution in the nation (and, to date, remains one of only three, the others being Indiana University–Purdue University Indianapolis and Miami Dade Community College) to embark on a *campus-wide* initiative to create "engaged departments." PSU embraced this strategy given our institutional commitment to continue to find effective ways to operationalize our university motto: *Let Knowledge Serve the City.*

Throughout this process, we have learned that an effective place to start with departments is to support the chair and loyal senior faculty in doing an organizational scan of current activities. We work with departments to help them develop a picture of their current and recent scholarly work, with a particular focus on community-based activities. This is relatively easy, can be accomplished in a variety of ways over the course of a couple of months, and then brought to the attention of the full departmental faculty during one or two unit meetings. We have found that faculty appreciate this activity; indeed, in many cases, it energizes them. An easy and simple place to start is to identify all the courses taught by departmental faculty, highlighting the ones that are required for the major and for various minors supported by the unit. Simultaneously, invite unit faculty to provide a list of all publications that are "works-in-progress" or that they have completed in the last three years. Finally, gather a list of the community partners that faculty are working with. These partners may include private enterprises, nonprofit organizations, and neighborhood, political, student and/or other advocacy groups both on and off of campus. We have found—over and over again—that by keeping the definition of "community engagement" broad, inviting faculty to share their accomplishments and works-in-progress with colleagues, and aggregating the data in a low-tech, transparent manner can be very energizing for most, if not all members of the department.[1]

Next, one of several things may take place, depending on the climate and context of the department. Some units have intentionally chosen short articles to read and discuss together—focusing on core disciplinary values, or on the integration of civic learning into core curricula, for example. Other units have chosen to re-visit their departmental mission, or in some cases, to rewrite it completely. Many advanced departments have found it useful to specifically re-analyze their overall curriculum to identify where key civic or other applied learning outcomes emerge. Once collective thinking amid the faculty takes place, a developmental approach to student learning within the major can emerge; and in many cases, erstwhile individualistic faculty orientations can give way to a sense of collectivity. Where the community is involved, commitments by *one* faculty member to a key community partner may transform into a deep *departmental* commitment. Students taking a variety of classes, over the course of years within the major, may engage in community placements

Erstwhile individualistic faculty orientations can give way to a sense of collectivity. Where the community is involved, commitments by one faculty member to a key community partner may transform into a deep departmental commitment.

that connect to and build upon each other. Relationships between faculty, students, and community members become durable; learning can deepen, and applied disciplinary research can have greater impact. The following model is one way to delineate some of the relationships in an engaged department.

Summary of Findings

Our emerging research at Portland State University suggests several key learnings about the departmental engagement process:

- Curricular changes takes time
- Institutional support is critical
- Identifying one or more required community-based courses for the major that intentionally integrate key civic engagement concepts—independent of the instructor—will facilitate the institutionalization of departmental engagement
- Utilizing a developmental framework to sequence community engagement aspects within a range of courses for the major can be very powerful
- Central Office support is critical
- Leadership involvement is critical
- Recognition of efforts is important
- Like people and institutions, departments each operate in their own climate and contexts. Recognizing, affirming, and building from that foundation is *essential;* therefore,
- Flexibility, adaptability, and creativity are more important than proposing a "template" approach

- Even if all faculty are not adopters of service learning, this effort enhances individual and departmental familiarity with service learning, and other civic engagement strategies

- Promotion of institutional vision and mission can increase commitment to and broaden understanding

- After three years of institution-wide implementation, we now see emerging a *continuum of depart-*

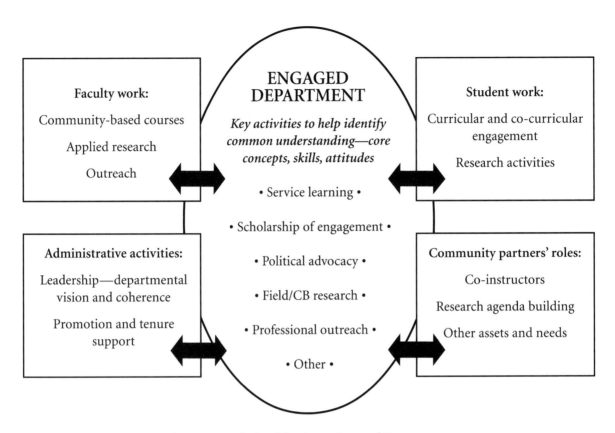

Figure 5.1. Relationships in an Engaged Department

mental level engagement, from a barely aggregated set of individual faculty efforts, on one end of the scale, to . . .

• The emergence of groundbreaking collective thinking, planning, and action on the other end of the continuum

Notes

This article is based on previously published work: Kecskes, K., 2004. Engaging the department: Community-based approaches to support academic unit coherence. In *The department chair.* Bolton, Mass.: Anker Publishing, Inc.

1. To learn more about the "Engaged Department Program" supported by the Center for Academic Excellence at Portland State University, see Kecskes and Spring, 2004.

References

Battisonti, R. M., S. B. Gelmon, J. Saltmarsh, J. Wergin, and E. Zlotkowski. 2003. *The engaged department toolkit.* National Campus Compact, 2003.

Kecskes, K. and A. Spring. 2004. Creating engaged departments: Moving faculty culture from private to public, individual to collective focus for the common good. In *Sixth annual continuums of service conference proceedings,* edited by G. Daynes. and H. Weaver: *http://www.wacampuscompact. org/publications.html.*

Sax, L. J., A. W. Astin, W. S. Korn, and K. M. Mahoney. 1999, 2000. *The American freshman: National norms for fall 1999 & 2000.* Los Angeles: Higher Education Research Institute.

Sigmon, R. 1998. Building sustainable partnerships: Linking communities and educational institutions. Alexandria. Va.: National Society for Experiential Education

Creating and Sustaining a Culture of Engagement

Christie J. Brungardt and Jill R. Arensdorf
Fort Hays State University

An engaged department is a collection of faculty who are committed to collaborating with one another as they make positive change in both their students and their communities. We believe the Department of Leadership Studies at Fort Hays State University (Hays, Kans.) exemplifies an engaged department. This department has been engaged in community-based teaching and learning since its inception in 1993. At that time, one full-time faculty member worked with forty students. To date, five full-time faculty members work with nearly 2000 students both on-campus and around the world. The Department of Leadership Studies' mission is to educate and nurture citizens to lead our communities, state, nation, and beyond. We believe that involvement in creating social change and civic engagement is critical for both students and faculty. These experiences are provided by the delivery of a comprehensive educational experience based on theory and practical application. Students and faculty learn leadership through the traditional classroom experience, experiential learning activities, and faculty collaborative efforts on campus and in the community. These activities create a culture that encourages the institutionalization of civic engagement.

Experiential Learning Activities

At the center of an engaged department is a curriculum that connects students with their communities. We do this by offering three service-learning courses: Youth Leadership Facilitation, Ethics and Leadership, and Fieldwork in Leadership Studies. A unique aspect of our program is the element of engaging our distance education students in service learning. Our bachelor's degree in Organizational Leadership is offered both on-campus and via distance. Structuring the Fieldwork course for off-campus delivery was a challenge, but we feel it has proved highly successful. These students identify a need and team within their home community. Reflection is done via the on-line course management system (Blackboard). The instructor facilitates reflection sessions as well as requires an individual reflection paper upon completion of the course. Every semester we have a number of projects that take place in the U.S., but we have also had service-learning projects implemented on Navy aircraft carriers and on military bases around the world. For example, in the fall of 2004 a Navy sailor stationed in Japan implemented an intense voter education and registration drive on his base to increase voting of all U.S. sailors on the base, as well as their families.

Institutionalization of Civic Engagement

The Department of Leadership Studies' faculty members have a strong passion for civic engagement. That passion is reflected in our active roles in community and university organizations. We believe that we must be willing to do leadership, as we ask our students to do. By modeling these behaviors, our hope is that students will be civically engaged both now and in the future. Some of the methods we use to create and sustain this culture of engagement are as follows:

- Mission driven—With the mission of our department being educating and nurturing future citizen leaders, the attitudes and culture of our department are embedded in everything we do. A major consideration when undertaking new initiatives is how well they align with our civic mission.

- Learning Objectives—Our curriculum strives to instill new thinking, attitudes, and behaviors in our graduates. The curriculum concentrates on the importance of both understanding and action.

  - Understanding Leadership—The students will be knowledgeable regarding the role leaders and followers play in making changes for the collective and common good.

  - Competencies in Leadership—Students will be able to demonstrate and perform both personal and collaborative leadership skills.

  - Commitment to Leadership—As leaders and followers, students will assume responsibility by actively engaging in service as agents of change for the purpose of making their organizations and communities a better place.

- Hiring of faculty—A critical element in creating this culture is to carefully select new faculty members who believe in, as well as practice, our philosophy of civic leadership development. The vitae of each new hire is carefully examined for evidence of both the understanding of leadership theories, as well as application of theory to practice.

• Collaborative team teaching—Our department believes strongly in the importance of the team approach to educating citizens. We maintain informal lines of communication between faculty members to assist one another when needed. We collaborate on ideas, projects, presentations, and teaching. We draw on the expertise of individual research interests to enhance the depth of our own classroom lectures and activities.

• Merit and Tenure Evaluation—Faculty are evaluated annually. A major component of this evaluation process is how well faculty members' teaching, research, and service activities are aligned with the department's civic mission.

• Continuous Improvement Plan—Twice annually our entire department collaboratively reviews and revises the continuous improvement plan during off-site departmental retreats. Giving all faculty members ownership in this process fosters greater depth of understanding and encourages creative input from all. This process assures continuous self-monitoring that our department's actions align with our goals of civic engagement.

• Organized Outreach Unit—As the department has grown, so has demand for civic leadership-training programs across the state of Kansas. To help meet this demand, the Center for Civic Leadership was created in 2002 as the outreach program of the Department of Leadership Studies. This has allowed for integration of civic engagement activities in the classroom, as well as the community.

• Assessment—The goal of our assessment efforts is to ensure we are achieving desired outcomes. Qualitative and quantitative assessment of students, faculty, and community outcomes is completed on a regular basis. Longitudinal assessment is an area in which we must improve. The ultimate question in this assessment process is whether we instill a sense of civic responsibility in our graduates beyond their collegiate experience.

Conclusion

The Department of Leadership Studies lends itself well to an engaged department. However, whether in a Department of Mathematics, Business Administration, or Psychology, many of these same methods can be applied. As departments strategically plan for an enriched culture of engagement they should evaluate their mission and student learning outcomes, hiring and promotion practices, community outreach activities, and continuous improvement plans. These practices promote the institutionalization of civic engagement, which aligns with an original goal of higher education.

A specific characteristic we hope our graduates will possess is that of civic-mindedness—a sense of community and a commitment to civic responsibility through action. Regardless of the program from which students graduate, the habit of engagement will encourage them to serve as architects and catalysts for change in their respective organizations and communities. These individuals will challenge the status quo and initiate and sustain transformational change for the collective and common good.

Maximizing Collaboration for Sustainable Innovation

Darlene Hantzis and Debra Worley
Indiana State University

The challenge to create sustainable civic engagement practices points to a tension between event-driven engagement activities and efforts to infuse experiential learning through curricular and co-curricular "infrastructures." Identifying and promoting individual activities as opportunities for engagement is easy; integrating engagement in the curricula and co-curricula is more complex. Events can establish campus rituals that contribute to a culture of engagement; however, events alone will not sustain curricular and co-curricular transformation.

Indiana State University designed an "infusion"

model of civic engagement that took advantage of the 2004 national election to accomplish sustainable curricular changes, successful co-curricular collaboration, and the immediate goal of increasing the number of students who vote in national elections. In this essay we identify the strategies utilized to develop this collaborative approach to civic engagement.

The goal of increasing voter participation was captured in the title, "4002 in 2004." Because we chose to pursue long-term learning goals under the auspices of the national election, we were able to make use of many programs developed externally and the natural energy that gathers around a presidential election.

Curricular Dimensions

We initiated the campaign with classroom-based research in spring 2004. Graduate students designed and completed three kinds of primary research: archival; in-depth interviews and focus groups with students, faculty, and staff; and a survey to measure voting knowledge, attitudes, and behavior of students. Undergraduate students in public relations summarized prior research on student voting behavior and analyzed the findings utilizing contemporary communication theory. Collectively, the graduate and undergraduate work helped identify effective communication strategies to encourage students to vote. Students in advanced case analysis developed a strategic communication plan to reach the campaign goal, and students in a media writing course developed specific "tactics" to enact the plan. Work in the courses was coordinated and sequenced so that students relied on and benefited from the research and planning accomplished by others.

The comprehensive research report completed in the spring served as text in several fall courses. Students in strategic planning utilized the prior research, and two first-year learning communities included the research in units designed to focus on aspects of college students' political participation.

Critical to this design was the willingness of faculty to utilize content specific to the campaign, while maintaining the integrity of the learning goals of their courses. Contributing faculty in this project found that most course content includes a higher degree of flexibility than initial resistance indicates. In particular, faculty teaching introductory courses in economics, political science, and environmental science successfully incorporated activities and discussion related to the campaign within their courses. Overall this project demonstrated that there is persuasive weight to the argument that faculty can accommodate experiential and service learning into courses without sacrificing content coverage.

The coordinators of three general education courses —writing, psychology, and communication—integrated attention to student political participation in their courses. Writing and psychology included assignments focused on voting and offered participation points for involvement with campaign activities.

Co-Curricular Dimensions

ISU has a strong collaborative infrastructure linking Academic and Student Affairs, based primarily in our first-year programs. The 4002 in 2004 campaign was explicitly co-sponsored by several Student Affairs departments, student organizations, and key administrative offices (e.g. Office of Diversity and Affirmative Action and the Center for Public Service and Civic Engagement). Residence hall staff integrated campaign themes into routine programming. The student newspaper created a weekly report entitled "Vote Watch 2004" and requested guest editorials from faculty in an effort to increase the use of the newspaper as a site for campus dialogues. The campaign was co-chaired by the president of the Student Government Association.

In addition to supporting pedagogic programming in residence halls, we scheduled co-curricular events. We created "Pizza and Politics," a weekly program intended to provide a place for student-faculty dialogue around current issues (identified in earlier research). The event concluded with an Election night "Party with the Parties" to watch the returns. Pizza and Politics has continued with an intensified focus on promoting effective civic argument.

Utilizing the national election allowed us to take advantage of externally resourced programming. We integrated Banned Books Week into the first Pizza and Politics, which focused on freedom of speech on college campuses. Our recognition of Banned Books Week featured a day of out-loud reading from banned books.

ISU registered as a Debate Watch site. We chose not only to organize public viewings, but to engage the community in "debriefing" discussions focused on the debate structure and content. Faculty, staff, students, and community members acted as citizen-peers, watching and commenting on the debates. ISU participated in two national research projects focused on the debates, providing students opportunities to administer survey instruments, results from which were utilized in work cited in national press releases and published research.

The co-curricular dimension of our project created opportunities for our students to speak to the media. Every event was well-covered, and students working on the campaign were sought for comment and benefited significantly from this laboratory about effective communication with the media.

The Results

Our focused effort continues to be assessed. We saw significant student participation in voting, and while identifying exact numbers of students who voted is complex, we know that the polling place designated for campus residents experienced a 400% increase in turnout. Over 1,000 students participated in the "Pizza & Politics'" discussions; more than 60 students and the president of the university participated by reading banned books. In a university with over 50% of eligible voters registered, we increased the numbers by more than 500. The campus media participation was also significant, with public service announcements (developed by students) run continuously throughout the campaign, and more than six weeks of front page coverage in the university newspaper. Finally, the Student Government Association "imitated" this effort when they held a campus-wide vote surrounding a new recreation center proposal.

We believe it is possible to raise the profile of national decisions that seem less "local" in their focus, and to also raise the profile of "local" decision making with the potential for long-term and national implications.

Conclusions

While it would be significant enough to marshal institutional resources to encourage students to exercise their right to vote, we sought to create experiential learning opportunities, promote learning about key issues, increase the knowledge base about political participation, and initiate sustainable changes in the campus culture. Our experience argues for leveraging national and local events in designing campus cultural transformation projects. We believe it is possible to raise the profile of national decisions that seem less "local" in their focus, and to also raise the profile of "local" decision making with the potential for long-term and national implications.

In this successful program, students, faculty and staff learned that text content can be applied to real-world problems, opportunities, and solutions. We all became more convinced that courses which appear to be content inflexible, can utilize active learning opportunities for engaging civically and still accomplish content goals. Our common identity was "4002 in 2004" and this call to action served to build the collaborative bridge between departments, units, curricular and co-curricular programs, learning communities, faculty and staff, administration, and the surrounding community. We firmly believe that establishing quality models of flexibility (in and outside of classes) contributes to ongoing efforts to involve the campus community in experiential learning.

Rethinking the Boundaries of the Classroom

Diana Cardenas and Susan Loudermilk-Garza
Texas A&M University–Corpus Christi

Our program in Technical and Professional Writing (TPW) at Texas A&M University–Corpus Christi focuses on helping students address needs, problems, and issues in the community to effect solutions. We base our program on the model of service learning put forth by Bowdon and Scott (2003). They advocate a "hands-on approach" where "students learn through active participation in thoughtfully organized service," an approach where service learning "is conducted in, and meets the community; is integrated into and enhances the academic curriculum; includes structured time for reflection; and helps foster civic responsibility" (1–2). It is this sense of fostering civic responsibility that makes what our students do more than just work in the community. As students become involved in trying to effect change, often they begin to reconsider their roles as citizens and their investment in the community's future.

When we first came to the university the common perception among students was that no opportunities existed for technical and professional writers in our community. In order to address these false perceptions, we surveyed the community to identify opportunities. As part of the survey, we asked if the organizations would be interested in working on projects with students. From contacts with those who said yes, we were able to organize several successful civic engagement projects. As a result of those initial projects, word in the community spread, and organizations began to contact us. Students also identified organizations with needs, and we now have an overabundance of projects.

When we started our focus on civic engagement we asked students to choose projects within each course, and as they became more involved in these activities, we realized they could benefit by working with students in other TPW courses. One of the main objectives of our program is to help students see that writing is a collaborative process that requires many kinds of connections. We realized that our program needed to support these connections, so we built flexibility and choice into all of the courses. And as students undertook a wider array of projects, such as technology related projects, they also began working with students in other disciplines. Be-cause of their interactions, we also developed connections with faculty members in many other departments, and they often become part of the collaborative network.

We have built several features into our program that encourage this sense of working as a collaborative network as opposed to separate classes:

- A centralized web site that lists projects students can engage in. Students from all classes begin with this source to determine what they will focus on.

- A policy that encourages students to work on different stages of a project in different classes. Thus, a student, or group of students, may complete the groundwork for a project by gathering data and creating a project plan in one class and then the following semester begin to develop the project. A third group might implement and conduct usability tests on the project.

- A policy that encourages students to rely on subject matter experts and skill experts to complete projects. Therefore, students may work with students from another class to meet the needs of a project that requires expertise outside their area.

- A restructuring of class management to allow time for meetings and other tasks.

- An advisory committee comprised of faculty and community members that oversees the program and offers suggestions for continued and improved collaboration between the university and the community.

- Continual contact with agency presidents, departmental supervisors, program coordinators, and many others to make decisions regarding projects and outcomes.

Some examples of collaborative work across the boundaries of the classroom include:

- Two students in a TPW class worked with students in a computer science class to create a database for the administrators at Catholic Charities who needed an effective method to register needy families and immigrants looking for a new start in our area, to identify their needs, and to deliver appropriate assistance.

• Two students assisted in the writing of a regional environmental plan for the director of Coastal Bend Bays and Estuaries. After studying the scope of their project, the students decided they would be able to complete only the first phase of the plan, which involved attending public forums to understand the need, working with city and county officials to obtain their ideas, and interviewing environmentalists to gather information about goals and procedures. From this information the students developed a plan for building collaborations among local entities and environmental groups. Two other students picked up the project and continued to work on it the following semester.

• Another student worked with a member of the Art faculty and some of the art majors to secure funds for an art exhibit that will bring experts in various areas to the university to conduct activities with students and the community.

When we first began to focus on civic engagement, we taught most of the courses within the program, so getting faculty involved was not an issue. Our program has grown and we now have four full-time faculty members who teach in the program. Before hiring new faculty, we determine their level of commitment to civic engagement and we also inform them of the history of our program so that they are aware of the program's focus. If they join our program, we provide support to help them make the transitions that this type of civic engagement requires of teachers. The program coordinator shares the philosophy behind the program, and the new faculty members work closely with experienced faculty during their first year to help them make connections in the community. The advisory group is also very bene-

ficial for new teachers as they hear first-hand from members of the community how excited they are to work with students, and what works and what does not work in setting up these collaborative efforts.

Students report in their project portfolios that in addition to increasing their writing skills, they feel a greater sense of investment in the community. Feedback from community leaders reveals positive outcomes for the organizations and agencies. Faculty members enjoy their new roles as coordinators partnering with their students. And as administrators and faculty engage in conversations about embracing civic engagement, they often call attention to our program as a successful model.

While we have been very successful implementing this approach, we have also faced challenges and have learned lessons. When people express interest in working with our students, we stress that this approach requires commitment on their part. We also find that students are challenged in new ways. Their contacts sometimes have conflicts, making it difficult to meet the student's schedule requirements. Sometimes students have to reconstruct plans or shift midstream to another project. Students who have less experience working independently require more attention. Because of these changes teachers have to adapt as well. They are no longer the sole experts; they become coaches and guides.

In spite of these challenges, we believe our students have benefited greatly and our program has become stronger.

References

Bowdon, M. and J. D. Scott. 2003. *Service-learning in technical and professional communication.* New York: Longman.

Infusing Service Learning in Teacher Education Programs

Trae Stewart
University of Central Florida

In 2004, the Office of Service-Learning at the University of Central Florida invited faculty to propose new or modified courses that would be designated as university service-learning courses. To merit this distinction,

student experiences must involve: 1) a minimum of 15 hours in a nonprofit or governmental agency that addresses a genuine need in the community; 2) reciprocity among university and community stakeholders that results in students' increased civic awareness and engagement while meeting course objectives; and 3) structured student reflection. In addition to the potential intrinsic benefits from the infusion of service learning (e.g., deeper command of subject matter, increased self-efficacy, development of reciprocal community-university relations), service-learning designated courses would receive an additional 0.15% of student credit hour funding for each student enrolled.

The Department of Educational Studies submitted 5 educational foundations courses for service-learning approval. Reasons for embracing this opportunity included:

1. The College of Education has felt a severe reduction in its operating budget. Designation of the five courses, central to the degree programs of all undergraduate, pre-service teacher education majors, would earn substantial more student credit hours, translating into more operating revenue.

2. Many requirements for the university designation already existed in the field-experience requirements of the five core courses. Field experiences needed simple redesign to ensure that: a) a genuine need was being met; b) civic awareness/engagement objectives were linked to class curricula; and, c) reflection activities specific to service experiences were included.

3. Faculty envisioned service learning as value-added to the educational opportunities for pre-service teachers. Previously, students' field experiences were tangentially connected to class topics, often left to the personal inclination and analysis of the student. In contrast, the infusion of service learning would provide a genuine means to teach pre-service teachers the philosophical foundations and pedagogy of service learning by framing lessons within their newly established "service schema." Students, in turn, could employ service learning within their internships and/or own classrooms after graduation.

4. Faculty sought to build more reciprocal relationships with community constituents and, in particular, neighboring school districts. Instead of indirectly exploiting the schools and willing teachers for students' graduation/course needs, a discourse of need and opportunity would be created.

Ultimately, the five courses received service-learning designation. A cohort of faculty attended an intense, four-day summer faculty development institute to finalize service requirements, accompanying reflections, and assessment strategies for implementation the following academic year. Myriad challenges have manifest since the implementation of the modified service-learning courses. From these challenges, education departments interested in infusing service-learning should consider the following lessons learned in their planning phases.

Lessons Learned and Tips

Lesson #1—Assuming Linearity

According to the university undergraduate catalog, students are to enroll sequentially in courses (e.g., 2005, 4323, 4603). Students would then have previous academic knowledge and service-learning experiences on which to build each semester. Instead, students have enrolled simultaneously in multiple courses, often out of sequence. Departments should check with their registrars to ensure that university computerized enrollment systems are programmed to reflect the catalog requirements. Furthermore, faculty must be diligent in their enforcement of prerequisite completion before allowing a student to remain in a course.

Lesson #2—Multiple Hours

Students who enroll in multiple courses with a 15-hour service-learning requirement must complete a significant field experience portion while juggling academic coursework. This heavy schedule concerns program designers in that students may complete all of their service-learning hours in one environment. Students then have the daunting task of examining their experiences through two separate epistemological lenses. Keeping track of students required to complete distinct types of service poses an additional accounting issue, particularly when funding hinges on students completing the separate service hours. By facilitating students' class enrollment per catalog requirements, this challenge can also be avoided.

Lesson #3—Policies about Volunteers

A new state policy requires that any individual volunteering, completing field experiences, or interning within a K-12 public school be fingerprinted every 90 days. Although the necessity for completing background checks on school volunteers is not disputed, students must incur a cost for each set of fingerprints and accompanying background investigation. In addition to the financial burden on students, there is concern that introductory classes will experience a severe drop in enrollment as approximately 30% of students enrolled in these courses are not intended Education majors and might frown upon paying additional fees for an elective class. Departments must remain up-to-date on policies that will affect students in their service requirements.

Lesson #4—"2+2" Model

A notable percentage of students enter UCF through the "2+2" model. Under this model, students attend a community college for two years to complete general education requirements and prerequisites, and then matriculate into a four-year university/college to complete a Bachelor's degree. Students who transfer in their sophomore or junior year have not developed a service schema to maintain the momentum as conceptualized in the service-learning infusion planning. Furthermore, the Department of Educational Studies could not ensure a common foundation of knowledge, experiences, and application among its students—a problem for upper level courses that require the same prerequisites. In this era of student credit hour competition, higher education institutions will find it difficult to overcome this challenge. Many students attending community college classes close to their full-time residences, some out-of-state, exacerbate this unlikelihood. Therefore, planning must account for this discrepancy in student background and preparation by potentially offering service-learning classes only after students have matriculated into the university fulltime.

Lesson #5—Faculty Comfort

With the infusion of service learning across the board, course curricula have begun to reflect a more essentialist philosophy—a danger vis-à-vis academic freedom. In addition, just because education faculty are familiar with service learning does not guarantee that they possess the knowledge of, comfort with, and buy in for service learning as a viable educational methodology. This pedagogical concern is heightened with the Department's growing number of adjunct instructors. Prior to an endeavor of such magnitude, departments should consider identifying particular sections of each course to pilot the service-learning infusion. Faculty most comfortable with service learning may then be assigned to teach these sections and subsequently serve as trainers for their colleagues. Faculty trainers should devote portions of the workshop to describing how service learning allows for the use of multiple epistemologies.

Conclusion

Although the development and implementation of new service-learning classes is daunting, the potential outcomes to all stakeholders involved are numerous and far outweigh the challenges. The efforts and experiences by the Department of Educational Studies simply further support past service-learning research that maintains that each program's design, implementation, and outcomes will be unique due to the subjectivity of the program, the mission and student populations of the institutions, and the immediate needs of the community.

Engaging Future Teachers about Civic Education

TONY FILIPOVITCH, CLARK JOHNSON, AND JOE KUNKEL
MINNESOTA STATE UNIVERSITY, MANKATO

This is the story of a departmental approach to civic engagement. The Social Studies Teaching program at MSU inserted a year-long Public Achievement service-learning experience (POL 382) and an associated year-long seminar in democracy and citizenship (POL 381) into the teacher-training program, between the first course (SoSt 200, Introduction to the Social Studies) and the methods course (SoSt 450, Teaching the Social Studies).

The students form a cohort of "coaches" who each lead a team of 4–8 middle-school children in Public Achievement (PA), a national program for teaching children and youth a democratic process for community involvement. Hildereth (1998) has also written a handbook for running a public achievement team. The emphasis is on process—teaching the skills of civic engagement and democratic process (for example, the children choose their team's focus, not the coach)—and on "policy"—the goal of the activity is to "make a change" in your community (which can be as local as the school community or as large as the globe). The teams (middle school students and their college coach) meet weekly, from October to April, for one 40-minute class period each week. The coaches also enroll concurrently in a seminar called Democracy and Citizenship, which focuses on concepts of democracy and civic engagement, and on skills useful in the classroom. There is also a small team of "mentors" (4–6 people), recruited from the previous year's coaches. These mentors observe 4–5 teams each week and meet with those coaches for debriefing, leading a general discussion and providing both written and oral feedback to each coach. The team of mentors also meets with instructor and site supervisor at end of each PA day to debrief and plan the following week.

This approach varies somewhat from the "standard" PA approach. While it stresses the same core concepts and leads the children through the same community-action process, it is integrated into the regular school day and extends for the better part of the entire school year. Further, the team coaches are simultaneously enrolled in a separate college course which includes both conceptual and pedagogical issues related to PA.

This approach is notable for the wide range of learning outcomes that it achieves—and the wide range of learners for whom it achieves them. There are at least five levels at which learning occurs: the children, the coaches, the mentors, the faculty, and the institutions.

Children

The children learn and practice a number of skills. They learn the skills for engaging in the democratic process—setting agendas, leading meetings, recording the decisions and actions of the group, writing mini-grants, and writing (and defending) action plans to authority figures. In addition, they learn the formal language for talking about the democratic process, repeatedly using terms like "citizenship," "public," "diversity," and "accountability." And they practice presenting their ideas, at first in small group meetings with school authorities, but finally by making a formal, public presentation of the outcomes at a Final Assembly. Further, in the process of researching and acting on their issue, the students develop some direct insight into how an issue

is brought to the public agenda and how that agenda is influenced.

Coaches

The coaches receive a closely mentored initial experience with a small group of middle school students. For many of them, this is their first experience leading a group of students on their own, and there is an advantage in having a small group rather than a full class of 25–30. The coaches also have the opportunity to reflect both on process and content of civic engagement activity. For many this is their first introduction to "action research" (Mills 2002), by which theory and practice are placed in dialogue with each other. The coaches also share their experience with other coaches—both in PA and in seminar—which leads to learning from others' experience. Finally, the coaches develop some skill in managing the interface between school and community. They learn to deal with issues of student responsibility (for example, what do you do when the team had an assignment to complete by the next meeting, and no one comes prepared), comportment (for example, how should the team behave as they walk through the halls on their way to make a presentation to the principal), presentation of self (for example, what phone etiquette should the team members practice when they call community businesses to request donations of goods or money for their project), and networking (for example, they often do "influence maps" which chart out who has an interest in their issue and who is in a position to influence what they can do about it).

Mentors

For the mentors, the focus of their action research shifts from community engagement to the skills of reflective teaching. Having already done it themselves, they now have the opportunity to observe and compare the teaching styles (and the resulting learning) of other coaches. Further, they must practice the skill of providing constructive criticism—every week, for 24 weeks. We have observed that this creates a significant maturing process in student teachers; as a result of this process, they understand better what their own teaching supervisor is doing and they take advice and correction much more positively. Finally, the mentors create and teach their own lessons as part of seminar that is paired with PA. This has the effect of moving them forward in their careers as teachers, and documents their ability to provide professional training to peers.

Faculty and Program

For the faculty, the PA project provides an excellent opportunity for "learning by doing." It is not enough to lecture and lead discussions on democracy and civic engagement; the ideas are immediately put to the test of practice. This leads to richer classroom discussion (every student has some experiences to contribute to the discussions) and greater student motivation (there is no question about what they are going to do with "all this theory"). It also gives the teacher some practice in moving concepts from the college level to middle school and (in the seminar) to high school. Often, after years of graduate study and teaching to adults, we become comfortable in the morass of detail and qualified propositions that are the stock of our professional discourse. Figuring out how to teach it to children (older, rapidly maturing children, but still fairly naïve and inexperienced) requires one to focus on the central ideas and to express them clearly. In the process, we have discovered that our own research has become more focused and the "so what?" question is more easily answered.

From the programmatic and institutional side, we are finding that the issues raised in PA have been diffusing to other courses in the social studies. The students themselves are raising issues (both of content and pedagogy) in their teacher-training courses, and the faculty have found PA a rich source of practical examples for other courses that we teach. Students from programs other than teaching (social work, community sociology, political theory) have been attracted by the Democracy & Citizenship Seminar, which has led to interesting discussions about how teachers learn and know and how students of other disciplines see it. The PA program has also required collaboration across institutions. The team coaches have had to learn (and enforce) the school rules, and must prepare their team to explain their issue and action plans for the principal's approval. There is also a project coordinator who is paid a stipend by the school district, but who is supervised by the PA faculty instructor as well as by the school principal. The need for funds (for the mini-grants that students write, as well as for underwriting the t-shirts and pizza for the final assembly) has required the program coordinator to "sell" the project to the community. This has not proven to be a hard sell—the local newspaper often does a story on one or more of the student projects, and the students themselves are making many community contacts.

References

Hildreth, R. 1998. *Building worlds, transforming lives, making history: A guide to public achievement.* 2nd ed. Minneapolis, Minn.: Center for Democracy and Citizenship.

Mills, G. 2002. *Action research: A guide for the teacher researcher.* 2nd ed. Upper Saddle River, N.J.: Prentice Hall.

Fostering Service Learning in a Small Department

SCOTT SMITHSON
PURDUE UNIVERSITY NORTH CENTRAL

A department cannot easily move forward with large service-learning initiatives without the support of campus administration and a climate and culture conducive to the task. The Department of Communication at our small Midwest campus now has four full-time faculty members and a growing number of communication majors. The Communication major is nearly three years old and the department presently has several different service-learning projects. The Communication faculty unanimously support these initiatives. Fundamentally, this faculty believes that higher education has an obligation to help students develop a fuller understanding of the importance of civic involvement and an enduring sense of accountability to their larger communities.

My experiences as chair of the Community Engagement Committee and acting chair of a department that prioritizes service-learning lead me to make the following suggestions for those intent on developing the culture of engagement within their respective departments:

1. *Walk the talk.* Encourage other faculty to consider service-learning initiatives and participate

yourself. I incorporate service learning in several of my classes.

2. *Don't go it alone.* Seek out the assistance and support of others on campus who share a similar vision and commitment to civic engagement. We began with a special interest group that met informally. Try a brown bag lunch and free conversation as a way to entice involvement.

3. *Recognize the effort.* Find ways to recognize and reward those who demonstrate a degree of effort and commitment in utilizing service learning. We often bring up individual efforts at faculty meetings and regularly mention our individual and departmental successes in annual reports to administration. Driscoll, Holland, Gelmon and Kerrigan (1996) found that institutional support played a significant role in encouraging faculty involvement with service-learning initiatives.

4. *Hire to inspire.* Driscoll and colleagues (1996) also found that many doctoral graduates sought out jobs where there was the potential for integrating their professional goals with their desire to be a positive force for change in their communities. As part of new faculty searches, recruit people who share a similar commitment to engagement. Our departmental search committee asks questions of interviewees related to this departmental priority.

5. *Take it to the top.* Seek out and nurture the support of those at the top of the institution. Connect service learning to discussions with those above you in the organizational hierarchy and share success stories whenever possible. Campus leaders are in good position to network with those in the community in need and may well relay opportunities to your department.

6. *Be proactive.* The department should identify service learning among their priorities whenever creating departmental goal statements. Our department consistently includes service learning among our top priorities.

7. *Network for success.* Connect with Campus Compact and related organizations. Let people know you are interested in service projects. The Campus Compact (campuscompact.org) provides listings of great ideas that work across disciplines. They include examples, contact people, and potential grant money, all of which could prove use-

ful in developing a departmental focus on service learning.

8. *Coordination is key.* A coordinator or director of community engagement can make a tremendous difference in the likelihood of success. This individual provides a touchstone for all service-learning efforts on the campus and can help any faculty member find resources and ideas. The regular and sustained development opportunities noted by Gelmon, Holland, Shinnamon, and Morris (1998) as being so critical to the establishment and growth of service learning can best be managed by giving the responsibility over to one individual.

9. *Quality is job one.* Find ways to ensure quality control for the service projects that the department undertakes. By establishing excellence as a priority, you guarantee that visibility received will be positive. There are numerous sets of "best practices" which may guide your efforts toward quality control. Gibson, Kostecki, and Lucas (2001) provide one model for instituting best practices for service learning into the standard communication curriculum. They base their suggested best practices on a model provided by the National Society for Experiential Education Foundation's Document Committee (www.nsee.org).

These ideas are but a few of the most important things I have gleaned from a few years of experience assisting in the development of various departmental service-learning projects. The following paragraphs briefly describe some of these projects. In each case, our overarching goal is to make the learning more intense, and more likely to be remembered.

For the course Approaches to the Study of Interpersonal Communication, students are given the option of participating in a School Buddies Mentoring program for one hour per week.

In the course Introduction to Public Relations, students study and apply the principles of effective public relations by forming small groups and taking on one area nonprofit organization as a semester public relations campaign project.

In the course Business and Professional Communication, students must participate in a team project in which they design and deliver a training session on a communication topic to children participating in a large area after school program.

For Communication and Emerging Technologies, students are divided into groups to create web sites for various nonprofit groups or organizations.

In the final analysis, incorporating growth and development of service learning is in part a function of setting related departmental goals and working to attain buy-in from key departmental faculty. Existing faculty should be encouraged to develop their ideas, seek out support, and submit for small grants that may be available on campus or through Campus Compact affiliates. They should also be recognized periodically for their efforts. Consider adding service-learning interest as a criterion for new faculty searches. If your campus does not have someone already cast in the role of directing community engagement efforts, then push for this step to be taken. Ultimately, this person will help to focus efforts and channel resources in a more efficient way than any one faculty member working independently.

References

Driscoll, A., B. Holland, S. Gelmon, and S. Kerrigan. 1996. An assessment model for service-learning: Comprehensive case studies of impact on faculty, students, community and institution. *Michigan Journal of Community Service-learning* 3:66–71.

Gelmon, S., B. Holland, A. Shinnamon, and B. Morris. 1998. Community-based education and service: The HPSISN experience. *Journal of Interprofessional Care* 12, no. 3:257–272.

Gibson, M. K., E. M. Kostecki, and M. K. Lucas. 2001. Instituting principles of best practice for service-learning in the communication curriculum. *Southern Communication Journal* 66, no. 3:187–200.

Service Learning in Asian American Studies

CHRISTINE S. CHOI AND AJAY T. NAIR
UNIVERSITY OF PENNSYLVANIA

Introduction

Civic engagement has been variously defined to include "participation in public life," "individual and collective actions designed to identify and address issues of public concern," and "exercising personal agency in the public domain" (Campus Compact Raise Your Voice 2005). In this paper, we define civic engagement to encompass these goals for students, as well as civic consciousness and responsibility at the community level. Particularly for universities, civic engagement constitutes an institutional commitment to the communities in which they operate. As Ira Harkavy asserts, "Universities cannot afford to remain shores of affluence, self-importance and horticultural beauty at the edge of island seas of squalor, violence and despair" (Bringle and Hatcher 1996, 221).

The interest in service learning as a means of meeting civic engagement outcomes has grown significantly over the past 25 years, and there is a growing body of literature about incorporating service-learning pedagogy in a range of disciplines (for examples, see the American Association of Higher Education *Series on Service-Learning in the Disciplines*). Nevertheless, the perception remains that there are some disciplines for which service learning is a "natural fit," and others, such as "business disciplines and natural sciences as well as several important interdisciplinary areas" for which service-learning pedagogy seems "less obvious" (Zlotkowski 1996, Foreword).

Asian American Studies is an example of an interdisciplinary field which, like many others, should be considered a "natural fit" for service learning and consideration of civic engagement goals, despite limited incorporation in the field at present. After all, arguments for actively engaging with the community and addressing community needs through relevant curricula echo the founding principles and mission of Asian American Studies. Asian American Studies, like other ethnic studies programs, emerged within the context of the Civil Rights Movement when students of color demanded the establishment of ethnic studies programs as a means of mobilizing students to take up community and societal problems, and "redirect university resources to promote social justice" (Omatsu 2002). A look at how Asian American Studies programs have leveraged service-learning pedagogy can serve as powerful examples of achieving a range of civic engagement outcomes in an interdisciplinary field.

Asian American Community Fieldwork in Urban Education

In 2003, the University of Pennsylvania's Asian American Studies Program and the Pan-Asian American Community House partnered with two local community schools affected by recent Pennsylvania school reform mandates—Philadelphia's Franklin Learning Center High School ("FLC") and the Alexander Wilson Elementary School ("Wilson")—to implement a strategic, academically-based Asian American Studies service-learning course. The course strived to foster structural community improvement and developed in response to: 1) a movement for Philadelphia school reform; 2) a growing tension between racial/ethnic groups in Philadelphia public schools; and 3) a movement for strengthening partnerships between higher education institutions and local communities. As a reform mechanism, the service-learning model employed here can help communities of color find common ground by promoting the larger meaning of community. The model can also help urban K-12 public schools offer students the validation and personalized attention needed, without overextending the school budget or teaching staff.

High school students from Franklin Learning Center High School were selected to participate in the course and potential first-generation college students in their junior or senior year of high school were especially encouraged to apply. The majority of students enrolled in the course identified as Asian American. Together, the high school and college students identified issues facing Asian American students in the Philadelphia School District and designed change projects to address them. As well, they facilitated Asian American Studies lessons in a second grade class at the Alexander Wilson Elementary School in West Philadelphia using cooperative learning teams to promote intercultural understanding and to provide character education for the elementary

In the final analysis, incorporating growth and development of service learning is in part a function of setting related departmental goals and working to attain buy-in from key departmental faculty.

school participants (Clark 1985). During the pilot year of the program, 94.5% percent of the students enrolled in Wilson were African American and 86.5% were from low-income backgrounds (Welcome to Info Resources 2003). Activities at the elementary school bridged the oft-divided neighborhood and university communities and actively engaged the students at all levels in cross-cultural learning.

Two activities offered by the California State Polytechnic University, Pomona Teachers' Asian Studies Summer Institute website were adapted for use in these lessons. The activities explore friendship through jump rope activity and the creation of friendship bracelets. The jump roping activity served as a natural bridge between the literature and the experiences of the African American children, for whom jump roping and associated rhymes like "Miss Mary Mack" were common childhood activities. Most importantly, the activities were selected because they related directly to the story-line in the selected book and it provided students with an opportunity to apply prior knowledge in a real world setting (Nair 2005).

However, prior to exploring concepts such as teamwork and friendship, it was critical that students build a strong classroom community. The lessons preceding the friendship bracelet and jump roping activities sought to develop a sense of community that transcended racial and socioeconomic barriers. The lessons here moved beyond volunteerism and community service by helping elementary school students, high school students, and college students develop a better understanding of multicultural societies and the larger meaning of community (Moore and Sandholtz 1999).

Through the service-learning course, ties between the university and schools in the community were strengthened and students were offered the opportunity to practice civic engagement through structured activities. Preliminary findings indicate: positive attitudes among students towards civic participation. Students at both high school and college levels reported increased awareness of issues facing Asian American and other minority communities; a sense of urgency around resolving these issues; renewed commitment to community service; and a belief that they can serve as agents of change (Nair and Nakiboglu 2003).

References

Bringle, R., and J. Hatcher. 1996. Implementing service-learning in higher education. *The Journal of Higher Education* 6, no. 2:221–239.

Campus Compact Raise Your Voice. 2005. What is civic engagement? http://www.actionforchange.org/getinformed/civic-engagement.html

Clark, M. L. 1985. Gender, race, and friendship research. Paper presented at the Annual Meeting of the American Educational Research Association, Chicago, Illinois. ED 259 053. Cooperative-learning teams can increase cross-race friendships in school settings.

Nair, A. T. 2005. Bridging Asian American and African American communities. In *Teaching about Asian Pacific American communities: Effective activities, strategies, and assignments for classrooms and workshops.* Lanham, Md.: AltaMira Press.

Nair, A. T. and H. Nakiboglu. 2003. Back to the basics: Service-learning and the Asian American community. *Journal for Civic Commitment* 3. http://www.mc.maricopa.edu/other/engagement/Journal/Issue3/Nair.jsp.

Omatsu, G. n.d. Defying a thousand pointing fingers and serving the community: Re-envisioning the mission of Asian American Studies in our communities. http://www.sscnet.ucla.edu/99F/asian197j-1/Omatsu.htm.

Welcome to Info Resources. 2003. *West Philly Data Info* [online]. Philadelphia: University of Pennsylvania. http://westphillydata.library.upenn.edu.

Zlotkowski, E. 1996. Foreword [online]. In L. Adler-Kassner, R. Crooks and A. Watters, eds., *Writing the community: Concepts and models for service-learning in composition.* http://www.aahe.org/service/series_new.htm#Foreword.

EDUCATING CITIZENS THROUGH RESEARCH

Immersing the Student Researcher in Community

LORI A. WALTERS-KRAMER
PLATTSBURGH STATE UNIVERSITY OF NEW YORK

This article addresses the value of moving the student's body off campus and into the surrounding environs to collect data about and/or for a community. Asking students to physically enter onto the material and cultural landscape of non-college students allows them opportunity to interact meaningfully with diverse people and, ideally, assess their own relationship to the community. In order to illustrate the power of immersing students in a community, I turn to a participatory action project integrated into my Small Group Communication course—a project that could be adopted by instructors in disciplines such as anthropology, history, mathematics, and sociology.

Many universities and colleges have more or less strained relationships with the cities or towns in which they are embedded. Tension between year-round and transient (usually student) residents is not uncommon and many institutions of higher education have implemented activities or procedures that aim to reduce problems that exist in spaces where college students and residents exist in close proximity. For example, Georgetown created the Student Neighborhood Assistance Program (Murugesan 2004) and MIT created the Town and Gown Team (Atwood 2003) to address problems between non-student and student neighbors. Community members, too, have been active in working to create spaces where students and residents can peacefully coexist (Murugesan 2004). In my city, a neighborhood association was created approximately 20 years ago to address growing concern about the declining quality of the neighborhood that encircles the university. This decline, the association members argue, is a result of student behavior (alcohol consumption, noise, improper

disposal of garbage, etc.) as well as the failure of landlords of student housing to maintain properties. After some years of inactivity, the association was re-energized due to an investor's proposal to turn a recently vacated school into a large student housing complex.

As the instructor of Small Group Communication—a course that is well suited for service-learning projects—I approached one of the officers of the association prior to the start of the semester to discuss the possibilities of developing a project that would allow my students to do something meaningful for the association. Instructors at other universities might approach a campus organization such as those at MIT and Georgetown. The neighborhood association with which I worked was incredibly enthusiastic about working with college students and, most significantly, was eager to hear students' perspectives. As such, the association chose to not prescribe the activities for the students (survey students who live off campus, interview residents, etc.) because they wanted the students to manage the project in a way that made sense to the students. This approach was my preference as well given the fact that the students were enrolled in a small group communication course in which a primary objective is learning how to make decisions in a problem-solving group. Although this organic approach led some students to feel as if they were not getting direction from the community partner, most were put at ease regarding their project after reading about and following the agenda-setting process articulated in Young, Wood, Phillips, and Pedersen's (2000) textbook *Group discussion: A practical guide to participation and leadership* (3rd ed.). This is a student-friendly text that could be utilized in many courses and in many disciplines. At the end of the second stage of the agenda-setting process the students crafted their initial guiding question: *How can the neighborhood association reach its goal of creating a "good neighborhood"?*

Throughout the semester students created and distributed surveys to on- and off-campus students; surveyed residents using a random sampling method; attended meetings of the neighborhood association; interviewed local politicians, college administrators, and police officers; facilitated a focus group comprised of members of the neighborhood association; and researched other cities' and universities' approach to improving student-resident relationships. Decisions about what data to gather were made by the students. The research process required students to become deeply familiar with the community—much more familiar than they had been prior to taking the course. The work of the students was revealed at a presentation at the end of the semester and the completion of a one-hundred-page report given to the association and other interested stakeholders (such as the dean of students). The neighborhood association implemented at least two of the suggestions made by the students.

A priority at many institutions of higher education is to be responsible to the community and, as a result, improve town/gown relationships. Indeed, individuals in the neighborhood association indicated that they valued the perspective of the students and commented that the students in the course changed their (negative) perception of college students. This perception shift is a significant accomplishment. Institutions that aim to be engaged, want students to be aware of their role in the community. At the end of the semester, students revealed that they did feel more connected to and knowledgeable about the community in which the college is situated, and several said that in the future they would like to be involved in a neighborhood association. Students also indicated that they had a better understanding of residents. When interviewed about the project by a reporter of the local paper, one student said, "We tend to forget that there are babies and working people who live on these streets. I think I assumed that there are only students" (Jolly 2004). This statement validates Murugesan's (2004) claim that students are "simply not aware of the extent to which their actions affected neighbors' quality of life."

In order to understand the ramifications of student behavior on others' quality of life, students needed to immerse themselves—physically and cognitively—in the community. One of the values of service learning (of which participatory action research is a form) is that students often encounter ("serve") people who are different from themselves. As this particular project progressed, I could not help but talk to the students about how their interactions with residents paralleled episodes of intercultural communication in which conflict and misunderstanding are present (Hall 2002). While most of the students looked like the residents (in terms of race), the residents and the college students had sometimes radically different perceptions of events as well as different standards by which to evaluate communication and other behaviors. It was only through the intensive process of gathering data that students were able to connect with and better understand the diverse individuals in their neighborhood and be engaged with and in the community at large.

> *Indeed, individuals in the neighborhood association indicated that they valued the perspective of the students and commented that the students in the course changed their (negative) perception of college students.*

References

Atwood, S. 2003. MIT News: Between town and gown. *Technology Review.* [Electronic version.] http://www.technologyreview.com/articles/03/06/atwood0603.asp?p=0.

Hall, B. J. 2002. *Among cultures: The challenge of communication.* Orlando, Fla.: Harcourt College Publishers.

Jolly, A. 2004. Students study downtown: PSU class promotes communication. *The Press Republican* (December). [Electronic version.] http://www.pressrepublican.com/Archive/search/.

Murugesan, V. 2004. Residents target problem houses. *The Hoya* (March 2, 2004). [Electronic version.] http://www. thehoya.com/news/ 030204/news3.cfm.

Young, K. S., J. T. Wood, G. M. Phillips, and D. J. Pedersen. 2000. *Group discussion: A practical guide to participation and leadership*. 3rd ed. Long Grove, Ill.: Waveland Press.

Using the Research Process to Enhance Civic Engagement

Luciana Lagana'
California State University, Northridge

To address the need to link research and civic engagement, this essay discusses relevant methodological and conceptual issues. It also highlights potential research topics for future community-based studies intended to stimulate students' civic engagement. A curriculum-based research model proposed by Lagana' and Rubin (2002) suggests engaging in the following five steps for the development and sound implementation of SL research: 1) define preliminary research objectives and operationalize the research variables of interest; 2) plan community collaboration and select a research sample; 3) design the course and its SL research component; 4) guide students to conduct the community intervention, reflect on their experience, and create a "deliverable" (i.e., a product that is donated to community partners for their future application); and 5) perform baseline and post-community intervention assessment and evaluation.

SL projects could easily follow all the steps of the model in question while focusing on maximizing students' civic engagement. This model could be used by research-focused professors as a vehicle to guide them through the research process, steering them in the direction of a methodologically well-planned and sound research.

Students' Civic Engagement Outcomes

Before proposing potential SL research endeavors, it is important to recognize several outcomes associated with students' involvement in SL projects. Some of the latest research on this topic has been conducted at CSU—Bakersfield by the research team of the Center for Community Partnerships and Service-learning (Marty and Rienzi 2005). The authors' qualitative assessment of reflection papers/diaries written by students engaged in SL projects focused on identifying the outcomes of SL participation. Although the research participants were psychology students, the outcomes identified apply to students from many other majors. Most pertinent to the present discussion, students provided examples of several core concepts, including diversity and citizenship/civic engagement. Diversity examples included learning about: diverse groups, such as various age groups; diverse needs of the community; cultural diversity; people with disabilities; and diversity related to physical and medical health. Ideally, students should master these topics prior to their engagement in SL research endeavors, to make sure that they are prepared to handle diversity issues when they arise. To address this need, professors could choose to cover such topics in class at the beginning of the academic term—just prior to starting community-based SL projects, to provide students with the needed awareness to tackle diverse community issues in an appropriate and sensitive manner. Ageism, sexism, racism, and homophobia, among other delicate issues, should be topics of particular importance, since students need to be sensitized to those somewhat controversial subjects and prepared to deal appropriately with minority populations of all kinds.

Based on Marty and Rienzi's (2005) findings, examples of citizenship/civic engagement outcomes include learning about: the importance of giving back to the community; the benefits and values of community organizations; the negative impact of limited resources; teaching others the value of volunteerism; and helping underserved populations. It is obvious that SL initiatives are the perfect vehicle to increase students' understanding and appreciation of organizations and communities. In particular, what types of SL research projects could foster students' enhanced civic engagement? The paragraphs below provide relevant examples on this topic; the proposed projects could be used as research templates and appropriately modified by faculty interested in SL research targeting other research populations or different civic engagement outcomes.

Potential Areas for Service-Learning Research that Could Promote Students' Civic Engagement

The proposed SL research targets contemporary social issues often neglected in academia. Before starting any of these projects, faculty needs to provide thorough training to students, beyond preparing them on diversity issues. Examples of activities aimed at achieving this goal are: a) read and critique articles on the social issue(s) in question; b) receive training on how to professionally and respectfully interact with the SL clients in question; c) if applicable, engage in role-play with faculty and other students to practice how to involve clients in the SL interventions; as well as d) anticipate project-related challenges and plan ways to handle them.

An area of potential investigation through sound SL research is the victimization of those who are particularly vulnerable, including (but not being limited to) children, women, older adults, and people with disabilities. Pioneer SL projects could be dedicated to conducting empirical analyses of critical factors involved in these crimes (of a physical or non-physical nature). For example, students could analyze crime scene attributes and the characteristics of the crime victims, including the severity of their injuries. SL law students could collaborate with law enforcement agencies on these challenging endeavors and identify important information regarding the characteristics of the offenders, in preparation for the design and implementation of SL preventive workshops for groups at particular risk of physical victimization and brutality. Furthermore, this topic could become the focus of SL projects conducted by departments such as Women's Studies, Gerontology, Health Sciences, Psychology, or various mental health-related ones. For instance, SL students could set up workshops for people with disabilities at community sites, in order to educate them on what constitutes abuse of all types, and to provide information on where to go and how to handle these challenges if the need arises.

The preventive SL projects mentioned above could help avoid, or at least minimize, victimization among those who cannot easily defend themselves. Furthermore, secondary prevention workshops could be offered through SL classes on how to minimize people's psychological vulnerability once they have been exposed to traumatic events of an abusive nature. Novel SL applications could also focus on pairing up students with abused individuals in order to get a personal account of the abuse experience. As suggested by Sleutel (1998), we could better understand how to help survivors by gathering this kind of data.

SL studies should also be conducted on important health-related topics usually neglected in research efforts. For example, SL students could survey various research populations on the topic of sexuality, to find out whether they subscribe to sexual myths; interested faculty could subsequently design SL projects aimed at dispelling them. In this regard, a commonly held myth is that those involved in steady relationships are not at risk for contracting the human immunodeficiency virus (HIV). In reality, regardless of their level of commitment to their intimate partner, many individuals do engage in high-risk sexual behaviors and are likely to become HIV-positive. Therefore, it is critical to conduct innovative SL training endeavors that emphasize the importance of safer sex. Community partners for such projects could be found among local hospitals, clinics, and mental health centers.

SL studies could also help identify solutions to institutional discrimination within communities where SL clients reside long-term; for instance, social factors such as attitudes towards the sexual expression of chronically medically or mentally ill patients can profoundly affect the latter. Therefore, the attitudes of personnel working in health care facilities should be researched and addressed in sound SL applications. These investigations could target negative attitudes held towards patients being sexual; this could be done by offering training on sexuality to health providers, administrators and other staff of long-term care centers. For example, students could assess pre- and post-SL workshop attitudes held by personnel, offering training on the physiological changes affecting patients' sexuality if applicable, and on their need to be regarded as sexual individuals who are entitled to their sexual privacy. Again, it should be kept in mind that SL endeavors of this nature require extensive training of the students and their thorough supervision at all stages of the SL project.

Sound training programs for administrators and caretakers of the residents of health facilities can elicit significant interest and participation. Misconceptions and value judgments about the sexuality of those with physical or mental conditions could negatively influence the staff of such institutions. This provides an opportunity for SL scholars to become involved in projects that address the need to offer such training to caretakers and administrators working in long-term care facilities.

Sexuality training curricula that target the staff working at such locations are already available, such as the one outlined by Walker et al. (1998) for geriatric institutions. Pioneer SL projects like the one proposed above could follow empirically-based curricula and provide community services that would benefit both the SL clients and their care providers. It would be best to involve in SL endeavors of this level of complexity only advanced students, such as graduate students or those with significant prior experience in training and evaluation projects.

Conclusions

Several kinds of SL research projects can have a profound impact on students' civic engagement. Those addressing the aforementioned topics could be directed by a single SL professor, or in collaboration with scholars from various disciplines, including Law departments and those specializing in the legal rights of minority populations whenever applicable. Other collaborators could include faculty from Psychology, Women's Studies, Gerontology, and various health-related departments. The involvement of SL scholars with different perspectives would provide an even more diverse foundation on which to establish the success of the proposed SL research.

Note

This research was supported by a National Institute of Health Grant, 3 So6 GM048680-0851, Luciana Lagana', Principal Investigator. Requests for reprints may be directed to Luciana Lagana', Ph.D., Associate Professor, Department of Psychology, California State University, Northridge, 18111 Nordhoff Street, Northridge, CA 91330–8255, luciana.lagana@csun.edu.

References

Lagana', L. 2003. Using service-learning research to enhance the elderly's quality of life. *Educational Gerontology* 29, no. 8:685–701.

Lagana', L., and M. Rubin. 2002. Methodological challenges and potential solutions for the incorporation of sound community-based research into service-learning. In A. Furco and S. H. Billig, eds., *Advances in service-learning research. Volume I: Service learning: The essence of the pedagogy.* Greenwich, Conn.: Information Age Publishing.

Marty, J. R., and B. Rienzi. 2005. *Assessment of students experiences in service-related psychology programs.* Poster presented at the 85th Conference of the Western Psychological Association, Portland, Ore., April 14–17.

Sleutel, M. R. 1998. Women's experiences of abuse: A review of qualitative research. *Issues in Mental Health Nursing* 19:525–539.

Walker, B. L., N.J. Osgood, P. H. Ephross, J. P. Richardson, B. Farrar, and C. Cole. 1998. Developing a training curriculum on elderly sexuality for long term care facility staff. *Gerontology and Geriatrics Education* 19:3–22.

Cultivating Commitment: A Role for Ethnography in Teacher Education

JANET L. FERGUSON AND KATHLEEN M. FOSTER
EAST STROUDSBURG UNIVERSITY OF PENNSYLVANIA

What is the obligation and role of the university and college domain in the preparation of students as citizens of engagement and responsibility? The simple answer is: to fulfill an ethical responsibility as an institution of higher education. The more complex answer is: we are not sure. Much of what we focus on in our professional roles as university and college faculty is a production-function approach to educating students.

What is needed, in addition to quality professional skills preparation, is for programs to provide for our undergraduates a campus climate that nurtures the development of "habits of the mind." The development of the ideals of civic responsibility and citizenship as "hab-its of the mind" are as much a part of our responsibility in higher education as the development of professional/vocational skills. This perspective becomes even more focused if we revisit the notion that the ideals of citizenship and civic responsibility are the birthright of higher education in this country.

This concept is certainly easier to discuss than do. Higher education can be an agent and architect of democracy but the blueprint for the design needs to emerge from the constituents of the community. One method for turning the blueprint into a framework for engagement and responsibility is the use of action research by undergraduate students in courses related to their professional goals. And certainly, a way to extend the development of habits of engagement is to integrate action research into the coursework of undergraduate teacher education students. These students becoming teachers who are habitués of civic responsibility then achieves the ultimate diffusion model of active engagement.

At East Stroudsburg University of Pennsylvania, we have, in the Elementary and Secondary Education Departments, begun to utilize ethnography as a framework for student-conducted action research. This practitioner research conducted by undergraduate students enrolled in East Stroudsburg University of Pennsylvania's Elementary Education Teacher Certification Program comprises continuing work which began in the spring of 2004. In Ferguson's course, Principles and Practices of Teaching, this work-in-progress began with an investigation of and response to the No Child Left Behind Legislation that puts tremendous demands on teachers and students to perform at predetermined, standardized achievement levels (Grayson 2005). A group of undergraduate students, enrolled in the course Principles and Practices of Teaching, developed concerns about possible discrimination of children of poverty and children with disabilities as an outcome of the NCLB testing requirements. As these class discussions were linked to the required observations of real classrooms, the legislation took on a reality based critique of how policy plays out for individuals in specific contexts (Bronfenbrenner 1977).

Background: Seeds of Interest

Stage I of the investigation of NCLB legislation began with a review of the literature and accompanying concerns regarding the potential harmful affective outcomes for groups of children. The students presented their projects in class. These students decided to form an extracurricular group to continue their investigation of outcomes of NCLB. They refer to themselves as Future Teachers for Social Action.

Stage II: Future Teachers for Social Action

Stage II of the research involved extending the initial projects and coordinating results into a panel presentation/discussion. The presentation consisted of four sections: An overview of the NCLB Act with a review of the literature discussing potential discriminatory outcomes. The second section of the presentation reviewed the statistics on children of single parent families, children of poverty and minority status, and chil-

dren with disabilities and reviewed how these factors play a role in achievement levels. The third section of the presentation offered insights into constructivist approaches to education, specifically instruction grounded in Montessori theory and how teachers find these methods difficult to maintain in a climate of high stakes standardized testing—teachers are teaching to the test rather than to the children. Finally the panel presented emerging understandings of how the NCLB Act discriminates again cultural diversity. The presentation concluded with information on how undergraduate students and others can become advocates for equity in our local communities.

This work was presented at the ESU Frederic Douglas Institute (FDI) Conference on Brown v. Board of Education on March 30, 2004, with a follow-up invitation to the Bloomsburg University 4th Annual FDI Conference, April 19 and 20, 2004.

Stage III: Mini-Ethnographies as Action Research

The Future Teachers for Social Action group continued their investigation of the outcomes of NCLB-mandated testing procedures. To gain a deeper understanding of the affective outcomes of testing on individual children they conducted a variety of mini-ethnographies of six elementary school children who were exposed to the high stakes testing environment. Building on the previous critical reviews of demographic, historical, and research literature, the participants conducted six micro-ethnographies which revealed how individual children experienced NCLB-mandated testing.

The six mini-ethnographies presented findings based on participant observation of the children before, during, and after testing periods; field notes of observations and interviews with the child; interviews with the child's parent(s) and teacher(s); as well as general demographic information for each type of child (Wolcott 1995).

Analysis of data adhered to standard ethnographic methods of inductive, grounded theory (Glaser and Strauss 1967). Analysis sought to reveal and understand the different actors, the child, the parent, and the teachers, and whether their lives were interrupted by high stakes tests. Questions put to the data included: How does this child experience testing? What are the specific reactions? What do children say about the experience of being tested? To what extent is testing stressful or debilitating? Is testing ever experienced as rewarding or personally gratifying? Does teaching to the test ease the tension or heighten it? What do children learn about themselves because of the tests?

Findings offered rich descriptions of how a child labeled ADHD, a child of a single parent family, a child of poverty, a child of a minority status, a child labeled gifted, and a child with disabilities experienced high stakes testing.

Relevance of Student-Conducted Action Research

Student-conducted action research is relevant on two important levels. Investigation of NCLB legislation revealed to education students the potentially negative responses of individual children to high stakes testing, offering a critical foundation for opposing high stakes testing and insights into how to buffer children from the negative affective impact of such practices. If, or when, children are not affected adversely, a close-up view of the context will provide guidance for replicating these conditions for other similar children. Secondly, this student-conducted action research has and will continue to foster critical inquiry habits of mind in the undergraduate teacher-education students who have conducted the research. It supports the importance of including modes of inquiry, particularly ethnography, in teacher education courses and programs.

References

Bronfenbrenner, U. 1977. Developmental research, public policy, and the ecology of childhood. *Child Development* 45:1–5.

Glaser, B. G., and A. L. Strauss. 1967. *The discovery of grounded theory*. Hawthorne, N.Y.: Aldine

Grayson, N. 2005. The Education Trust press release of January 19. http://www2.edtrust.org

Wolcott, H. F. 1995. *The art of field work*. Newbury Park, Calif.: Sage.

Involving Students in Campus-Wide Assessment of Civic Engagement

CHRISTINE M. OLSON AND PAUL G. NIELSON
SOUTHWEST MINNESOTA STATE UNIVERSITY

This article will describe the structure, process, and outcomes of involving students enrolled in an applied research course in a campus-wide assessment of civic engagement. It will conclude with a consideration of how the course could be improved by assuming an interdisciplinary format.

Context

Recognizing the improbability of securing outside consultants to conduct a campus-wide assessment of civic engagement and also recognizing the significant ways in which students' learning might be enriched by providing them with an opportunity to serve the campus, members of a campus assessment committee asked students to assist with data gathering and analysis. With the guidance of a professor of psychology and the assessment committee, students initiated a semester-long effort to collect qualitative and quantitative data that would, they hoped, stimulate a campus "conversation" about civic engagement.

Structure and Process of Course

The applied research course was offered as a 3-credit upper-division psychology class. Because students had some background in statistical analysis and research design, a relatively brief period of time was devoted to distinguishing between quantitative versus qualitative data gathering and analysis processes. More time was devoted to providing assistance with developing assessment surveys, interview protocols, and content analysis coding schemes. Surveys were distributed to all faculty and residential hall staff, as well as a random sampling of students. Class members also conducted structured interviews with a random sampling of faculty, led focus group discussions with self-selected student club leaders, and did a content analysis of student club activity reports, student club websites, and admissions office materials.

In addition to guidance with research processes, students were oriented to the notion of campus civic engagement and related concepts such as service learning and volunteerism. For this purpose, readings from several Campus Compact publications were useful in providing students with a shared language for discussing these concepts and developing assessment measures.

Prior to the data gathering and analysis phase, students were asked to select one of two projects to work on, depending upon whether they wished to enhance qualitative or quantitative research skills. Throughout the process of developing surveys, interview protocols, and content analysis coding schemes, students received feedback from their professor and classmates; additional feedback was provided by assessment committee faculty.

Each class period allowed time for problem solving related to data gathering and analysis, discussion of the strengths and limitations of quantitative and qualitative methods of evaluation, and reflections on student learning. For example, students had assumed that a majority of faculty would be enthusiastic about the prospect of completing a survey on civic engagement. They were surprised to discover otherwise! Responding creatively to the challenge of low faculty response rates, students identified faculty with whom they had a good relationship and hung around their offices (some with candy!) requesting that they complete the survey. This resulted in a very strong response rate of 85% (versus the original 15%).

An additional example illustrates how enhanced self-knowledge can result from regular reflection on learning. Some students learned that they enjoyed and were skilled with interpersonal data-gathering processes such as conducting structured interviews and focus groups; others learned that they preferred the more solitary data entry, interview transcription, and content analysis tasks. Collectively they learned the value of "triangulation" or the identification of themes that occurred across the various methods of data collection and analysis that were used.

After data was gathered and analyzed, students worked in pairs to produce summary reports, which were later distributed to all participants in a campus-based Learning Outside the Classroom Conference. Following the conference, the summary reports were posted on the campus civic engagement website and have been used by faculty, staff, and students for strategic-planning purposes.

Student Learning Outcomes

Drawing from Eyler and Giles' (1999) articulation of desired service-learning outcomes, students' development was enriched in several ways. Through taking responsibility for various subprojects within the overall effort to assess campus civic engagement, students reported enhanced skills and efficacy related to leadership; in fact, half of the students enrolled in the course

went on to assume leadership roles in campus clubs the following semester.

By the end of the semester, students were better able to identify multiple, interacting factors that influence motivation for civic engagement. For example, instead of simply attributing low levels of enthusiasm for volunteerism to intrinsic disinterest, they considered the influence of such factors as competing demands for time with heavy course and work loads, not having an office of civic engagement, and not highlighting opportunities for service in promotional materials.

In addition, students expressed a deepened sense of connection with other students, faculty and the campus community as a whole. Similarly, they expressed satisfaction with the fact that what they were involved with an effort that seemed worthwhile. In fact, all of the students indicated an interest in taking other service-oriented courses in the future and several had begun to explore further opportunities for volunteerism. Moreover, a few students indicated an interest in pursuing a profession that would involve social change. Collectively, these changes indicate a heightened commitment to civic engagement.

Value of Interdisciplinary Format

While students and faculty had a strong positive reaction to the course, both student learning and campus "buy-in" for addressing the topic of civic engagement in higher education could be enhanced by assuming an interdisciplinary format versus one primarily geared to the interests and skills of students majoring in the social sciences. Some examples of how other disciplines might be involved include the following: math students could assist with statistical analysis; graphic design and technical writing majors could aid in the development of brochures and websites to communicate the outcomes of the study to the broader campus community; history majors could provide a historical context for the role of civic engagement in democratic societies; and, students majoring in philosophy and theology could contribute a basic language for discussing ethical and moral concepts such as "the common good." Beyond gaining the knowledge and skills offered by these disciplines, the process of involving faculty and students from a variety of academic areas could have the added benefit of fostering support for institutionalizing the concept of civic engagement; faculty and students would recognize, through their participation, the relevance of their disciplinary knowledge and skills for the shared objective of making civic engagement part of the fabric of the institution.

References

Eyler, J., and D. E. Giles, Jr. 1999. *Where's the learning in service-learning?* San Francisco: Jossey-Bass.

Increasing Political Efficacy through Community-Based Research

ELIZABETH A. BENNION
INDIANA UNIVERSITY SOUTH BEND

This essay explains the value of randomized field experiments for enhancing student learning, faculty research, and civic engagement. During the Fall 2002 semester, I required students in my political science courses to participate in a three-precinct, non-partisan voter mobilization campaign. Students studied campaigns and elections. However, it was not until they actually participated in a voter mobilization campaign that they truly understood the intense effort required to educate and mobilize voters. Student reflection papers and surveys indicate that participating in this hands-on field experiment increased students' understanding of the campaign process, developed their understanding of social sciences research, and heightened their sense of political efficacy. This experimental approach can be easily replicated by instructors in diverse fields with a wide variety of research interests.

The field experience was designed as a fully randomized *field experiment*. In this way, I was able to combine a hands-on student-learning experience with actual social science research. Using randomized field experiments, instructors can involve students in faculty research, while also engaging them in the community. It is an ideal way for faculty to combine (and enhance) their teaching, research, and service commitments. First, I collected the names and addresses of all registered voters in a neighborhood adjacent to our campus. I then used a computer to randomly assign voters to a contact group or a control group. I explained this process to the students so that they could understand the nature of a randomized experiment and would not attempt to contact citizens in our control group. Each student participated in a one-hour training session before heading out to canvass. I matched each student with a partner (pairing men with women, conservatives with liberals, and Caucasians with minority students whenever possible). Each pair of students received a walk list and walked door-to-door with a partner, contacting voters on their list. Trained Political Science Club interns supervised the student canvassers. Students kept careful records of their contacts so that we were able to analyze the effectiveness of our mobilization campaign.

In order to insure that students would participate fully in the experiment, I included a variety of incentives within the structure of the courses themselves. The field experiment was *required* of all able-bodied students. The experiment was written into the course syllabus; students were allowed to sign up for their own (Saturday, Sunday, or Monday) time slots; and students were awarded 100 points for completing the assignment. This allowed students who ordinarily struggle on exams to earn a grade of A+ on an assignment worth the same number of points as an in-class examination. I stressed the importance of this project for the community. I encouraged students to think about this as an opportunity to actually make a difference in the community and to get involved in politics. I also reminded them that their effort would be rewarded with a major boost to their course grade. Paid student auditors called select voters after the experiment to insure that student records were accurate. All students were told about the auditing process ahead of time to insure full cooperation and accurate record-keeping.

After the congressional election, I collected 2002 turnout data for individual voters in our treatment and control groups and measured the effectiveness of our campaign. To measure the effectiveness of the mobilization campaign, I ran a two-stage least squared regression (see Gerber and Green 2000 for more information on this methodology). In the end, our mobilization campaign had little effect on voters over 30 (as might be expected during a competitive congressional election in which campaign volunteers were also going door-to-door). However, we had a large effect on younger voters—those least likely to be contacted by partisan campaigns. We boosted young voter turnout by 18 percentage points. Although the fall semester had ended, I used an e-mail distribution list to send the results to students participating in the research. Even before they received the results of the study, students were convinced that the campaign had made a difference, both in the community and in their own lives.

This research encouraged civic engagement among students (who described their learning experiences in reaction papers) and among citizens in the local community (who were contacted by the students and reminded to vote). In 2003, I expanded this study to a ten-precinct door-to-door and telephone experiment, again using students as canvassers. I used students' 2002 reflections about the best and worst parts of the experience to construct a learning-outcomes survey administered to all participants in the 2003 study. Students took the survey anonymously using an online survey tool. A strong majority of students felt that this experience increased their interest in, knowledge of, efficacy about, and excitement toward politics. Most also suggested that they acquired a deeper level of knowledge about voter attitudes and campaign procedures than they could have learned in the classroom (Bennion 2006).

This research should be attractive to many faculty members. It led to research presentations and publications in traditional social science journals concerned with voter mobilization (Bennion 2005) and in the scholarship of teaching and learning (Bennion 2006). It also led to numerous research grants (Yale Institute for Social and Policy Studies, Indiana Campus Com-

By using randomized field experiments, instructors can involve students in faculty research, while also engaging them in the community. It is an ideal way for faculty to combine (and enhance) their teaching, research, and service commitments.

pact, Student Government Association, Alumni Association). Finally, it strengthened IU South Bend's partnership with the community and encouraged civic engagement and political efficacy among college students who might otherwise never understand the inner workings of election campaigns or social science research.

Although my experiment focused on voting, instructors in other fields could adopt an experimental approach to study a wide variety of topics. Education professors might study the effectiveness of study skills workshops on student success. Sociology professors might study the effectiveness of diversity training programs in fostering cross-cultural relationships. To enhance civic engagement and active learning, each professor might use students as *teachers* as well as learners. By involving students in community training programs, instructors can measure the educational effectiveness of these programs for both students and community participants. Of course, research need not be limited to randomized field experiments. Chemistry professors have involved students in testing the lead content of paint in the homes of economically disadvantaged families. Community-based learning experiences need not even be limited to research. Student practicums, in which students are required to apply the skills and knowledge they have gained in a course, would be equally useful in serving the community and fostering civic engagement among students. Several counties, including my own, could use an updated county website that would include high quality, reliable information for voters about elected officials, polling places, and voting instructions. This would be an ideal project for computer science or informatics students. There are a wide variety of ways that faculty members can involve their students in meaningful community-based learning. The added value of the randomized field experiment is the ability to actually *measure* the impact of students' engagement in the community.

References

Bennion, E. A. 2005. Caught in the ground wars: Mobilizing voters during a competitive congressional campaign." An-nals of the American Academy of Political and Social Science 601:123–141.

———. 2006, forthcoming. Civic education and citizen engagement: Mobilizing voters as a required field experiment." *Journal of Political Science Education* 2, no. 2.

Gerber, A. S., and D. P. Green. 2000. The effects of canvassing, telephone calls, and direct mail on voter turnout: A field experiment. *American Political Science Review* 95, no. 3:654–663.

Teaching Race and Politics through Community-Based Research

Saundra J. Reinke
Augusta State University

Service learning, a form of experiential learning that combines classroom study with community service, is often proposed as one way to rebuild the sense of civic engagement in the younger generation. By involving students in the process of identifying and creating solutions for community problems, service learning helps instill in students a sense that we are all responsible for the future of our community and our nation (Mendel-Reyes 1998). Service learning promises to improve critical thinking skills, the integration of theory with practice, and general work-life skills such as communication, tolerance, and civic engagement (Battistoni 1997; Jacoby 1996).

Description of the Course and Project

Introduction to Research Methods is a required undergraduate course for all Political Science majors. The course provides basic instruction in designing research questions and hypotheses, collecting data, and testing hypotheses using appropriate statistical techniques. To make the course more interesting and enhance students' ability to grasp the material, the instructor chose to structure the course around a community problem or issue. The students are challenged to work together to design a research project, collect and analyze the data, and present the results.

Topics for the course are chosen in one of two ways. In some cases, community agencies or individuals approach the instructor with a request for research on a particular subject. The second way to select topics is simply by observing what problems or concerns surface in the community. Observations can come from reading the local paper, or through involvement in community volunteer work. The topic that is the framework for this article—race and politics—was chosen using this method. Race and race relations problems are mentioned frequently in local news articles and in conversations with local politicians and other community leaders.

The students began the semester by reading one local newspaper article that explored racial conflict in their community. This was followed by two assigned readings in peer-reviewed journals on race and politics. The students then wrote short papers on each of the articles. With this necessary background, the students were ready to learn how to "do" research. The course proceeded in this sequence:

- Reading literature on race and politics
- Developing a research question
- Designing an instrument
- Sampling (or selection of interviewees for elite interviewing)
- Data collection and analysis

The students participated throughout this process in developing the research question and the instrument, drawing the sample or selecting interviewees, and did all the data collection and input themselves. The instructor double-checked this data entry against the actual surveys to insure the data set was accurate, then passed the data sets to both classes. This gave each student access to all the elite interviewing and telephone poll data. From this data, each student wrote an individual research report, in the same format as a peer-reviewed journal article for an individual grade.

Outcomes

Although the students found the project challenging, they thoroughly enjoyed the topic and the course, and were convinced they had learned a great deal about how to conduct research. Students experienced researchers' frustrations as they attempted to organize meetings with interviewees or contact citizens for the telephone poll. They genuinely felt like "real researchers," and understood how to more critically analyze research results encountered in popular media and on the internet.

From the standpoint of civic engagement, the most important outcome of this project was what the students learned about their community. The students' were amazed to discover how disconnected local politicians seemed to be from their constituents on this topic. Black and White politicians interviewed were united in claiming that racial issues were important, but those issues did not divide them as a commission or keep it from being a productive force for change. The political poll results, and the elite interviews of other community leaders painted a far different picture. This led to a first for this instructor—two undergraduate classes where every student claimed to have voted in the local commission elections.

In addition, the students learned a great deal about how the media affects perceptions of public problems. Students repeatedly commented on one of the poll's findings: Black and White citizens believe that the local media, especially the local newspaper, plays a major role in encouraging racial tensions and divisions. Ironically, the local newspaper's own poll, conducted by professional pollsters, had the same results.

Problems, Pitfalls and Prevention Strategies

This particular project was highly successful, and the instructor experienced few problems. However, this has not always been the case. The two most common problems with research-based service-learning projects are:

- For agency-initiated projects, a lack of involvement or commitment on the part of the agency itself. This has practical consequences—delays in getting access to needed data, for example. Worse, if the agency is not fully committed to the project,

students have difficulty committing themselves wholeheartedly.

- Interpersonal conflicts can erupt in any type of group work, with possible negative consequences for the project.

The instructor can do several things to prevent or mitigate the damage from these problems. These strategies have proven effective:

- Get the agency's commitment to the project in writing prior to beginning work.
- Provide ample opportunity for individual assessment using tests and individually-written papers.
- For classes where group grades are used, include specific instruction on group dynamics and peer evaluations as part of the assessment process (Reinke 2001).

Conclusions

Using service learning to teach research methods has numerous benefits. The students get the invaluable opportunity to actually apply what they learn, which enhances their retention and understanding of the course material. Moreover, in the process of doing the project, the students learn about the problems and challenges facing their community. In some past projects, they also have had the opportunity to help craft solutions.

From these projects, students learn that we are all collectively responsible for our communities. This collective responsibility is the essential foundation for civic engagement which in turn lies at the heart of democracy. Without such engagement, democracy cannot long survive.

References

Battistoni, R. M. 1997. Service learning and democratic citizenship. *Theory Into Practice* 36:150–157.

Jacoby, B. 1996. Service-learning in today's higher education. In B. Jacoby, ed., *Service learning in higher education*, 3–25. San Francisco: Jossey-Bass Publishers.

Mendel-Reyes, M. 1998. A pedagogy for citizenship: Service learning and democratic education. In R. Rhoads and J. P. F. Howard, eds., *Academic service learning: A pedagogy of action and reflection*, 31–38. San Francisco: Jossey-Bass Publishers.

Reinke, S. J. 2001. Teachable moments: Teaching teamwork through research. *Journal of Public Affairs Education* 7: 153–160.

OVERCOMING BARRIERS TO EDUCATING STUDENTS FOR CITIZENSHIP

7

From Oblivion to Engagement: Dissolving Barriers to Thoughtful Response

NAOMI JEFFERY PETERSEN
INDIANA UNIVERSITY SOUTH BEND

Oblivion is a happy place, for ignorance is bliss. It confounds every instructor laboring to change students into wiser, more skilled graduates. Oblivion may be seen in students who focus exclusively on the concrete tasks required in the syllabus. This isn't just a matter of low level thinking about extrinsic rewards. It is deeply rooted in competition and fear of failure. It is manifested by overreaction and risk avoidance. It is alleviated by civic engagement experience, by conscious awareness of oblivion and engagement, and by developing skills of contemplation and preparation. Let's consider your profoundly influential role as the teacher, and how you can confront oblivion and foster thoughtfulness.

First of all, you may unintentionally encourage the narrower perspective by framing your syllabus in exclusively concrete, individualistic terms. You are not alone. Most instructors respond to the demand to "Just tell me what I have to do "—borne of a desire to limit the scope of the course to a manageably confined list of tasks. This avoids a larger, integrated understanding of the world. Therefore, your first strategy is to *include language that connects the objectives to the greater knowledge base and benefit to humanity.* Mention the way the course supports the larger mission of the university. Include at least one objective that applies the knowledge of the course to real world decisions, based on principles of professional organizations in the field or even the university's mission statement. In this way, you demonstrate that you are not oblivious to the intellectual context of your content.

Your next strategy is to discuss the background of the discipline or the approach you are teaching with regard to the *multiple contributors to the final knowledge base,* and emphasize the dialectical process required to arrive at new understanding. Your students should know the names of organizations currently refining that understanding, and they should be encouraged to join professional organizations related to their majors. There are always *current events* related to the topic, and they need to be used to trigger interest in an ongoing debate and awareness of the universal problem of egocentrism.

This tendency (to reduce the complex and the unknown to concrete, familiar tasks) may be seen as the systemic cancer it is. The impulse to avoid change is a barrier in itself, and you must introduce an alternative path. It is important to help your students rehearse the new path and to be aware that it is not so scary after all. It is helpful to illustrate this for your students, sketching out the path as in figure 7.1. This shows the chronic recycling effect of returning to oblivion after impulsive overreaction or mindless habit.

The alternative path does require two steps, and is therefore slower and more demanding than the knee-jerk habits you are trying to modify. The steps are a) contemplation, i.e., considering possibilities; and b) preparation, i.e., making decisions and choosing a strategy before acting. The civic engagement here is that the first step, contemplation, requires awareness of other possibilities. The second step, preparation, is a rehearsal that includes perspective.

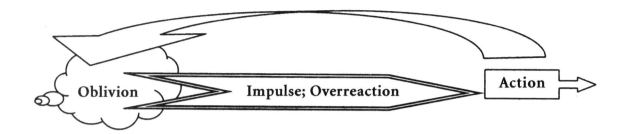

Figure 7.1. Maintaining the State of Oblivion

Figure 7.2 may be help you explain to your students the dynamic state of affairs they find themselves in. The visual metaphor of a cloud represents the state of oblivion you are trying to dispel. The emphasis here is on the *choice of paths* leading to action, and the resulting paths following the action. Present each aspect of your course as part of a continuous, integrated process of responding to new demands for action: there are multiple opportunities to self-correct if the thoughtful path becomes a habit. Eventually—as they become more alert to more information, and less satisfied with narrow explanations—they will be less likely return to the state of oblivion as readily.

Oblivion is a safe retreat from the complexities and vagaries of a changing world. *Requiring your students to talk to each other* helps dissolve the artificial cocoons they construct in the hope of emerging transformed at the end of the season. The demand for action inspires the oblivious to resist, or to impulsively over-react. In both cases, the individual returns as quickly as possible to the happy state of oblivion.

Through practice, your students can develop this skillful disposition. This requires having to explain and support one's logic. Include at least one *essay question* in every test requiring students to consider others' perspectives of the same problem. An essay question by definition requires the connection of several thoughts to a single theme, and the criteria for success should include the logic of linking these thoughts. For instance, a mathematics problem could be presented with an incorrect answer and this prompt:

> Explain to your colleague where the opportunities were to make different decisions and to arrive at a more accurate answer. Coach your colleague by referring to lectures and readings that you both have experienced.

Using interactive strategies throughout the course will alleviate the tension of catastrophic thinking that prevents a more flexible approach. By the time they have done this several times throughout the course, students develop an awareness of others' approaches to problems and a perspective on their own approach. Students who are panicky about revealing they don't know everything will relax and regard the content in a more collaborative and therefore civil way. Students who are impatient with lesser intellects will realize there is a lot of thinking going on that isn't expressed in quite the same way, and will see more value in others.

Here is an example of an *interactive experience.*

1. Prepare and number three examples of incorrectly worked problems.

2. Students number off by three. Each sequence becomes a small group.

3. Students use the "coach your colleague" prompt to prepare a script for their problem.

4. In one-minute "stand up" conferences, students consult other students working on the same problem, rehearsing and troubleshooting their logic.

5. Returning to their original groups, they proceed to "coach" each other through the problems.

6. Students give feedback to each "coach", i.e., "Thank you for reminding me that. . . . (insert useful information)."

It is no stretch to point out that dogmatic insistence on one approach is not only undemocratic, it is self-destructive. Your students are compelled to seek "one right answer" because they suffer from *catastrophic thinking*—the fear that one small error will render the entire effort disastrous. They cling to the hope of guaranteed success. By contrast, engaging in the larger perspective helps them see the course in perspective: one

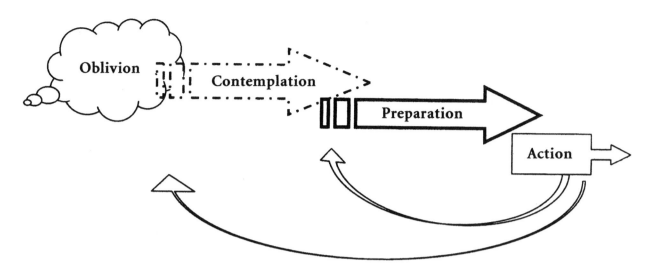

Figure 7.2. Developing Dynamic Opportunities for Healthier Action

unit of study integrated into a whole education preparatory to future complexity. Although difficult (because novices will always prefer a rigid application of known formulas), it is possible, even with large classes. You need strength of character to assert the transitions, and trust that this is in your students' best interests. It is also in your best interest: the more students become aware of their own learning progress, the greater the likelihood they will attribute their advances to your inspired instruction.

Creating Classrooms as "Safe Space"

PAMELA JEAN OWENS
UNIVERSITY OF NEBRASKA OMAHA

In light of the claim that conservative students are being discriminated against by liberal faculty, it has never been more important to learn how to create safe space in our classrooms. But safe space does not happen accidentally, and it is not a by-product of other activities or goals. If one wants a "safe space" classroom, then creating it must be a pedagogical starting point. Given the desire, how do we start?

Since I teach controversial subjects in a conservative state, and since my most conservative students and my most liberal students equally affirm the safety they enjoy in my classes, I know that if my classroom can be safe space, anyone's classroom can. In a move characteristic of safe-space pedagogy, I asked my students what they perceive that I do. They had no trouble giving me the answers, and they were quite unanimous:

1. "You start out the first day telling us this is going to be safe space and you never go back on that promise."

2. "You tell us what you think and why, and then you listen to what we think and why. You don't hide behind some idea of neutrality or objectivity. You don't allow us to not think. You tell us when there is no 'right' answer and when there is, and when you don't know if there is."

3. "You don't force people to talk, but you watch for the ones who aren't saying anything and when they do speak up you encourage them and make sure the rest of us listen."

As the students recognize, to create the classroom I want, I start with the syllabus itself; in every syllabus I include a list called "Very Essential and Seriously Important Stuff to Remember." The somewhat silly and re-dundant title is my attempt to catch students' attention and communicate that this section has a different kind of importance. Here is a typical list:

- I expect absolute academic integrity from every member of this class.

- If you have any special needs, please see me ASAP.

- Help each other in every possible way, but de-mand that your classmates do their own work when it is asked for.

- There are no dumb questions. Some questions may be outside the scope of what we can do in this class, but in that case I will always do my best to tell you another avenue to find an answer.

- There are no dumb people.

- Smart people can seem dumb when they make un-supported arguments. This includes all of us, so let's not let each other do it!

- I care a lot about this mate-rial and I hope you will too.

- Always be respectful of me and each other.

- Always be respectful of all peoples, those who are most like you and those who seem very different from you.

While a list in a syllabus is only a starting point, it is an essen-tial and important starting point. Students notice that I take the time to make these points explicit and that I highlight them in a special way. As a result of self- consciously demanding respect, our class-room is bracketed off from the rest of the world as "safe space." Putting the chairs into a circle makes this process easier, but even a crowded lecture hall can become safe space, with a little work.

The second point the students made came as no surprise to me, but I am keenly aware that it defies com-mon faculty practice and risks making other faculty sus-picious, or even hostile. "Common wisdom" tends to as-sume that the teacher should always "remain neutral." According to this assumption, once the teacher reveals "biases," students holding diverging views will be afraid to speak up. In class after class, and confirmed in post-

class focus groups, I have found that this widely held assumption is dead wrong!

Students know that few subjects are without nu-ance. They know that teachers hold opinions, whether expressed or not. Students report that teachers' attempts at neutrality often produce the opposite of what is intended. Students who think they disagree with the teacher are hesitant to express their views for fear of be-ing told they are wrong, or even being ridiculed. Stu-dents who think they agree with the teacher may not speak up, for fear of being seen as seeking the teach-er's favor, or they make a point of trying to reflect the teacher's opinions. When this latter group receives praise for participating eagerly, they come to be seen as more involved, and the students with other views become even more silent. In both cases, the teacher receives a less-than-accurate picture of what stu-dents could and would contribute, were they to speak up. And the stu-dents learn not to think, but to try to guess what the teacher thinks.

For students to feel safe, they need to know their teacher and they need to know one another. I don't wait for this to happen by ac-cident. I tell students who I am and what has brought me to this topic and to this perspective on it. I do this in a series of increasingly de-tailed "introductions" of myself over the first few class periods. I provide similar opportunities for the students to get to know each other, taking a similar series of small steps.

For example, I plan several "getting to know each other better" learning activities for the first weeks of class. I start with an introductory topic worth discussion and ask students to form small groups to "turn and talk" with each other. Often I find several related questions and give a different question to each section of the room.

When we regroup for discussion, I invite volun-teers to share good ideas they heard in their group. They don't give *their* ideas, but someone else's. Such a simple technique has powerful results: students know they have been heard, they receive the affirmation of hearing their idea voiced by someone else as a "good idea," and the persons speaking know what they say is safe, because they are not risking themselves alone.

> *For students to feel safe, they need to know their teacher and they need to know one another. I don't wait for this to happen by accident.*

In whatever way works for the subject, I begin to elicit the variety of views held by reasonable people, showing how they are supported by reasoned arguments. At the same time, I point out how opinions advanced without reasoned arguments will be challenged and pushed. In this process I continue to reveal my own thoughts, as they fit in, while welcoming the ideas of the class. This is where I search for the hook to bring out the reticent students and affirm their participation. Students often do not realize that reasonable people can reach different conclusions based on exactly the same factual data. When I sense that a quiet student and I share a starting point but may have arrived at different conclusions, I suggest that possibility and see what happens. I know that recognizing the nuance in issues is a learned skill; I understand that part of my job is to teach that skill and to give students opportunities to practice it in the safe space of the classroom.

Experiencing a truly democratic classroom offering safe space may be the first place students have had such an experience. If we as teachers are both diligent and lucky, it will not be the last.

Faculty Development for Facilitating Civil Discourse

Patrick J. Ashton and Jeanette Clausen
Indiana University–Purdue University Fort Wayne

In order to engage in useful dialogue around contentious issues, students and faculty must respect each others' rights to free and open speech and learn how to deal with conflict, tension, and strong emotions. This is easier said than done. The ability to facilitate civil discourse must be acquired—and often, barriers to initiating discussions must first be overcome.

Perhaps the largest and most invisible barrier to integrating civil discourse into teaching is the culture of academia itself, which rewards individual achievements, encourages competitiveness, celebrates "experts," and discourages or denigrates the expression of personal values. Small wonder that faculty may shy away from controversy in the classroom. Another barrier is created by fear that discussion of difficult issues may erupt into verbally or even physically violent episodes. No one wants an unsafe classroom. Yet safety is created by dialogue about differences, not by suppressing them.

Critical thinking skills and the ability to participate in civil discourse are mutually reinforcing. Fundamental to critical thinking about an issue is the ability to identify one's own perspective and position, to identify and consider other salient perspectives, and to identify underlying assumptions. Skills such as active listening, paraphrasing, purposeful questioning, and centered communication can keep the discussion from getting out of hand and contribute to a deeper understanding of the issues.

One of the keys to creating a classroom where civil discourse is possible is establishing ground rules: those you, as the educational leader of the class, create in advance and those you and the students collectively establish. Ground rules established in advance should appear on the syllabus, as part of your contract with students. Here is a sample statement of mutual respect:

> Each person in this course has unique prior experiences and a unique viewpoint to share. Though disagreement and even conflict may occur, I expect your cooperation in maintaining an atmosphere of mutual respect. When participating in discussions, it is perfectly acceptable to have strong opinions—in fact I encourage you to do so. I also encourage you to discuss your own personal experience and relate it to that of others. In the process, however, I expect you to respect the basic intelligence and humanity of each participant in the discussion. Conflict is not necessarily a bad thing, as long as there is a commitment to mutual respect. Hateful and demeaning speech will not be tolerated.

In order to create a safe environment for discussing controversial topics, it is also important to establish in advance that the rights of individuals will be protected and that discrimination will not be allowed. Your university undoubtedly has an official anti-discrimination policy, probably in the Student Handbook, which can be reprinted on the syllabus. If your institution has an official statement supporting diversity, include that as well. If not, craft your own and print it on the syllabus.

Figure 7.3. The Components of the Written Chinese Word, *Tin*

You will also want to discuss other possible ground rules with your students, for example, how individuals will obtain the floor (raise hands, possess a talking stick) and who will moderate discussion (teacher, student volunteer, rotation among all students). Having this discussion will (1) empower students to take responsibility for what goes on in the classroom; and (2) increase buy-in, making it more likely that they will not only abide by the rules but help to enforce them as well.

During discussion of controversial issues, make sure that you model for the students—and encourage them to use—active listening. Consider the components of the written Chinese word *tin,* to listen (see fig. 7.3).

Use all of these elements to tune in to a speaker's message and demonstrate respect—regardless of whether or not you agree with what they are saying.

In order to make sure that people are heard, you should model and practice paraphrasing. Paraphrasing lets the speaker know that you really heard them. To paraphrase correctly, restate the core message you heard and also reflect the emotion(s) underlying the statement. Paraphrases should be brief. After the speaker says the equivalent of three to five sentences, the listener should paraphrase them with three to twelve words. Contrary to popular belief, a short paraphrase is *not* an interruption. People like to know that they are being heard. If your paraphrase is off the mark, the speaker has an opportunity to clarify. Also, students who think out loud will appreciate feedback that allows them to refine their thought.

As a listener, you should concentrate on getting the speaker's message and feeding it back. Don't worry about formulating a response, judging, evaluating, or adding your own examples—just hear the speaker. This technique is particularly effective with angry or deeply emotional speakers. People calm down when they know they are heard and their emotion has registered. One good index of the need to paraphrase more is when people keep repeating themselves or rehashing the same argument. This means they don't think that they've been heard. Paraphrasing will reassure them and allow the discussion to move on. Especially with controversial issues, paraphrases are far more effective than questions for allowing the speaker to be heard but not put on the defensive.

Civil discourse requires students and teachers to take responsibility for their own positions and statements. This notion flies in the face of much academic discourse, which is often conducted in the third person and in the passive voice. Discussion of controversial issues and the values and beliefs that underlie them requires centered communication in which speakers use "I-statements." Among the most important are those in which the speaker expresses agreement, a preference, puzzlement, or states their purpose. Examples are sentences that begin "I agree that . . . ," "I prefer to . . . ," "My purpose is to . . . ," and "I'm puzzled by. . . ." The latter technique is particularly effective when students express stereotypes. Expressing puzzlement allows the speaker to realize the stereotype without getting defensive or feeling like they have been charged with a politically incorrect crime, while still being held accountable for what was said.

Some of these techniques are amenable to practice

by individuals; some are better practiced as part of a professional development workshop. Some resources are listed below.

References

Ashton, P. J. 2005. *Transformative conflict resolution and mediation: A sociological approach*. Training Manual. 8th ed. Department of Sociology. Fort Wayne: Indiana University-Purdue University Fort Wayne.

Association for Conflict Resolution. http://www.acrnet.org.

Study Circles Resource Center. http://www.studycircles.org/.

Timpson, W. M., et al. 2005. *147 practical tips for teaching diversity*. Madison, Wisc.: Atwood Publishing.

Warren, L. 2002–2004. "Managing Hot Moments in the Classroom." Derek Bok Center for Teaching and Learning, Harvard University. [Online Document]. http://bokcenter.harvard.edu/docs.html.

"Writing" the Civic into the Curriculum

HEATHER SPEWEIK
BOWLING GREEN STATE UNIVERSITY

If, as Jeff Smith (1994) claims, "The quality of students' knowledge and thinking should be the concern of the whole college faculty" (217), then we need a pedagogy for teaching the civic to our students in all classes. Without blaming the students themselves, Smith refers to today's college educated as still wholly "illegerate," a term that he uses to signal an inability to see choices worth arguing about within their culture and an "abdication" by students of responsibility for the direction society will take (201–210). For some of this "illegeracy" Smith blames departmentalization; the problem originates in our awareness that *someone* should be teaching civic matters, but someone *else* whose disciplinary conventions lend themselves to it.

As a teacher in rhetoric and composition, I have arrived at the position that civic engagement is a job we all must assume as educators. I will explain here some of the ways that teachers can overcome barriers to a civic pedagogy within the disciplines, outlining an approach that invites reflection by first encouraging students to recognize civic responsibility as it relates to their potential disciplines and then engaging them in civic or "participatory" writing in their major classes and across the curriculum.

> *[Faculty] should be encouraging a sense of agency in the student body and modeling how to handle disciplinary and civic debates with maturity, fairness, and civility.*

Civic "Answerability" in the Disciplines

A pervasive obstacle to civic initiatives is the assumption of faculty and staff that higher education, and the critical thinking associated with it, instills civic values in students without further pedagogical theorizing of the civic. As the editors of this volume point out, "Research indicates, however, that where teaching and learning activities are not intentionally linked to learning objectives, the learning we want for our students is unlikely to occur" (see the introduction to this volume, xix). For this reason, and because of declining enrollments in disciplines that seem to be losing their relevancy to students' lives and careers, teachers have a responsibility to implement the civic. Because teachers are accustomed to the debates that characterize their fields and how these debates affect the public, they should be encouraging a sense of agency in the student body and modeling how to handle disciplinary and civic debates with maturity, fairness, and civility.

"Participatory" Writing

Writing is often at the heart of civic pedagogy, whether it is integrated as informal logs of service-learning activities, full papers reflecting on field experiences, or public documents that meet the needs of organizations or individuals (Herzberg 2004). However, some instructors find a full integration of service learning too "messy" because of extra legwork required, or they find service learning inaccessible for other reasons related to curricula, ethics, the administration, or resources. Whatever the reason, these individuals are not excluded from civic pedagogies, and by using some practical teaching theories borrowed from composition scholarship, instructors can work civic writing into the classroom in relatively unobtrusive ways.

For instance, Sandra Stotsky (1999) advocates "Participatory Writing" which she describes as the "unpaid writing that citizens do as [a necessary and inseparable] part of the process of democratic self-government" (Para. 2). The purposes Stotsky outlines for such writing include generating common ground with other citizens or with officials; providing public information; obtaining information; evaluating public programs, services, or personnel; or advocating for people or causes. Stotsky advises teaching this type of writing by assigning students to read and analyze samples to help them "think carefully and clearly about basic questions of purpose and audience and appropriate ways to communicate in public" (Para. 2). In their analysis of these writings and any accompanying visual texts, students might be asked to consider whether the author presented the issue responsibly and fairly. This should lead to fruitful class discussion and lay the groundwork for students to produce their own "participatory" documents.

Utilizing Real Audiences

Another civic writing pedagogy implements genre theory. Teachers can provide students with examples of opinion/editorial page entries, asking that students complete research on disciplinary issues with civic relevance and compose an editorial based on their research. (For instance, a student could propose revision to legislation on cloning within a biology class.) At the end of the exercise, students can choose whether they want to submit their entries to a local, campus, or national forum or just share them with classmates. Some teachers may see opportunity within this exercise to teach conventions of disciplinary discourse such as style sheet considerations and may prompt students to write about a civic issue and format it as a submission to a disciplinary journal or other specialized publication in their field. In cases where students will not be circulating writing

to external audiences, the teacher can still collect entries and either assemble and duplicate them or post them to web space, asking students to read and provide feedback for one another's work.

Finally, Writing the Civic across the Curriculum

In a large class environment or where writing is used to supplement other course assignments (pre-writing for an end-of-term research paper, for instance), teachers can assign some of this work as ungraded writing. With ungraded writing, success of communication with one's classmates can take the place of rigorous teacher comment. Students can be asked to write at the beginning of class, as a transition between discussion topics, to capture questions on paper that they may have, or to make connections among the content of two or more of their classes. Imagine this scenario: students begin class by writing for five minutes about reactions to a civic issue discussed at the end of the previous class and swap papers, reading and providing a response to their partner's writing. Then, the class briefly discusses the writing exercise and students' observations about it. (With ungraded writing, it is important that it always have a clear use in the class environment, whether it be to generate discussion or help students concretize their questions.) Writing across the curriculum (WAC) research has shown this type of writing, while not reviewed by the teacher, is still useful in helping students solidify learning, enabling teachers to better match their curriculum aims to actual learning outcomes (Bean 2002).

Creating "Civic Space"

Some teachers may find that no large, coherent "public" exists for student writing or that the class does not respond to peer activities. There are other options that will enable teachers, with minimal risk, to create smaller publics where students can actually make a difference (Wells 1996). Students can create blogs on the Internet as part of a class assignment, participate in class discussion boards, or post web pages as components of larger class assignments. (Some guidance in using the technology will be required with these methods.) Or, to borrow an approach often taken in technical writing curricula, students might be asked to draft or edit a piece of technical writing to make a disciplinary concept more user friendly or accessible to the public, or seek out a public need and remediate that need using disciplinary methods. The tricky part of such work is guiding students to recognize real needs and determine fruitful projects that can be completed in the scope of a semester. Especially when set within relevant disciplinary discussion, these teaching techniques offer real potential for preparing students to make a difference.

References

Bean, J. 1996. *Engaging ideas: The professor's guide to integrating writing, critical thinking, and active learning in the classroom.* San Francisco: Jossey-Bass.

Herzberg, B. 2004. Civic literacy and service learning. In *Coming of age: The advanced writing curriculum,*. Portsmouth, N.H.: Heinemann.

Smith, J. 1994. Against "illegeracy": Towards a new pedagogy of civic understanding. *College Composition and Communication* 45, no. 2:200–219.

Stotsky, S. 1999. Civic writing in education for democratic citizenship. (ERIC Document Reproduction Service No. ED431706). ERIC/E*Subscribe database.

Wells, S. 1996. Rogue cops and health care: What do we want from public writing? *College Composition and Communication* 47, no. 3:325–341.

Reaching Out to Tomorrow's Scientists, Technologists, Engineers, and Mathematicians

Josué Njock Libii

Indiana University–Purdue University Fort Wayne

For ten consecutive years, an outreach program involving several departments has been run on the campus of Indiana University–Purdue University Fort Wayne. The program consisted of a math-and-science camp held on campus during the summer and small service projects at a selected Middle School during the academic year. Four types of barriers were identified and overcome during the integration of this outreach program into the engineering curriculum.

I. Barriers

A. Curricular Barriers

It is estimated that, on average, only about sixty percent of the engineering curriculum is actually dedicated to engineering subjects. Faculty are protective of this percentage, for they need and must utilize all of it to teach engineering subjects.

B. Concerns of Faculty

Faculty expressed reservations and concerns about how to integrate civic engagement into their courses and its impact on accreditation.

C. Concerns of Students

Part-time students expressed the view that they had obligations at work, at home, and at school. They anticipated that civic engagement activities would require extra commitments from them.

D. Characteristics of the Campus Culture

Faculty look for the relation between the investment of their precious time and the potential rewards that could be reaped at the end, as indicated by the prevailing values of the campus and departmental cultures.

II. Civic Engagement in the Curriculum

Two key issues were found to be important.

A. Identification of Appropriate Courses

In engineering, courses with design content are good candidates for civic engagement because course projects can be geared specifically to the particular interests of faculty and students, as well as to the needs of the service area. The phrase "design component" means that part of the course content must be allocated to teaching and learning the design process, where students are given the opportunity to work on a design that is both appropriate to the contents of the course and commensurate with the allotted time.

B. Use Open-Ended and Flexible Assignments

- In each course, divide students in small groups.
- Give statements of specific (design) problems that need to be solved, some of which were related to civic engagement.
- Require each group to choose one, and only one, assignment from those listed.
- Allow students to design their own problems.
- Make these assignments open-ended, flexible,

and, more importantly, amenable to the interests and input of the students involved. This allows students to take ownership of the assignment.

If possible, give examples of successful projects done in the past. We listed:

• Hot-air balloons: used to demonstrate buoyancy and Archimedes principle;

• Water rockets and compressed-air rockets: used to demonstrate momentum, propulsion and ballistics;

• Smoke-ring generators: used to demonstrate rotation, vorticity, and diffusion;

• Suspension bridges and model elevators: used to demonstrate action and reaction using forces along cables; and

• Battery-operated wooden propellers: used to demonstrate thrust and lift.

The designed products could be used by teachers in their classes and resource rooms or during the math-and-science camps held on campus. The assignments that generated these projects had several components that are compatible with accreditation criteria: hands-on activities in which analysis is combined with design, building, and testing; work in small groups; report writing and presentation; and project management.

III. Interaction with the Community to be Served: Recommendations

Several practical issues are important to keep in mind.

A. Planning Ahead

• Identify a school early: start with a school where one has contact with teachers.

• Proximity of the school to the university is essential. Choose a school that is close to campus. This makes access easy and reduces travel time.

• Determine what the needs of the teachers, the school, the curriculum, and the pupils are.

• Develop working relationships with teachers before starting the program to identify goals and objectives of the programs, potential schedules, methods, expected outcomes, and an inventory of resources that would be needed, as well as time frames.

B. Working with the Teacher

It is important to:

• Respect the teacher's classroom philosophy and style.

• Integrate the work to be done into the Middle School's science, math, and technology curriculum.

• Taking the work schedule of the Middle School into account is important. Although school may be open from 8am to 3:30 pm, only certain time slots are available for instruction. Also, a given teacher may have classes that meet at different times during the day. Generally, a teacher would prefer to expose all of her/his classes to the same learning experiences.

• Review the compatibility between the expected outcomes of university courses and the learning objectives that the teacher has in mind.

C. Recruiting University Students

• Participation in civic engagement activities should not be mandatory.

• Students in a given class should be given a choice whether or not to participate.

• Civic engagement is not well served if students engage in it grudgingly.

• If done reluctantly, the quality of the interactions with Middle Schools are neither as successful nor as rewarding as they would be otherwise.

Conclusion

Practical barriers make integrating civic engagement into the engineering curriculum a serious challenge. They stem from the structure of the curriculum, the concerns of the faculty and of the students, and the low rank of importance that these activities have in the structure of rewards in engineering schools. Nevertheless, as described above, it is possible to overcome these barriers. Although this process takes time, energy, and considerable commitment, the rewards can be very good for the students involved. They gain valuable insight into the needs of society and gather tangible evidence on how relevant the application of what they are learning can be to solving problems that face the communities around them.

Using Organizational Writing to Engage Engineering and Business Students

Stevens R. Amidon

Indiana University–Purdue University Fort Wayne

Engineering and business students taking advanced courses in writing tend to resist efforts to bring the political into the classroom. One source of this resistance is the fact that most of these students have already chosen careers, and are focused upon reaching individual career goals. Unfortunately, most textbooks in technical and business writing (a field I will henceforth refer to as *organizational writing*) reinforce this instrumental viewpoint by presenting the conventions and genres of organizational writing as a fixed set of tools for accomplishing routine organizational tasks. More frequently than not, when the individual focus of our students meets a pedagogy that focuses on the conventions of organizations, students become even more likely to develop an ideological identification with a status quo which emphasizes passivity and obedience to rules, rather than the sort of critical thinking that citizenship in a democracy requires.

A better approach to teaching organizational writing is one that emphasizes the local and contextual nature of such writing by demonstrating the fact that writing occurs within the muddy waters of organizational politics. In other words, a better approach is one that teaches students that written communication within the hierarchy of most organizations occurs in a space of asymmetrical power relations in which cultures and ideas clash, a space that has been called a "contact zone" (Pratt 1996).

Teaching Methods

The method I am suggesting is one that moves away from rote learning of genres and other writing conventions, and instead focuses upon giving students an "inside look" at the ethical and political nature of organizational writing. It teaches the importance of resisting the kind of "groupthink" that often characterizes such writing. Students acquire this knowledge by reading a series of historical narratives about writing in organizational contact zones, and reflecting upon those narratives in class discussions and writing.

The first narrative begins with a simple technical document, a memo written by a German engineer to his superior that proposes improvements to the vans being used by the Nazis to transfer Jews to extermination camps. After reading this horrifying memo, which exemplifies the kind of clear, concise, and correct writing advocated by their textbook, students read and discuss an article that criticizes the "ethic of expediency" often seen in such writing (Katz 1991).

From this disturbing narrative, they read about a more recent event where the lines between "good and evil" aren't quite so starkly drawn. This article analyzes the correspondence between managers and engineers at NASA and Morton Thiokol, which led NASA to ignore warnings about possible O-ring failure that led to the 1985 "accident" on the *Challenger* space shuttle (Winsor 1988). This article demonstrates the difficulty writers face in resisting internal pressures to conform to "groupthink," as well as the asymmetrical nature of power relationships between readers and writers of organizational documents.

In the third narrative, I use a story that demonstrates that, despite those power relationships, writers in the lower levels of a hierarchical organization retain some measure of agency they can use to enable political change both inside and outside these organizations. This article describes the work of a civilian wildlife biologist working at the White Sands Missile Range in New Mexico. In reading and reflecting on this article the students learn how the official format for writing environmental impact statements constrained this biologist from reporting the detailed environmental threat posed by some military initiatives. We learn how the biologist bypassed those conventions to allow herself the space she needed to detail the impact of these threats. Her letters pointed out problems that military commanders could not ignore, and demonstrate how she successfully overcame some of the obstacles posed by the structure of official genres of writing (Herndl 1996).

In the final narrative, I tell a story which challenges students to go further and become "boundary crossers," showing them how organizational writing can move from the sphere of the workplace to the public sphere. In this narrative I tell the story of submarine engineer who used his institutional writing as a springboard to enter the 1993 debate on the military's "Don't Ask, Don't Tell" policy. The engineer saw a disconnect between the ideology of the military hierarchy, which opposed lifting the ban on military service by gays and lesbians, and his own experiences supervising gay sailors aboard a submarine. The engineer began writing letters to his elected representatives in Washington, and eventually testified before the U.S. Senate Armed Services Committee. This narrative becomes even more powerful when I later show students video of that testimony, and students realize that the engineer in the scenario was their "professor" during his military career.

Outcomes

The movement of these narratives from the dangerous passivity of Nazi technical discourse to the political activism of the final narrative is designed to teach students to see that the choices they will make in their professional lives have political and ethical consequences. Organizational communications can affect the public stakeholders beyond the walls of the corporation where students may work. And while my students tend to be materialistic and pro-business, they are not naïve. I have followed the advice of Herndl (1996) who suggests that if professors avoid the trap of indoctrinating their students, experience will bring those students to the realization that there is often a "dark side" to institutional communication practices. My students are becoming ethically sensitive to groupthink that leads to "the prob-

lem of a common good becoming a totalitarian evil" (Porter 2003, 213). And while my students still learn the conventions of business writing genres and style, I believe they are also learning to challenge those conventions.

Not all professors have the example of their own Senate testimony to use as a pedagogical tool. However, even that testimony grew out of discontent with a situation I saw as local—the attempt by the military hierarchy to mischaracterize the contribution of homosexual sailors I worked with on a routine basis. Many of us have stories of our own encounters with "dark forces" within institutions. One way we can help our students negotiate the challenges of dealing with these forces is by telling stories—both our own, as well as those of others.

References

Herndl, C. G. 1996. Tactics and the quotidian: Resistance and professional discourse. *Journal of Advanced Composition* 16:455–470.

Katz, S. B. 1991. The ethic of expediency: Classical rhetoric, technology, and the holocaust. *College English* 54:255–275.

Porter, J. A. 2003 Framing postmodern commitment and solidarity. In T. Peeples, ed., *Professional writing and rhetoric: Readings from the field*, 202–217. New York: Longman.

Pratt, M. L. 1991. Arts of the contact zone. *Profession* 91:33–40.

Winsor, D. A. 1988. Communication failures contributing to the challenger accident: An example for technical communicators. *IEEE Transactions on Professional Communication* 31:101–107.

Cal Campaign Consultants: An Interdisciplinary Approach to Civic Education, Leadership, and Community Involvement

Melanie J. Blumberg, Greg Harrison, Richard J. Helldobler, Jesse G. Hereda, Robert M. Mehalik, Michele A. Pagen, Emily M. Sweitzer, and Margo Wilson
California University of Pennsylvania

California University of Pennsylvania, like other colleges and universities, has a relatively small number of politically active students who hold leadership positions in influential campus organizations. Two political science majors who are board members of the Student Association, Inc., a student-funded and controlled corporation, decided that an organization to give students practical experience in campaigns and elec-

tions would be a natural extension of the university's new Leadership Studies Minor. The underlying objectives included instilling a sense of community among students, increasing student participation in campus elections, giving students an understanding of the political process, and creating the awareness they can make a difference.

The two students sought the advice of a political science professor and, together, they envisioned an interdisciplinary organization, Cal Campaign Consultants, which would appeal to students from a variety of majors and draw on the expertise of faculty in political science, psychology, sociology, communication studies, journalism, theater arts, graphic design, public relations, and marketing. Professional campaigns, after all, incorporate theories and techniques in each of these fields.

Campaign Strategies and Election Outcomes

Cal Campaign Consultants (CCC) recruited members fall semester, structured the organization, and learned campaign techniques. The two founders lobbied Student Government and convinced members that CCC should run the campaigns. Candidates could accept or reject having CCC strategists design and implement a campaign plan; however, funding depended on using the operatives.

Declared candidates were invited to CCC meetings. One candidate, who had attended the first session, argued that he should be able to select his own consultants. He chose the most aggressive group, thinking it was his ticket to success. His opponent, not completely convinced CCC would make a difference in the election outcome, agreed to accept its help after some coaxing.

The two candidates were opposites. One was overly confident, even bombastic, while the other was quiet and open to suggestions. The former was his consultants' nightmare, although they were sure they could mold him into a winner. The latter was the perfect candidate in many respects, willing to adhere to the game plan.

Both consultant teams devised similar strategies, but one was faster out the gate and slightly more creative than was the other. Both teams obtained permission to post campaign signs in prohibited areas, such as the library and on glass entrance doors, and one even placed handbills in lavatory stalls and above hand-dryers. The most innovative signs were two-inch squares taped on doors to classroom buildings, as students paused to read the messages before entering. On the day of the candidate debate, the team responsible for the miniature signs hung a sheet-sized banner from the mezzanine above the student center lobby. A consultant was there when the doors opened, trumping the opposition.

The candidate debate, outside the student center, was taped and shown on the university television station. Prior to the debate, both teams worked with their candidates, reviewing possible questions and answers. On debate day, the teams had "plants" in the audience, asking their candidates questions not covered in the debate and raising other questions to discredit the opposition. (This tactic was not discussed in the CCC meetings.) The debate was rebroadcast through the close of the polls. The student newspaper had run a full-page feature and campus radio had run public service announcements previously.

During campaign week, consultants and candidates visited classes, targeting political science and history classes where the most likely voters were believed to be. The candidates also visited club meetings, the athletic training facility, and the food court. Both candidates were schooled to shake hands firmly, arrive at events early, look people in the eye, and not scan the room to see whether there was someone "more important" present. One candidate jotted people's suggestions in a notebook thereby demonstrating interest in their concerns.

There was electronic balloting at sites across campus. One team had members at each polling place, asking students for their votes. It was surprising to watch ordinarily shy students become aggressive campaigners.

A few tension-filled days passed before the election results were announced. The election outcomes were as anticipated for the down-ticket candidates, but the contest for president was so close that it took days to certify. The candidate who hesitated using CCC won the election by 33 votes. He admits that his consultants' advice and hard work made the difference. During the week of the election, one strategist even knocked on this future winner's dorm room door at dawn in order to get him on the campaign trail ahead of the competition. The candidate likened it to being in boot camp. Voter turnout increased by 21 percent from the previous Student Government election.

Summary

CCC members came to understand it is possible to make a difference in election outcomes and help develop policy positions. It was a heady experience for some; their first foray into electoral politics. As a result of their immersion into campaigns and elections, the students took active roles in other campus events, such as voter registration drives.

For the 2004 general election, returning CCC members held an issue expo; sponsored a voter registration booth at Academic Excellence Day; offered rides, within a 50-mile radius, to the polls; and co-sponsored events featuring public officials, party operatives, and campaign consultants. Others were involved in Rock the Vote, serving as area field directors. One of the charter members won a seat on city council and another CCC member plans to run for school board. Some are interested in pursuing graduate degrees in campaign management and others may one-day practice campaign finance law. The lessons are invaluable for students. The awareness and understanding students gained about campaigns and elections may have a lasting effect on their political involvement.

Students are not the only ones who benefited from CCC. Professors who advise the group now are applying what they learned from their colleagues, as well as from the students, in the classroom. For example, a faculty member in the English Department, who has extensive experience as a journalist, indicates she now alerts her students to psychological and marketing strategies used by candidates to "sell" themselves. Journalism students, according to the professor, must understand how suc-

cessful campaign consultants brand their clients by schooling them on everything from what to wear, to how to make eye contact, to what to say and how to say it.

It is not so much that students and faculty have never been exposed to these tactics, but that the exposure has been fragmented. The organization met its objectives: It instilled a sense of community among students, increased their participation in campus elections, gave them an understanding of the political process, and created the awareness that they can make a difference. The project convinced the dean and participating faculty that an interdisciplinary approach to campus campaigning can enhance the quality of life both in and outside the classroom.

Authors' Note

The chapter is based on a paper presented at the 2005 Meeting of the Midwest Political Science Association.

CONTRIBUTORS

Stevens R. Amidon
Assistant Professor
Department of English and Linguistics
Indiana University–Purdue University Fort Wayne
amidons@ipfw.edu

Jill R. Arensdorf
Instructor, Department of Leadership Studies and
    Chair, FHSU Service-Learning Committee
Fort Hays State University
jrarensdorf@fhsu.edu

Patrick J. Ashton
Associate Professor of Sociology and Director,
    Peace and Conflict Studies
Department of Sociology
Indiana University–Purdue University Fort Wayne
ashton@ipfw.edu

Arcea Zapata de Aston, Ph.D.
Assistant Professor of Spanish
Foreign Language Department
University of Evansville
Aa113@evansville.edu

Matthew R. Auer
Associate Professor
School of Public and Environmental Affairs
Indiana University Bloomington
mauer@indiana.edu

Elizabeth A. Bennion
Assistant Professor
Department of Political Science
Indiana University South Bend
ebennion@iusb.edu

R. Todd Benson, M.Ed.
Coordinator of Community Service and
    Volunteer Programs
Residence Life and Housing
East Stroudsburg University of Pennsylvania
tbenson@po-box.esu.edu

Melanie J. Blumberg
Associate Professor
Department of History and Political Science
California University of Pennsylvania
blumberg@cup.edu

David Boyns
Assistant Professor
Department of Sociology
California State University, Northridge
david.boyns@csun.edu

Christie J. Brungardt
Instructor, Department of Leadership Studies
and Coordinator, American Democracy Project
Department of Leadership Studies
Fort Hays State University
cjbrunga@fhsu.edu

Katharine Byers
Associate Professor and BSW Program Director
School of Social Work
Indiana University
kvbyers@indiana.edu

R. B. Campbell
Associate Professor
Department of Mathematics
University of Northern Iowa
campbell@math.uni.edu

Diana Cardenas, Ph.D.
Assistant Professor
Department of English
Texas A&M University—Corpus Christi
Diana.cardenas@mail.tamucc.edu

Vivian Chávez
Assistant Professor
Department of Health Education
San Francisco State University
vchavez@sfsu.edu

Dr. Janet Cherrington
Associate Professor
Urban and Regional Studies Institute
Minnesota State University, Mankato
janet.cherrington@mnsu.edu

Diane Chin
Assistant Director, Chicago Civic Leadership
    Certificate Program
Office of the Vice Provost for Undergraduate
    Studies
University of Illinois at Chicago
dianchin@uic.edu

Christine S. Choi
Master's Candidate
International Educational Development Program
Teachers College, Columbia University
csc2110@columbia.edu

Linda Christiansen
Assistant Professor of Business
School of Business
Indiana University Southeast
lchristi@ius.edu

Jeanette Clausen
Associate Vice Chancellor for Faculty Affairs
    and Professor of German
Indiana University–Purdue University
    Fort Wayne
clausen@ipfw.edu

Mary Ange Cooksey
Humanities Lecturer
Humanities and Fine Arts Division
Indiana University East
mcooksey@indiana.edu

Michael DeCesare
Assistant Professor
Department of Sociology
California State University, Northridge
mdecesare@csun.edu

Lisa Dicke, Ph.D.
Assistant Professor
Department of Public Administration
University of North Texas
ldicke@unt.edu

Ronald J. Duchovic
Associate Professor
Department of Chemistry
Indiana University–Purdue University Fort Wayne
duchovic@ipfw.edu

Ann M. Feldman
Faculty Director, Chicago Civic Leadership
    Certificate Program
Department of English
University of Illinois at Chicago
feldman@uic.edu

Janet L. Ferguson, Ph.D.
Assistant Professor
Department of Early Childhood and
    Elementary Education
East Stroudsburg University of Pennsylvania
jferguson@po-box.esu.edu

Joan Ferrante
Professor
Department of Sociology, Anthropology,
    and Philosophy
Northern Kentucky University
ferrantej@nku.edu

Tony Filipovitch
Professor
Urban & Regional Studies Institute
Minnesota State University, Mankato
tony@mnsu.edu

Kathleen M. Foster, Ed.D.
Associate Professor
Department of Professional and Secondary Education
East Stroudsburg University of Pennsylvania
kfoster@po-box.esu.edu

Joanne R. Gilbert
Associate Professor of Communication and
    Co-Director, Women's Studies Program
Communication Department
Alma College
Gilbert@Alma.edu

Elizabeth M. Goering
Associate Professor
Department of Communication Studies
Indiana University–Purdue University Indianapolis
bgoering@iupui.edu

Nathan Hand, BA
Coordinator
Student Activities and Leadership Programs
University of Idaho
Nathan@sub.uidaho.edu

Darlene Hantzis
Associate Professor of Communication and Associate
    Dean of the College of Arts and Sciences
Indiana State University
dmhantzis@indstate.edu

Greg Harrison
Assistant Professor
Department of Art and Design
California University of Pennsylvania
harrison_g@cup.edu

John C. Hayek
Senior Associate Director
Center for Postsecondary Research and National
    Survey of Student Engagement
Indiana University Bloomington
jhayek@indiana.edu

Richard J. Helldobler
Dean
College of Liberal Arts
California University of Pennsylvania
helldobler@cup.edu

Jesse G. Hereda
Department of History and Political Science
California University of Pennsylvania
jess1280@aol.com

Michelle Salinas Holmes
Project Associate
Center for Postsecondary Research and National
    Survey of Student Engagement
Indiana University Bloomington
msholmes@indiana.edu

Juan Carlos Huerta
Associate Professor
Department of Political Science
Texas A&M University–Corpus Christi
jhuerta@falcon.tamucc.edu

Clark Johnson
Professor
Social Studies Teaching
Minnesota State University, Mankato
Clark.Johnson@mnsu.edu

Daniel J. Jorgensen
Associate Professor of Public Administration
Department of Social Science
Texas A&M University–Corpus Christi
dan.jorgensen@mail.tamucc.edu

Joseph Jozwiak
Assistant Professor
Department of Political Science
Texas A&M University–Corpus Christi
joe.jozwiak@mail.tamucc.edu

Kevin Kecskes
Director, Community-University Partnerships
Center for Academic Excellence
Portland State University
kecskesk@pdx.edu

James T Knauer
Professor Emeritus of Political Science and Founding
    Director, Pennsylvania Center for Civic Life
Lock Haven University of Pennsylvania
jknauer@lhup.edu

Brenda E. Knowles
Professor of Business Law and Director,
    Honors Program
Indiana University South Bend
bknowles@iusb.edu

Katharine Kravetz, JD
Assistant Professor and Academic Director,
    Transforming Communities Seminar
Washington Semester Program
American University
kkravet@american.edu

John W. Kraybill-Greggo, Ph.D.
Coordinator-Social Work Program and Assistant
    Professor Department of Sociology
East Stroudsburg University of Pennsylvania
jkgreggo@po-box.esu.edu

Michael C. Kuhne, Ph.D.
English and Urban Teacher Program
Minneapolis Community and Technical College
Michael.Kuhne@minneapolis.edu

Joe Kunkel
Professor
Deparment of Political Science
Minnesota State University, Mankato
Joseph.Kunkel@mnsu.edu

Luciana Lagana', Ph.D.
Associate Professor
Department of Psychology
California State University, Northridge
luciana.lagana@csun.edu

Heather Laube, Ph.D.
Assistant Professor
Department of Sociology, Anthropology, and
    Criminal Justice
University of Michigan–Flint
hlaube@umflint.edu

Josué Njock Libii
Associate Professor
Engineering Department
Indiana University–Purdue University
    Fort Wayne
Libii@engr.ipfw.edu

Susan Loudermilk-Garza, Ph.D.
Associate Professor of English
Department of English
Texas A&M University—Corpus Christi
Susan.Garza@mail.tamucc.edu

Joan Mandle
Associate Professor (Emeriti)
Department of Sociology
Colgate University
joanm@democracymatters.org

Megan Marie
Graduate Teaching Assistant, Chicago Civic
    Leadership Certificate Program
Department of English
University of Illinois at Chicago
mmarie2@uic.edu

Linda S. Maule
Associate Professor Political Science
Director, Legal Studies Program
Interim Director, Women's Studies Program
Indiana State University
lmaule@indstate.edu

Gera McGuire
MPA Student
Department of Public Administration
University of North Texas
GMcGuire@scs.unt.edu

Robert M. Mehalik
Department of History and Political Science
California University of Pennsylvania
meh2482@cup.edu

Ajay T. Nair, Ph.D.
Associate Director
Asian American Studies Program
University of Pennsylvania
atnair@sas.upenn.edu

Paul G. Nielson, Ph.D.
Campus Religious Center
Southwest Minnesota State University
paulniels@aol.com

Christine M. Olson, Ph.D.
Associate Professor
Psychology Program
Southwest Minnesota State University
olsonc@southwestmsu.edu

Pamela Jean Owens
Assistant Professor
Department of Philosophy and Religion
University of Nebraska Omaha
powens@mail.unomaha.edu

Michele A. Pagen
Professor
Department of Theatre and Dance
California University of Pennsylvania
pagen@cup.edu

Naomi Jeffery Petersen, Ed.D.
Assistant Professor
School of Education
Indiana University South Bend
NJP@iusb.edu

Chapman Rackaway
Assistant Professor of Political Science
Fort Hays State University
crackawa@fhsu.edu

Candice Rai
Graduate Teaching Assistant, Chicago Civic
    Leadership Certificate Program
Department of English
University of Illinois at Chicago
crai1@uic.edu

Gerald Lee Ratliff
Associate Vice President
Academic Affairs
SUNY Potsdam
ratlifgl@potsdam.edu

Saundra J. Reinke
Associate Professor and Director, MPA Program
Department of Political Science
Augusta State University
sreinke@aug.edu

Cynthia Roberts, MSOD, MSTD
Assistant Professor and Section Coordinator of
    Organizational Leadership and Supervision
Purdue University North Central
croberts@pnc.edu

Nancy Brattain Rogers
Associate Professor Recreation and Sports
    Management
Director, American Humanics
Acting Director, Center for Public Service and
    Community Engagement
Indiana State University
nancyrogers@indstate.edu

L. Sullivan Ross
Project Manager
Democracy Lab
Lock Haven University of Pennsylvania
lross@lhup.edu

Nadia Rubaii-Barrett, Ph.D.
Associate Professor
Masters in Public Administration Program
Binghamton University
nbarrett@binghamton.edu

Jennifer S. Simpson, Ph.D.
Assistant Professor
Department of Communication
Indiana University—Purdue University
    Fort Wayne
simpsonj@ipfw.edu

Thomas A. P. Sinclair
Assistant Professor and Director
Masters in Public Administration Program
Binghamton University
sinclair@binghamton.edu

Scott Smithson, Ph.D.
Associate Professor and Acting Chair of
    Communication
Purdue University North Central
ssmithson@pnc.edu

Heather Speweik, M.A.
Graduate Assistant, Rhetoric and Writing
Department of English
Bowling Green State University
hspeweik@bgnet.bgsu.edu

Trae Stewart, Ph.D.
Assistant Professor
Department of Educational Studies
College of Education
University of Central Florida
pbstewar@mail.ucf.edu

Emily M. Sweitzer
Assistant Professor
Department of Psychology
California University of Pennsylvania
sweitzer@cup.edu

Ruby Turalba
Health Education Department
San Francisco State University
ruby2006@sfsu.edu

Lori A. Walters-Kramer, Ph.D.
Assistant Professor
Department of Communication
Plattsburgh State University of New York
Lori.walterskramer@plattsburgh.edu

Adam Weinberg
Senior Vice President
Academic Affairs/SIT Provost
World Learning
adam.weinberg@worldlearning.org

Laurie Wermuth
Professor
Department of Sociology
California State University, Chico
lwermuth@csuchico.edu

Mollie Whalen, Ph.D.
Professor of Women's Studies
Women's Studies Program
East Stroudsburg University of Pennsylvania
mwhalen@po-box.esu.edu

Katy Wigley
Instructional Design and Technology Specialist
Institute for Learning and Teaching Excellence (ILTE)
Indiana University Southeast
kwigley@ius.edu

Christopher Wilkey
Assistant Professor
Department of Literature and Language
Northern Kentucky University
wilkeyc@nku.edu

Sabrina Williamson, Ph.D.
Assistant Professor
School of Social Work
Indiana University
sabawill@indiana.edu

Charmaine E. Wilson, Ph.D.
Associate Professor
Department of Communications
University of South Carolina Aiken
charw@usca.edu

Margo Wilson
Assistant Professor
Department of English
California University of Pennsylvania
wilson_m@cup.edu

Debra Worley
Associate Professor of Communication and
    Coordinator of the Public Relations Program
Department of Communication
Indiana State University
cmdebra@isugw.indstate.edu

INDEX

THE EDITORS

STEVEN G. JONES is the Coordinator of the Office of Service Learning in the Center for Service and Learning (CSL) at Indiana University–Purdue University Indianapolis. Prior to joining CSL, he was the Associate Director of the Integrating Service with Academic Studies project at Campus Compact from 2002–2004. Steven received a Ph.D. in political science from the University of Utah in 1995 and was an associate professor of political science at the University of Charleston from 1995–2002 where he also served as the Director of the Robert C. Byrd Institute for Government Studies. He edited the second edition of Campus Compact's *Introduction to Service Learning Toolkit* and is a co-author of two other Campus Compact monographs, *The Community's College: Indicators of Engagement at Two-Year Institutions* and *The Promise of Partnerships: Tapping into the Campus as a Community Asset.* Steve lives in Indianapolis with his wife Rebekah and their two cats, Yonah and Lila.

JAMES L. PERRY is Chancellor's Professor in the School of Public and Environmental Affairs (SPEA) and Senior Scholar in the Center for Service and Learning at Indiana University–Purdue University Indianapolis. He also holds adjunct appointments in Philanthropy and Political Science. He directs the Indiana University American Democracy Project. He has held faculty appointments at the University of California Irvine, Chinese University of Hong Kong, University of Wisconsin Madison, and Indiana University Bloomington. Perry's research focuses on service motivation, national and community service, and government reform. He is author and editor of many scholarly articles and several books, including the *Handbook of Public Administration,* Second Edition. His most recent book is *Civic Service: What Difference Does It Make?,* co-authored with Ann Marie Thomson. In 1999–2000, he was senior evaluator in the Corporation for National and Community Service. He is chair of the Indiana Commission on Community Service and Volunteerism and an advisor to the Points of Light Foundation.